The Politics of Gender and Education

D1477877

Also by the Editors:

Suki Ali, MIXED RACE, POST RACE: New Ethnicities and Cultural Practices

Suki Ali, Kelly Coate and Wangui wa Goro (eds), GLOBAL FEMINIST POLITICS

Shereen Benjamin, THE MICROPOLITICS OF INCLUSIVE EDUCATION: An Ethnography

Melanie Mauthner, SISTERING: POWER AND CHANGE IN FEMALE RELATIONSHIPS

Melanie Mauthner, Maxine Birch, Julie Jessop and Tina Miller (eds), ETHICS IN QUALITATIVE RESEARCH

The Politics of Gender and Education

Critical Perspectives

Edited by

Suki Ali
*Lecturer, Department of Sociology,
London School of Economics and Political Science,
University of London*

Shereen Benjamin
*Lecturer in Difficulty in Learning
Birmingham University*

and

Melanie Mauthner
*Lecturer in Social Policy
Open University*

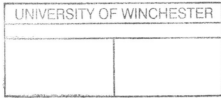

Editorial Matter, Selection and Introduction © Suki Ali,
Shereen Benjamin and Melanie Mauthner 2004
Text © Palgrave Macmillan Ltd 2004

First published 2004 by
PALGRAVE MACMILLAN
Houndmills, Basingstoke, Hampshire RG21 6XS and
175 Fifth Avenue, New York, N.Y. 10010
Companies and representatives throughout the world

PALGRAVE MACMILLAN is the global academic imprint of the Palgrave
Macmillan division of St. Martin's Press, LLC and of Palgrave Macmillan Ltd.
Macmillan® is a registered trademark in the United States, United Kingdom
and other countries. Palgrave is a registered trademark in the European
Union and other countries.

ISBN 1–4039–0489–8 hardback
ISBN 1–4039–0490–1 paperback

This book is printed on paper suitable for recycling and made from fully
managed and sustained forest sources.

A catalogue record for this book is available from the British Library.

Library of Congress Cataloging-in-Publication Data
The politics of gender and education:critical perspectives/edited by
    Suki Ali, Shereen Benjamin, Melanie Mauthner.
      p. cm.
    Includes bibliographical references and index.
    ISBN 1–4039–0489–8 (cloth) — ISBN 1–4039–0490–1 (paper)
    1. Sex differences in education—Congresses. 2. Educational
    equalization—Congresses. 3. Feminism and education—
    Congresses. I. Ali, Suki, 1962– II. Benjamin, Shereen, 1965–
    III. Mauthner, Melanie L., 1964–

    LC212.9.P65 2003
    370'.82—dc21   2003050905

10   9   8   7   6   5   4   3   2   1
13 12 11 10 09 08 07 06 05 04

Transferred to digital printing 2005

Contents

Notes on the Editors and Contributors

The editors

Suki Ali teaches Gender and Social Theory in the Sociology Department of the London School of Economics and Political Science. Her current research interests include the use of Cultural Theory in studying co-constructions of gender, ethnicity and class, and how these terms are understood in everyday contexts. She has also published in the field of visual methodologies and the politics of 'mixed-race' identifications. Recent publications include *Global Feminist Politics* (2000) co-edited with Kelly Coate and Wangui wa Goro. Her monograph *Mixed Race, Post Race: New Ethnicities and Cultural Practices* will be published by Berg.

Shereen Benjamin is Lecturer in Difficulty in Learning at the University of Birmingham where she is responsible for distance education courses for teachers in schools and further education colleges. She is interested in the intersections of gender, ethnicity and social class in the construction of meanings and practices surrounding disability and 'special educational needs'. Her recent publications include *The Micropolitics of Inclusive Education: An Ethnography* (2002).

Melanie Mauthner is Lecturer in Social Policy in the Faculty of Social Sciences at the Open University. She is part of the course teams writing *U130 Get Connected: Studying with a Computer* and *DD305 Personal Lives and Social Policy*. Her research explores cultures of friendship and kinship, especially among siblings. She has written *Sistering: Power and Change in Female Relationships* (Palgrave Macmillan, 2002) and co-edited *Ethics in Qualitative Research* with Maxine Birch, Julie Jessop and Tina Miller (2002).

The contributors

Jacky Brine has taken a class and gender analysis to the education and training policy of the European Union. She is interested in the social, economic and political context of education policy as framed by the processes of globalisation and neo-colonialism. This has been explored throughout journal articles and books (1999, 2001). Returning to her home town as Professor of Education at the University of the West of England, Bristol, she is now exploring the life histories of pupils educated within the post-war tripartite secondary modern system.

Marianne S. Castano has been involved in the issues that intersect human development, psychology, education and technology as a researcher, graduate school faculty member, facilitator and trainer. These issues include gender, race, ethnicity, language and disability. At the Gender and Diversities Institute at EDC she is doing research on how gender equity issues are learned from an online course. She is also working with teachers to develop strategies that promote gender equitable practices in their classrooms. Currently, she is completing her doctoral dissertation at the Harvard Graduate School of Education's Human Development and Psychology program.

Sue Clegg is Professor of Educational Research and Deputy Director of the Learning and Teaching Research Institute at Sheffield Hallam University. She has a long-standing interest in gender dynamics in education and has drawn on a critical realist framework in developing her ideas about social relations in technology. She has recently published on gender dynamics in computing in *Gender and Education, British Educational Research Journal* and *Higher Education*. She has worked extensively on the continuing professional development of research degree supervisors and has an ongoing interest in understanding and improving the experiences of research students.

Miriam David is Director of the Graduate School of Social Sciences and Professor of Policy Studies in Education at Keele University. She is a sociologist of education and policy sociologist and has an international reputation for her studies of gender, families, education and policies. She is an executive editor of the *British Journal of Sociology of Education*, on the editorial board of *Gender and Education* and co-chair of the Gender and Education Association. Her publications include (with Madeleine Arnot and Gaby Weiner, 1999) *Closing the Gender Gap: Post War Education and Social Change*, and (forthcoming). *Personal and Political: Feminisms, Sociology and Family Lives.*

Kevin Davison is a doctoral candidate with the Department of Education at the University of South Australia, Adelaide. His doctoral research is in the area of masculinities and bodies in schools. He is currently a part-time faculty member with the Department of Education at Mount Saint Vincent University in Halifax, Nova Scotia, Canada. He teaches graduate courses on masculinities and literacies, research literacies and educational foundations.

Linda Eyre is Professor in the Faculty of Education, University of New Brunswick, Canada, where she teaches courses in feminist theory and education, and sexuality education. Her recent publications have appeared in *Canadian Journal of Education, Atlantis, Gender and Education,* and edited collections. She is co-editor with Leslie G. Roman of *Dangerous Territories: Struggles for Difference and Equality in Education* (1997).

Sundra Flansburg is director of the Women's Educational Equity Act Resource Center at EDC, a national project that promotes gender equitable education in the US. She earned an M.S. in women's studies from the University of Costa Rica, and co-ordinates, for the Gender and Diversities Institute at EDC, several inter-American initiatives with Costa Rican and other Latin American universities and women's organisations.

Blye Frank holds a PhD in Educational Foundations. His doctoral thesis is entitled 'Everyday Masculinities'. He has taught and researched in the area of Gender and Masculinities and presently holds his third Social Science and Humanities Research Council grant in this area (Post-Colonial Masculinities and Schooling in the New Millennium 2002–2005). He is presently a Full Professor in the Division of Medical Education and Director of Faculty Development in the Faculty of Medicine at Dalhousie University in Halifax, Canada.

Katherine Hanson directs the Gender and Diversities Institute at EDC, a global education research and development organisation, located near Boston, Massachusetts. She is currently principal investigator for two National Science Foundation grants; one on developing a better understanding of how adults learn in online courses, and the other the creation of a global digital library on gender and science. She directed the Women's Educational Equity Act (WEEA) Resource Centre, a major national technical assistance and dissemination centre as well as a number of school reform projects. She recently helped develop a series of international exchanges that bring educators and researchers together to discuss critical gender and diversity topics, bridging the boundaries of geography. All her work has focused on the integration of gender and diversities into the development of innovative and effective education. She is a nationally recognised speaker, writer and workshop presenter.

Trudy Lovell is a doctoral candidate at the University of South Australia in Adelaide. Her research interests include poststructural analyses of sexual harassment in elementary schools, 'at risk' student discourses and the 'boy' question in education. Current research projects include an examination of policies and practices regarding sexual and gender-based harassment in primary (elementary) school, masculinities in schooling, and education for students who are identified as being 'at risk'. She has been a public school teacher and part-time faculty member at Mount Saint Vincent University, Nova Scotia, Canada.

Helen Poulsen is a social development consultant working in the education sector. She has a strong interest in 'North-South' learning and conducted research on the gender implications of learning from the South in the UK. Recently, she has been working on gender and equity issues in education projects in China, Bangladesh and Sri Lanka.

Jocey Quinn is currently Research Fellow at the Institute for Access Studies, Staffordshire University, a research centre dedicated to widening participation, lifelong learning and social inclusion. She has recently completed an ESRC-funded PhD at Lancaster University entitled 'Powerful Subjects: Women Students, Subjectivity and the Higher Education Curriculum'. She previously had many years' experience as a lecturer, equality officer and researcher in universities and the public sector.

Melissa A. Rychener is a PhD candidate in the Higher Education programme within the School of Educational Policy and Leadership at the Ohio State University, Columbus, Ohio. She is engaged in research about the acquisition of intercultural sensitivity by graduate students in medicine and education. Melissa has worked in the field of international education, advising US and international students about education abroad. She served as the resident co-ordinator for the Lancaster University-Ohio State University higher education internship programme.

Mary Ann Danowitz Sagaria is Associate Professor and Interim Director of the School of Educational Policy and Leadership at the Ohio State University, Columbus, Ohio. She directs the Lancaster University-Ohio State University higher education internship programme. Mary Ann earned a doctorate in higher education from the Pennsylvania State University and has been a Fulbright Scholar in Indonesia and a visiting scholar at Edith Cowan University in Australia. She has published extensively on gender and racial equality in education, administrative performance, leadership, and the experiences of academic women.

Carol Ann Smith is an independent scholar. Her research interests include the practices of teachers' unions and professional organisations in gender equity policy and public school education.

Ann Vibert is an Associate Professor in the Department of Education at Mount Saint Vincent University in Halifax where she teaches Literacy Education at the graduate and undergraduate levels. Her research and teaching interests focus on critical literacies, school and educational change, and equity issues in education. She is currently involved in a national research project looking at schooling for social justice across issues of class and diversity.

Sue Webb is Senior Lecturer and director of the Institute for Lifelong Learning in the School of Education at the University of Sheffield, where her research interests are in educational policy sociology in the context of social change in post compulsory education and social justice. She has a specific interest in access and participation in higher education and co-authored a collection edited by Jenny Williams entitled *Negotiating Access to Higher Education: The Discourse of Selectivity and Equity* (1997). Currently she is researching participation, equity and gender issues in relation to on-line learning, and has published a number of articles in this area.

Introduction

In April 2001, the Centre for Research in Education and Gender at the Institute of Education, University of London, hosted the third international 'Gender and Education' conference. Entitled 'The Politics of Gender and Education', the conference attracted over 200 delegates from around the world. The high levels of response to the theme revealed that gender is indeed still high on the agenda, but the kinds of debates and struggles that are in play about gender issues in education take many new forms which reflect changing political positions.

Recent years have seen major developments in the politics of gender and education. Globalisation, the marketisation and commercialisation of education and new forms of corporate managerialism have profoundly altered the political contexts that shape the formal and informal sites of education (Apple, 1995; Blackmore, 1999; Kenway and Bullen, 2001). Inter/national concerns, such as the moral panic over boys' perceived 'underachievement' (Epstein *et al.*, 1998; Raphael Reed, 1999), dominate the gender agenda, and channel debate into a narrow set of perspectives associated with the policy drive to raise 'standards' in education (Slee *et al.*, 1998). Alongside these political shifts, theoretical developments, notably those associated with poststructuralism and postcolonialism as well as with feminist theory, are increasingly influential in shaping our understandings of changing political contexts and policy imperatives (Walkerdine, 1997; Tsolidis, 2001). The book is a collection of papers that, taken as a whole, engages with the politics of gender and education in its widest sense. The collection illustrates current practice and research across a diverse range of educational sites, and exemplifies the use of theory in work for egalitarian change in education.

In their introduction to the *Feminist Educational Thinking* series, Weiler *et al.* (2001) note that 'feminist educational thinking views the intersection of education and gender through a variety of lenses'. Such variety is very evident in this book. The contributors share a common concern with how micro-politics and macro-politics act on, inform and shape each other in space produced by the intersection of education and gender. The somewhat overburdened feminist adage 'the personal is political' is here reconfigured within a range of discursive registers. Of increasing interest to feminist and pro-feminist educational thinkers are the production of student identities and the centrality of gender in the complex processes of subjectivity (Cherland, 1994; Hey, 1997; Kenway *et al.*, 1997; Walkerdine, 1997; Burke, 2002). The challenge here is to keep macro-political contexts not just clearly in view, but central to any analysis of and for change. Our intention in drawing together this collection of papers is to juxtapose work which is situated at the personal – 'micro' – end of the spectrum, with work that takes in a broader sweep of policy in the 'macro' context.

The Politics of Gender and Education brings together recent empirical work from a range of perspectives and contexts. The collection presents a provocative mixture of work from well-established academics with that of less well-known writers, who are working at the cutting edge of educational research. The chapters come from authors based in Northern countries, but address issues from both global and local perspectives, making explicit the location of the work and its relevance to cross-cultural perspectives where appropriate. The book uses recent theoretical developments, and the international base of its contributors, to demonstrate the links between the macro- and the micro- in educational policy and practice. To this end all of the writers utilise the concept of 'gender', but do so with an awareness of its inter-dependency with other social positionalities, most notably 'race', ethnicity and class.

In Part I, 'Political and Policy Contexts', the chapters reflect a concern with assessing the ways in which particular political interventions into policy changes in education have impacted in recent years upon those working at 'ground level'. All the authors use a wide-ranging analysis of educational policy, from the use of counter-hegemonic models of knowing (Helen Poulsen) through to the more conventional approaches to 'equity'. Miriam David looks at the consequences of liberal discourses about parental involvement, when 'parents' are in fact most often disadvantaged mothers, whilst Blye Frank *et al.* are interested in the ways in which 'failing boys' are an inevitable result of rigid policy interpretations. For Helen Poulsen, even the non-traditional arenas of learning which utilise 'radical' approaches have produced negative effects for those in oppressed circumstances. In all the chapters, relations of power between those who are gendered, classed and racialised come to the fore. For Frank *et al.*, concerns with gender incorporate concerns with the production of hetero-normative masculinities which are also 'raced'. Poulsen argues that the term 'women' is overwritten by so-called First/Third world relations at the level of epistemology and of practice, whilst for David, economic and social disadvantage makes the variables of 'gender' all the more important. These chapters share a concern with the production of broad discursive registers that produce educational policy reforms which have been detrimental to women and girls in their attempts to improve 'gender equity'.

Part I explores some ways in which policies intended to combat inequality are often failing in wide reaching ways, at the level of the epistemological, political and practical. In Part II, 'Macro Policies and Micro Effects', the implications of policy for practice are explored in specific sites. This Part is something of a bridge between the more broad sweeping analyses of Part I and the micro-environments of Part III. Again all the contributors are centrally concerned with investigating the ways in which gender equity in learning is differentially experienced through specific institutions and ideals. Linda Eyre *et al.* also write about Canadian histories and show that teachers have struggled with policies which they believe have failed girls and boys.

For Katherine Hanson *et al.* the area under scrutiny is the virtual space of the Internet. None the less, like the authors of the two other chapters in this Part, it shows that the ways in which studies of gender interaction on-line have so far been conducted, have again failed to account for the multifaceted aspects of gender, such as class and ethnicity. These inclusive analyses are also used by Mary Ann Danowitz Sagaria and Melissa Rychener to reveal that women administrators' progress in Higher Education in the US is limited to those who have access to networks of privilege that may countermand factors such as 'race'. All the authors argue that the evidence from research document the complexity of 'gender', which is elided in much educational theory.

In Part III, 'Politicising Educational Identities', the ways in which political decisions in education impact on individuals in immediate and localised ways comes under scrutiny. These chapters are linked by an analysis of how changing political discourses of gender and/in education individually and in relation to each other, directly influence learner and researcher identities. Sue Clegg and Jocey Quinn focus on the researcher subjectivity in their work with adult learners and those in Higher Education. Quinn investigates the impact of researcher identities in a more embodied realm by focusing on how changing aspects of her own physicality affected her research. For Clegg the interesting relationship between the researched and the researchers provides another more grounded understanding of what 'gendered research' means. The chapter explores how PhD research students draw on gender and class identities in describing their route into postgraduate research. She focuses on the experiences of non-traditional students and the challenge of inclusive education at PhD level. Both Jackie Brine and Sue Webb are interested in the ways in which class impacts upon the experience of education. Brine's autobiographical material takes us through from schooling to Higher Education, and Webb explores the world of adult returners to education. Webb's data show highlights between men and women who have made choices about study which are pragmatic and responsive to classed identifications.

The book does not aim to provide the definitive guide to the changing problem associated with being gender-aware and taking a pro-feminist stance within education and related fields. What we believe emerges from this necessarily small selection of papers is that the understandings of gender that are utilised by the contributors are indicative of the absolute necessity to take the politics of gender as fundamental to educational research. The authors reveal how a simplistic view of what constitutes gendered approaches is guaranteed to fail. The ways in which women and girls are materially disadvantaged by many educational institutions remains unchanged. Furthermore, boys from socially marginalised groups are also let down by such policies. The collection provides insight into the processes by which such failures and problems occur and as such provides a resource for change. The continuing agenda for educationalists is the critical and proactive engagement with both the theoretical and practical implications of 'gender sensitive' work. This engagement can only be useful when coupled with firm political commitment to transformative outcomes across all educational and related sites.

References

Apple, M. (1995). *Education and Power*. New York: Routledge.
Blackmore, J. (1999). *Troubling Women: Feminism, Leadership and Educational Change*. Milton Keynes: Open University Press.
Burke, P. J. (2002). *Accessing Education: Effectively Widening Participation*. Stoke-on-Trent: Trentham Books.
Cherland, M. R. (1994). *Private Practices: Girls Reading Fiction and Creating Identity*, London: Taylor and Francis.
Epstein, D., Elwood, J., Hey, V. and Maw, J. (1998). Schoolboy Frictions: Feminism and 'Failing Boys'. In D. Epstein, J. Elwood, V. Hey, and J. Maw, (eds.) *Failing Boys? Issues in Gender and Achievement*, Buckingham: Open University Press.

Hey, V. (1997). *The Company She Keeps: An Ethnography of Girls' Friendship.* Buckingham: Open University press.

Kenway, J. and E. Bullen (2001). *Consuming Children: Education, Entertainment, Advertising.* Milton Keynes: Open University Press.

Kenway, J., S. Willis, *et al.* (1997). *Answering Back: Girls, Boys and Feminism in Schools.* St Leonards, NSW: Allen and Unwin.

Raphael Reed, L. (1998). Troubling Boys and Disturbing Discourses on Masculinity and Schooling: a feminist exploration of current debates and interventions concerning boys in school. *Gender and Education,* Vol. 11, No. 1: 93–110.

Slee, R., Weiner, G. and Tomlinson S. (1998). Introduction: School Effectiveness for Whom School Effectiveness for Whom? *Challenges to the School Effectiveness and School Improvement Movements* London: Falmer Press.

Stone, L., Ed. (1994). *The Education Feminism Reader.* London: Routledge.

Tsolidis, G. (2001). *Schooling, Diaspora and Gender: Being Feminist and Being Different.* Milton Keynes: Open University Press.

Walkerdine, V. (1997). *Daddy's Girl: Young Girls and Popular Culture.* Basingstoke and London: Macmillan.

Weiler, K., G. Weiner and R. Yates (2001). Series Introduction to P. Dalton, Gendering Art Education: Modernism, Identity and Critical Feminism. Milton Keynes: Open University Press.

Part I
Political and Policy Contexts

1
A Feminist Critique of Public Policy Discourses about Educational Effectiveness

Miriam E. David

Introduction

This chapter provides a feminist critique of the development of public policy discourses about school effectiveness and improvement, in the context of globalisation and social transformations. The aim of achieving educational effectiveness and school improvements has become an international, or global, policy phenomenon, and is particularly associated with westernised and developed or late modern societies (Giddens, 1998; Slee, Weiner and Tomlinson, 1998; Avalos, 2001). Along with these developments, the social and political movement for educational improvement has shifted the characteristics of policy debates about school effectiveness away from a social welfarist perspective. There have been moves first, towards more fine-grained professional educational strategies, and second, to 'new managerialism', raising public policy discourses that ignore the social, economic and family contexts of education (Morley and Rassool, 1999). Two new and revised public policy discourses have recently emerged from the transformed political movement as strategies to achieve school effectiveness, namely, parental involvement in education and training for paid work. These two public policy discourses have developed from previous social welfare strategies that centred on political rather than professional approaches to education, and are now centred on a mix of social welfare and neoliberal strategies, or what have been named 'the third way' or modernisation project (Giddens, 1998).

Former social welfarist public policy strategies for education aimed to provide equality of educational opportunity by reducing the effects of parental or family backgrounds of either privilege or poverty (David,

1993). Drawing on the contentious debates from the origins of the educational improvement movement of the 1960s and 1970s, the revised public policies, and separately the professional approaches, disregard issues about gender, family and social transformations in the contexts of education (Tomlinson, 2001). They focus solely on professional and educational strategies for school improvement and social change, and the role of school in particular (Mortimore, 1998). Nevertheless, without paying close and detailed attention to the diverse and global contexts of education and social change, the various strategies may militate against the achievements that they hope to bring about. In particular, the strategies may reinforce inequities in terms of diversity – social class, gender, ethnicity and race – that the discourse of improvement aimed to alleviate (Phoenix, 2002).

Taking a feminist perspective, which foregrounds issues about gender equity linked to social class and race/ethnicity, I will provide a critique of these developments in debates about school improvement. At the same time, I will give consideration to an analysis that weaves concerns with economic and social changes, and familial and educational transformations. The debates and developments around educational effectiveness and school improvement have taken place at the same time as have political and social transformations. Forms of social analysis have consequently been developed to aid our understanding of the complexities, contradictions and challenges in those debates (Blackmore, 1999; Morley and Rassool, 1999). The shifts and changes are part of a far more complex pattern of restructuring and transformation in government, political values and policy changes in relation to social welfare, education and employment. They are also intimately linked to the revised ways of understanding and interpreting the shifts and changes by social and educational researchers, and social scientists in government.

Overall, there has been a shift in governance from the social welfarist and corporatist approach of the 1960s and 1970s, towards the new forms of managerialism, public management, introduction of markets, public–private partnerships and consumerism of the 1980s and 1990s. These were associated originally with neoliberalism and neoconservatism, and with what became known, in Britain, as Thatcherism (Arnot, David and Weiner, 1999), but are now also linked with New Labour in Britain and the New Democrats in the US. I want to illustrate the ways in which the debates and discourses about school improvement are both decontextualised, and at the same time being developed as responses to globalisation, whereby educational improvement is critical to social and economic changes on a global scale (Avalos, 2001).

In this chapter, I will focus first on the recent transformations in the emergent policy discourses about educational effectiveness, and the particular development of the two new public policy discourses, drawing examples from Britain and the US. Second, using the perspectives of feminist and poststructural analysis, I will discuss some international research evidence about the experiences of families, parents and children in relation to policy and implementation of educational effectiveness. This evidence is drawn from parents, children and young people's accounts and narratives, and illustrates some of the contradictory implications of the policy discourses for gender equity. By reviewing social and feminist evidence about the practices of families, and mothers especially, living in what are now considered socially excluded circumstances, it can be demonstrated how these public policy discourses do not attend to 'evidence' but remain ideologically and politically driven. I will show that strategies to deal with social exclusion and educational effectiveness in changing contexts militate against gender equity. They do so first, for families in poor economic circumstances, or for those who are socially excluded, especially mothers who are rearing children on their own; and second, for young people in regard to their education, their gender and sexual identities, and their future work and family lives.

The two public policy discourses

In developing new arguments about educational effectiveness and school improvement, current international policy debates have begun to take on a wider canvas especially amongst social democrats, such as New Labour in Britain and the New Democrats in the US. The initial and original movements for school improvement, called social welfarism, drew on social research and evidence from public policy debates in the late 1960s (Mishra, 1986). These heavily contested debates centred on the social relations between education, schooling and the contexts of education such as communities and families (David, 1993). Social scientific research was developed and used as part of the process of policy development around equality of educational opportunity. This research attained its high point in the 1960s in the US (see especially Coleman, 1966; Silver, 1994). The debates focused chiefly on issues of social class and individual opportunities, and raised questions about the balance between social and educational strategies, and how to achieve greater educational opportunities. Whilst one aspect of the policy debates focused on public policies around education and in relation to social class, others focused only on a variety of strategies

within education, aiming to enhance professionalism and educational policies, rather than to develop political and social democratic approaches to educational involvement. These academic and intellectual approaches have been the subject of numerous reviews within the social and political sciences, on the basis of social class, race, ethnicity or gender (Silver, 1994). Whilst the links between education and other issues such as family and employment have been analysed and debated politically, they did not feature as central in the developing policy and professional or research debates about school improvement (Morley and Rassool, 1999).

Historically, strategies to achieve educational effectiveness tended to be confined to education, and they became part of a professional educational movement for school effectiveness. The phenomenon of building school improvement thus treated schools as institutions in their own right, devoid of social context, and emphasised strategies within schools and amongst educators, teachers and educational professionals. This professional educational movement mapped on to wider economic, social and political changes that eventually surfaced as forms of globalisation, including economic, political and social transformations. In particular, these shifts can also be seen as part of a far more complex pattern of restructuring in governance and policy in relation to social welfare, education and employment.

Two key shifts may be identified away from the social welfarist approaches dominant in the 1960s and 1970s, whereby political responsibilities for social welfare and education centred on public and political strategies aimed at equality of opportunities. The first shift is to neoliberal strategies of the 1980s and early 1990s, in which governing responsibilities moved towards concerns with individualism and individual responsibilities for one's own welfare and education, along with moves towards private rather than public responsibilities, including privatisation and marketisation of public services. A feature of these developments was management of new forms of risk, as identified by Beck (1992). The second key shift is to strategies that have increasingly been referred to, in Britain, as 'the third way', balancing between public and private provisions, and responsibilities for social and educational needs. In this latter respect, these new approaches emphasise individualism and individual responsibilities, and downplay the role of collective and social approaches to education. However, they do give some recognition to family and community contexts of education for particular groups of individuals identified as 'at risk of social exclusion'. These notions draw upon developing

European, international and global notions of strategies to deal with social and economic changes.

These two key shifts, however, are identified chiefly from the perspectives of professional and political approaches to education, rather than from the perspectives of those now considered to be consumers in the educational marketplace (Morley and Rassool, 1999). More recently, attention is being focused on social change, on the effects of globalisation and on changing political and socio-economic contexts. And yet, the need to address social, family and cultural diversity amongst those involved has not become central, or even peripheral, to these developing policy discourses (Walkerdine *et al.*, 2001).

At the same time, there is recognition of the shifting responsibilities of government, leaders and managers of education to deal with these complex social, economic and cultural changes in traditional policy terms. Simply put, social and economic transformations have brought with them political shifts and policy changes that move beyond traditional left and right. Privatisation is occurring through the introduction of market forces into public services. Increasingly, the boundaries of responsibilities are shifting between government, education and individuals in different family contexts. This shift had also been identified in the balance between the personal, private and public, emphasising the need for individuals and families to take responsibilities for their own lives in terms of constructing their identities through education and work (Bullen, Kenway and Hey, 2000; Kelly, 2000). Social researchers have also begun to develop critical reflections and analyses of these complex social and political developments. Individualisation, risk and reflexivity have become the hallmarks of these developments as understood by sociological analysts (Beck, 1992; Beck and Beck-Gersheim, 1996). Understanding the risks associated with a range of social and political issues, which were formerly the collective responsibility of social welfare governments aiming to provide forms of social protection, has been identified as a key to social transformations (Mishra, 1986).

The language of policy-makers about these perspectives also draws on new forms of 'performativity' through commercialism and marketing, emphasising 'excellence' and 'high standards'. Fairclough (2000) has developed a cogent analysis of the 'language' of New Labour in Britain, arguing that 'the ... inherent importance of language in government is enhanced in the case of New Labour. New Labour's promotional way of governing means that language becomes an even more important part of the action of government' (2000, p. 157). In addition, notions of 'evidence' about performance and management have also become integral to the emerging discourses of public policy. These are predicated on concepts of social and public policy research as traditionally defined through positivist methods (Morley and Rassool, 1999). Although equity and change are issues that are addressed in the public policy discourses about school improvement and effectiveness, they have been defined in very specific and traditional ways. A series of discursive shifts has occurred in the identification and naming of these issues (Fairclough, 2000). These shifts tend to be about social and economic circumstances, and family backgrounds in terms of a focus on poverty and social exclusion; they are not about social class (Levitas, 1997). Indeed, Levitas has shown clearly the discursive shifts in policy developments over social class and opportunities for employment and social welfare. She identified three conceptually distinct social democratic perspectives through an analysis of the Labour Party's different approaches in the 1990s: the moral underclass debate (MUD); the social integrationist debate (SID); and the redistributive approach to equal opportunities (RED). Levitas's argument was that New Labour tended towards the middle path, or 'way', in developing its language of social inclusion and exclusion, rather than toward traditional approaches to social welfare with an emphasis on redistributive policies.

This kind of analysis has also been provided by other commentators on New Labour's developing approach, variously termed a modernization project, neo-liberal project, or as the 'third way' (Giddens, 1998; David, 1999). Although there is little consensus on the terminology used to describe the overall project, most commentators agree on the shifts from a social democratic and welfare approach, toward accommodation of the new right and Thatcherite approaches of the 1980s and 1990s. In particular, this shift in approach has included the growing development of market forces, consumerism and the involvement of the private sector in provision of public services. Nevertheless, there has also been some attempt to redefine the terrain of education, and the social, moving away from an emphasis on a collective definition of equality of opportunities, toward a much more individualistic notion with an assumption of individual responsibilities.

Moreover, the New Labour project has not taken up the revised forms of understanding and interpretation of sociologists; in particular it is not addressing questions of gender explicitly. However, within all the policy proposals and developments, the project implicitly retains a notion of 'family values', as specified originally through what Levitas called the 'moral underclass debate'. Here, commitment was retained to traditional patriarchal family values, and the underclass was regarded as those single parents who had not adhered to traditional values. Equity is viewed in terms of social, racial, ethnic and cultural differences and diversity, and is to be achieved in the context of global social change and economic transformations. The debates and texts recognise increasing social change, draw on particular kinds of evidence, and identify the need for more fine-grained strategies and solutions to the issues, with an emphasis on identifying standards of excellence in teaching and learning.

Thus the two policy discourses, which are both linked and yet mutually contradictory, have emerged to address how educational effectiveness can be achieved for all in these changing and increasingly complex circumstances. The first discourse specifies the greater involvement of parents, families and communities in education; the second emphasises education and training for forms of paid employment, thus advocating the necessity of paid work as a solution to poverty. In this latter debate, poverty is reconstructed according to social exclusion or inclusion, rather than social class. Specific groups are targeted, especially young women and mothers, in settings where educational standards appear to be failing or where they have avoided paid work through parenthood or gendered and potential motherhood.

The public policy discourse of family involvement in education

The first public policy discourse illustrates the discursive shifts in political rhetoric about how to ensure educational effectiveness and 'excellence' through a closer involvement of families and communities in education. This takes a very general form of developing home–school relations, or family and education partnerships. The terms of the discourse have shifted considerably over the last 30 years, from when notions of family and parental involvement were embryonic (David, 1993), and subject to close scrutiny and analysis, to assertions of the necessity of parental involvement and the elevation of that concept to a principle. This principle is 'a one size fits all approach', but with a plethora of initiatives and strategies within the more general educational discourse, all of which expect and require more individual involvement and responsibility, especially for socially excluded groups such as young and teenage mothers.

There is little review of the varied and diverse elements of parental involvement in the context of global, social and familial transformations (Duncan and Edwards, 1999). Policy proposals, texts and arguments draw on very particular public notions of evidence and research as critical to the development of more fine-grained policy proposals and forms of implementation through deeply significant shifts in the public discourses. These arguments have often been specifically constructed for this purpose. For instance, over a decade ago, at the height of the transformation in public policy discourses from equality to quality about how to achieve educational effectiveness, a selective approach to research evidence was intentionally used. The US Secretary of Education, prompted by the establishment of America's National Educational Goals of 1990, argued that parental involvement in children's education was vital for the strategy of educational effectiveness:

> Thirty years of research tells us that the starting point of putting children on the road to excellence is parental involvement in their children's education. (Richard Riley, US Secretary of Education, US Department of Education, 1996; cited in Shartrand *et al.*, 1997, Harvard Family Education Project, p. 3)

More recently, these public policy arguments, based on particular views of 'evidence' and often cited more as assertions than arguments, have been developed as part of New Labour's public policy discourse and subsequent strategies for educational effectiveness. Once in power, in May 1997, the first New Labour Secretary of State for Education in Britain, David Blunkett, expressed similar views in numerous speeches and addresses. It was perhaps best articulated as part of his introduction to promoting new policy proposals for education. Much of the rhetoric of new forms of educational governance was then less explicitly recognised, although the key elements were already being put into place. Thus, the initial developments mixed the languages of traditional social welfare with that of modernisation in relation to education and achievement (DfEE, 1997).

These emergent notions of family involvement in, or partnership between, families, communities and education, which draw on the growing social scientific literature and research, have also influenced public policy developments and reforms of education. In particular, the strength of the political arguments about parental involvement in education internationally has been growing with the development of new public policy discourses, associated with the more global developments of how to achieve educational effectiveness. This principle has been incorporated into various forms of legislation and/or become part of more official discourses in several countries in the last decade.

Within the last ten years, the concept of family involvement in education has become part of federal legislation in the US and a statutory requirement in Britain. For example, in 1994, the US Congress, under a neoliberal administration, formalised parent and family involvement as a key component of national educational reform toward educational excellence (Shartrand *et al.*, 1997). This trend has also become part of a wider development in transporting policies internationally and globally (Avalos, 2002). Through its colonialist or imperialist policies and strategies for education, associated with revised and neoliberal reforms, the US has exported notions of family involvement and parental partnerships with education. For example, in developing a strategy to rebuild the Balkans in the wake of the wars, the US government, together with various corporations and religious organisations, has proposed that parents need to be involved in building communities and schools for their own children (Smit *et al.*, 2001).

By contrast, in Britain, one of the first developments in educational policy under a New Labour administration was the School Standards and Framework Act 1998. This Act legislated for a whole range of home–school relations through statutory home–school agreements and homework policies that included the following: study support and homework centres; literacy and numeracy strategies; parental involvement at home and at school; and various forms of parenting education. Thus, public policy discourses about educational effectiveness, advanced by a range of political perspectives that incorporate a mix of public and private strategies, include the principle of family involvement and parental partnerships with education.

These public policy discourses have continued to assume a traditional patriarchal family model where both parents live together, ignoring the mounting international evidence about diverse social and family life changes. The array of evidence includes changes in family structures, forms and practices in relation to employment, personal relations within families, gender and generation. The discourses continue to draw selectively on concepts and principles about relatively traditional upper- and middle-class family practices in relation to their children's education. Parents or mothers are assumed to be involved with supporting education at home, through homework and other extracurricular activities; at school, through either monitoring or attending and contributing to school activities; and in the larger community by developing social networks and participating in community activities.

In Britain, there has also been an array of new strategies to extend forms of parental and family involvement to ensure the goal of educational 'excellence for the many, not just the few' (Blunkett, 1999). Although these strategies build on the general principle of parental involvement, they are aimed at particular parents in circumstances where they may be at risk of poverty and social exclusion, formerly known as educationally and/or socially disadvantaged. Levitas (1997) identified various revised educational strategies including the following: Education Action Zones (EAZ), which build on traditional forms of targeted policy initiatives; and Excellence in Cities, which develops new linked education and health measures for areas identified as socially and economically disadvantaged, whereby educational activities may be specifically targeted. In particular, the focus has been on involving parents either in their children's schools or in their own learning. In addition, there have been specific strategies, such as Sure Start (David, 1999), which link educational initiatives with health and social service measures, especially for very young children and their mothers.

Paid work as the solution: The second public policy discourse

The targeted strategies discussed above are also linked with the second public policy discourse about social inclusion and exclusion, and consequent educational effectiveness. This discourse advances training and skills for paid employment for young people – boys and girls alike – as specific measures to ensure educational effectiveness. Thus, paid employment has become the mantra for this public policy discourse (O'Connor *et al.*, 1999). A key element in the New Labour project is the re-emphasis on paid employment as necessary for ensuring equality of opportunity and avoiding poverty. This second shift harkens back to the neoliberal project rather than the social democratic approach of equality of opportunity. This shift has its roots in nineteenth-century approaches to poverty and welfare. Poor women, and women raising their children alone, are not entitled to special treatment in their capacity as mothers, but are to be seen as potential workers, alongside men.

The plethora of corresponding initiatives disregards gender and parenthood. It includes providing services to enable mothers of young children to seek and find paid employment. It aims to ensure paid work variously through an array of initiatives that borrow names and titles from poor law and US social welfare approaches, including what is now called the 'New Deal' (Fairclough, 2000). Financial and social service support is offered to families with young and dependent children through taxation, working families tax credits, child credits, child care services and early education initiatives.

This public policy discourse was revived and became dominant in the US in the early 1990s as part of welfare reform, drawing initially on experiments and experiences in Wisconsin (Bloch, 1999). It also drew on a moral debate about the growing underclass (Levitas, 1997). New Labour in Britain has borrowed and transported it back to Britain extensively. Interestingly, however, some other countries, traditionally dependent on borrowing British approaches to social welfare and education, have not adopted traditional measures with such zeal, but have modified the more punitive elements. For example, Canada, Australia and some European countries, whilst developing managerialist perspectives on social welfare, have developed new, contrasting and less punitive public policies for children.

The 'moral' discourse has become a key component of the New Labour project, where education has been carefully linked with these revised approaches to social welfare. In particular, revised views of what constitutes social class, and social disadvantage, have been adopted in keeping with a more individualistic stance and approach to public policies. Shifts in public policy terminology consequently centre on notions, also borrowed from European projects, about social inclusion and exclusion, and are part of a growing global discourse. This has become a key element of New Labour's modernisation project whereby social inclusion is used to ensure involvement of citizens with individual opportunities for paid employment. Thus, the New Labour government set up an inter-government body, called the Social Exclusion Unit, which was charged with responsibility for ensuring development of public policies across the spectrum. An expression of this public policy discourse can be found in a policy review document from the government's Social Exclusion Unit (SEU, 1999).

The government also evolved specific strategies targeted on groups of children and young people in schools and educational institutions deemed to be in danger of social 'exclusion'. Social inclusion is increasingly defined in terms of access to work or employment, rather than in relation to the traditional notions of social class, and for men and women alike, regardless of family responsibilities such as parenthood (Levitas, 1997). Education and training are identified as necessary to enable young people to learn how to find work rather than rely on social security to deal with potential poverty. There is a plethora of public policies that link education with social welfare, social security and health or medical strategies.

There is also concern about young people, especially when boundaries between parents and children are not in accordance with traditional approaches to family life and 'family values'. Indeed, a particular feature of these strategies in Britain is concern about teenage parenthood, defined in non-gendered terms, and yet identifying different strategies through education for girls and boys. Teenage pregnancy especially has been identified as a major social problem and has assumed the status of a moral panic (SEU, 1999; Bullen *et al.*, 2000; Kelly, 2000). The government has developed guidance for sex and relationship education as an educational strategy to prevent teenage pregnancies, aiming to ensure that schoolgirls and teenage girls avoid immature parenthood and that boys learn about the responsibilities of parenthood. It is also argued that there is a continuing need for young mothers to be in education, employment or training to avoid poverty and social exclusion.

Whilst the new language of public policy discourse about paid employment to avoid social exclusion and to achieve school effectiveness centres on both boys and girls, it focuses selectively on each, and articulates particular moral concerns about gendered parenthood. Mothers especially are targeted. Such young women are deemed to have behaved inappropriately, fracturing the balances between parenthood and childhood. Thus they are to be provided with special and specific treatment, differentiating them from socially included young people, in the hope and expectation that this will provide appropriate examples to avoid inappropriate forms of future parenthood. This differential treatment, however, is carried out in the name of new forms of educational effectiveness and social inclusion.

Research evidence about parental involvement, paid employment and educational effectiveness

Although the public policy discourses acknowledge the importance of research and evidence for developing detailed strategies for educational effectiveness, this evidence is drawn selectively and does not necessarily arise from academic social research (Morley and Rassool, 1999). The first public policy discourse argues that educational effectiveness can be achieved only by developing home–school relations or family involvement in children's education. This discussion draws on the evidence of developmental and social psychology and the assumption of a traditional patriarchal family form. It does not consider gender equity. It thus appears that the complex social and statistical evidence about changing families in a global context, such as the implications of changing patterns of marriage, divorce, cohabitation or consensual unions for patterns and practices of parenthood, have not influenced the practices of policy-makers. In particular, international trends towards divorce and lone parenthood, amongst all social classes, have received scant attention with respect to these general family-education policies and practices. Yet, there is considerable evidence about trends in divorce and lone motherhood internationally (Kiernan *et al.*, 1998; O'Connor *et al.*, 1999). In England, for instance, two out of five children are now born to mothers who are not married and may be living alone (Haskey, 1998).

The research evidence drawing on international and transnational scholarship, especially the increasing body of feminist work, demonstrates that it is usually mothers who have the regular responsibilities for their children's education, whatever their family circumstances and social, sexual or racial situations. Mothers may be living alone and/or divorced or separated, or may be cohabiting or involved in what the Norwegians call consensual unions (Clarke and Jensen, 2000). Equally, there are changing family patterns internationally that push for a greater involvement of mothers in paid employment. Mothers' various accounts from diverse families and settings from a range of studies in the US, Canada, Australia, Scandinavia and Britain demonstrate the constraints and pressures that educational reforms, policies and practices place upon them. In particular, they show the difficulties and pressures of the changing requirements on parents, especially mothers, to be involved regularly and routinely with both their children's education and with paid employment (Griffith and Smith, 1990; Luttrell, 1997; Crozier, 2000; Tsolidis, 2000; Phoenix, 2002).

All the studies reveal that strategies for parental involvement have complex implications for mothers in these varied circumstances. Diversities and differences in their practices in relation to schools and their children's education influence how effective they may be as parents in developing their children's education (Waggoner and Griffith, 1998).

Mothers' approaches vary as Ribbens-McCarthey (2000) has shown in discussing maternal mediations of children's education. However, all mothers struggle with helping and enhancing their children's education, despite their own prior involvement with education that may have left them devoid of appropriate resources and strategies. There is also evidence from research studies of mothers that they become involved in education as mature students specifically in order to improve their children's educational development (Tsolidis, 2000). Mirza and Reay (2000) have intriguingly demonstrated that Saturday schools are an educational strategy of black mothers to improve their children's schooling. The mothers engage in extracurricular activities, outside conventional schooling, and at times outside the traditional forms of paid employment, specifically aimed at educational effectiveness for their own children. Yet such strategies increase burdens on mothers, already in tightly constrained circumstances, especially with the added burdens of increasing marketisation and consumerism in education, to achieve educational effectiveness (Walkerdine *et al.*, 2001).

Comparisons between mothers' and fathers' activities with respect to extracurricular activities, homework and subjects also reveal the stronger roles of mothers in day-to-day involvement, with fathers' involvement confined to key decisions regarding school, subject choices, subject interest and regarding expertise in maths and computing (West *et al.*, 1998). These patterns of differential involvement appear whether parents live together, are separated or divorced, or are step-parents. There are complex issues in relation to involvement in the education of sons and daughters, and there is no simple equation, except that fathers are typically the more distant parent, whether or not they live with the children. Even divorced fathers may exert an influence on key educational decisions, for example, involvement and investment in higher education (Reay *et al.*, 2001).

The second public policy discourse acknowledges evidence of the global trends in changing families, and in particular, points to the increasing numbers of lone parent families who are in poverty (SEU, 1999). These strategies of encouraging paid employment to achieve educational effectiveness do not recognise the implications for the single mothers who have to find paid work and, at the same time, support their children's education. Thus, this policy discourse is at odds with that of the first policy discourse of an overarching general strategy of parental involvement in children's education to increase educational effectiveness. In particular, there seems to be no official recognition of the dilemmas that may be created for teenage and/or lone mothers with respect to paid work, and the necessity of parental involvement in their children's education. These dilemmas would indeed hinder educational effectiveness for their children, as much of the evidence about single mothers' strategies for education would indicate.

There is, however, a growing body of social research evidence that not all countries pursue the same strategies for mothers in poverty with attempts to alleviate potential social exclusion (SEU, 1999). There are diverse approaches internationally to single mothers' paid work that provide alternatives to social exclusion and inclusion (Duncan and

Edwards, 1997). This social research evidence highlights the dilemmas of the second public policy discourse of paid employment for mothers living in a variety of constrained circumstances and situations of poverty. In Britain, single mothers' accounts from a diversity of social, racial or ethnic backgrounds demonstrate how difficult they find juggling paid work and educational involvement with their children. This is particularly the case if they are living in poverty or constrained financial circumstances (David *et al.*, 1997; Standing, 1999). These accounts also confirm the evidence of Kelly (2000) and others in Canada and the US.

Further confirming social research evidence of the contradictory approaches to school improvement and effectiveness through parental involvement in education and lone mothers' paid employment can be found in Weiss's (2000) albeit small-scale but indicative study in the US. Weiss's ongoing longitudinal mixed methods study looked at how child, family, school and community factors shape the developmental pathways of diverse, young, low-income children in three contrasting American communities. She identified four maternal strategies to balance home, school and work connections, and has identified maternal employment as the critical determinant of both involvement with kindergarten children's learning at home and at school. Whilst some of the British official reviews (Hallgarten, 2000) of evidence about parental involvement and mothers' work with young children is more equivocal about their influences on children's attainment, they do not take account of the specific groups of mothers who may be identified as at risk of social exclusion. Yet, it is precisely this evidence that is crucial to understanding the twin effects of these discourses on gender equity for current parents and for future generations.

Thus the debates about family involvement in education to achieve educational effectiveness have not only ignored issues of gender equity with respect to parents, and mothers in certain family and socially excluded circumstances, but have also not fully considered the changing forms of gender equity amongst children and young people. There are new and complex ways in which gender equity in educational achievements has developed over the last two decades, as associated with social, global and economic changes, including markets and consumerism. Social research evidence would now indicate that boys' and girls' achievements in public examinations are very similar (Arnot *et al.*, 1999). However, in the policy arena this has created a moral panic about the question of the balance of achievements between boys and girls, where the gender gap has been closing. The debate has largely focused on boys' relative underachievement, rather than on improved standards for all (Epstein *et al.*, 1997). More complex questions about changing gender and sexual identities in relation to racialised, social and educational transformations are barely alluded to, yet the research literature is replete with fascinating examples (Mac An Ghaill, 1994; Mikel Brown, 1998; Walkerdine *et al.*, 2001). In particular, there is evidence from the perspectives, understandings, and narratives of new generations of boys and girls (Arnot *et al.*, 1999; Walkerdine *et al.*, 2001). These give voice to how young people develop new and more complex gender and sexual identities than previous generations, in relation to work and family (Kenway *et al.*, 1997; Lingard and Douglas, 1999). Some of this has to do with changing social contexts and with changing policy towards making individuals cope with their own emerging identities of masculinities and femininities in emerging new contexts of risk where reflexivity and self-assessment become more important (Whitehead, 1998). Thus, there are complex relations between gender equity for parents and children in the context of emerging policies to achieve educational effectiveness. The global transformations in social, economic and educational contexts have had differential impacts on children and young people in school such that they have begun to highlight and transform differential achievements between boys and girls, mediated by social class, race and ethnicity. In particular there is evidence of a growing polarisation between white working-class boys and middle-class girls in terms of school-based educational achievements (Epstein *et al.*, 1997). Yet, the official policy discourses about educational effectiveness have not attended to these nuanced differences but only to aiming to achieve ungendered educational effectiveness, whilst targeting girls' inappropriate sexual behaviour for specific treatment. Thus, parenthood takes on specific meanings in specific contexts, whilst official discourses appear to articulate an uncomplicated meaning about such issues (Walkerdine *et al.*, 2001).

Conclusions: Contradictory implications of policies of educational effectiveness for gender equity

In conclusion, the two public policy discourses about educational effectiveness, namely, parental involvement in education and paid employment, have been developed as key to the modernisation project of a socially inclusive society, but have been selective in the kinds of evidence that has informed their strategies. Whilst official discourses have raised issues and questions about equity, this has centred on social and economic matters, rather than issues about gender equity. These discourses have been directed at issues about social inclusion and exclusion, aiming to target key groups made up largely of women as mothers, especially young mothers. Global social and economic changes have been identified as crucial to such educational strategies, however, these have been identified in specific ways that have not noted the gender dimensions of such changes in family and economic life. Such dimensions have remained implicit, and yet the policies have in fact centred on gendered strategies, requiring in particular mothers' involvement in paid work and education at the same time. There is now substantial social research evidence to demonstrate changing patterns of family life and the emergence of gender and sexual identities that are influenced by such broad social changes. On the other hand, there is also targeting of specific groups of young people, especially young women, to carry the burdens of social and economic change in order to achieve educational effectiveness and school improvements for the next generations.

Public policy-makers have not attended to the array of social research evidence of the voices of mothers nor those of young people. The strategies have contradictory implications for mothers, who are increasingly expected to be involved in their children's education, in increasingly sophisticated ways. At the same time mothers, particularly those at risk of social exclusion, are also increasingly expected to be involved in paid employment, and thus are often supported with public policy strategies, such as child care and training programmes for paid employment. These all recognise the changing nature of the labour market and increasing skills. Additional burdens are placed on mothers living in poverty, especially on those who have little support and help from partners and family members. The complexities of family life are acknowledged in the discourse as being resolved through paid employment. Whilst this may be important and valuable, it cannot reduce social or gender inequities since such mothers are then not able to fully support and help their children's education. This paradox is abundantly clear in the increasing social research evidence from mothers in a diversity of social and economic circumstances. On the other hand, official public policy discourses about educational effectiveness rely on parental involvement both at home and in school to accomplish educational aims and goals. In particular, marketisation of schools and education has increased consumerism both within schools and families. This adds to the social and sexual differentiation of educational achievements and effectiveness.

Similarly, such mothers are frequently blamed for their children's lack of educational achievements, especially their sons' underachievement. Thus, strategies have become universal for all parents but do not deal with the specific needs of opportunities for all, or rather do not reduce gender inequities, or those based on social and racial diversity. Indeed, such strategies may increase gender inequities on a class and racial basis, for young single mothers and their sons from similar ethnic/racial and social circumstances. Given the global social and educational changes taking place, gender equity could become a central part of educational effectiveness for both parents and children of this and future generations who are increasingly expected to forge their own gender, sexual and work identities.

Finally, issues about gender equity in educational effectiveness in relation to families and young people have been occluded in official and public policy discourses about social inclusion. Yet, the strategies clearly have differential impacts and intended differential consequences for groups of men and women in different social and economic circumstances. Thus, parental involvement has very different impacts on mothers (and fathers where they share households) in diverse family and educational circumstances, and may enhance rather than eradicate social and gender inequities, and forms of social exclusion. Similarly, official discourses about paid employment as a key strategy for eradicating social exclusion and achieving educational effectiveness may have different consequences for gender equity especially for young women becoming young mothers and for their children, regardless of gender.

In the contexts of global social, economic and family changes, we as educational researchers could contribute to more effective public policies and practices by providing the social research evidence that highlights issues of social and sexual equity (Shartrand *et al.*, 1997). This could provide more nuanced and sophisticated evidence of the impacts, effects and influences of strategies for educational effectiveness in relation to the details of the specific local, national and international contexts of social, economic, and familial transformations. Public policy discourses might then tackle issues of gender equity for a diversity of families and future generations of children and young people, countering the differential and diverse effects of policies aimed at achieving educational effectiveness in a socially inclusive society. Current public policy discourses of educational effectiveness through parental involvement in education and paid employment exacerbate rather than eradicate inequities in relation to gender, sexual diversity, social class and race/ethnicity.

References

Arnot, M., David, M. and Weiner, G. (1999). *Closing the Gender Gap: Post War Education and Social Change.* Cambridge: Polity Press.

Avalos, B. (2001). Policy Issues Derived from the Internationalisation of Education: Their Effects on Developing Countries. Paper presented at ICSEI, *Equity, Globalisation and Change.* Toronto, 5–9 January.

Beck, U. (1992). *The Risk Society.* Cambridge: Polity Press.

Beck, U. and Beck-Gersheim, E. (1996). *The Normal Chaos of Love.* Cambridge: Polity Press.

Blackmore, C. (1999). *Troubling Women: Feminism, Leadership and Educational Change.* Buckingham: Open University Press.

Bloch, M. N. (1999). Welfare State Reform and Child Care: A Critical Review of Recent U.S. and International Trends. Presented at *The Child and the State: Restructuring the Governing Discourses of the Child, Family, and Education.* Conference held at University of Wisconsin-Madison.

Blunkett, D. (1999). Foreword to *Excellence and Standards in Education* (White Paper). London: HMSO.

Bullen, E., Kenway, J. and Hey, V. (2000). New Labour, Social Exclusion and Educational Risk Management: The Case of Gymslip Mums. *British Educational Research Journal* 26/3, 441–57.

Clarke, L. and Jensen, A.-M. (2000). Cohabitation in Britain and Norway: A Childhood Perspective. Paper presented at the final conference of ESRC Children 5–16 Research Programme, *Children: Making their Future?* 20–21 October, London.

Coleman, J. (1966). *On Equality of Educational Opportunity.* US Dept of HEW.

Crozier, G. (2000). *Parents and Schools: Partners or Protagonists?* Stoke-on-Trent and Sterling: Trentham Books.

David, M. E. (1993). *Parents, Gender and Education Reform.* Cambridge: Polity Press.

David, M. E. (1999). Home, Work, Families and Children: New Labour, New Directions and New Dilemmas. *International Studies in the Sociology of Education,* Vol. 9, No. 3, 209–29.

David, M. E. (2002). Teenage Parenthood is Bad for Parents and Children: A Feminist Critique of Family, Education and Social Welfare Policies and Practices. In M. N. Bloch and T. S. Popkewitz (eds), *Restructuring the Governing Patterns of the Welfare State.* New York and London: Routledge/Falmer.

David, M. E., Davies, J., Edwards, R., Reay, D. and Standing, K. (1997). Choice within Constraints: Mothers and Schooling. *Gender and Education,* Vol. 9, No. 4, 397–410.

DfEE (1997). *Excellence in Schools.* White Paper, London: HMSO.

Duncan, S. and Edwards, R. (eds.) (1997). *Single Mothers in an International Context: Mothers or Workers?* London: UCL Press.

Epstein, D., Elwood, J., Hey, V. and Maw, J. (eds.) (1997). *Failing Boys? Issues in Gender and Achievement.* Buckingham and Philadelphia: Open University Press.

Fairclough, N. (2000). *New Labour, New Language?* London: Routledge.

Giddens, A. (1998). *The Third Way: The Renewal of Social Democracy.* Cambridge: Polity Press.

Griffith, A. and Smith, D. E. (1990). What Did You do in School Today? Mothering, Schooling and Social Class. *Perspectives on Social Problems* Vol. 2, 3–24.

Hallgarten, J. (2000). *Parents Exist OK?* London: IPPR.

Haskey, J. (1998). Families: Their Historical Context, and Recent Trends in the Factors influencing Their Formation and Dissolution. In M. E. David (ed.), *The Fragmenting Family: Does it Matter?* London: The Institute of Economic Affairs Choice in Welfare No. 44.

Kelly, D. (2000). *Pregnant with Meaning: Teen Mothers and the Politics of Inclusive Schooling.* New York: Peter Lang.

Kenway, J., Willis, S., Blackmore, J. and Rennie, S. (1998). *Answering Back: Girls, Boys and Feminism in Schools.* London and Sydney: Allen and Unwin.

Kiernan, K., Land, H. and Lewis, J. (1998). *Lone Motherhood in 20th Century Britain: From Footnote to Front Page.* Oxford: The Clarendon Press.

Levitas, R. (1997). *The Inclusive Society? Social Exclusion and New Labour.* London: Macmillan.

Lingard, R. and Douglas, P. (1999). *Men Engaging Feminisms: Pro-feminism, Backlashes and Schooling.* Buckingham and Philadelphia: Open University Press.

Luttrell, W. (1997). *School-Smart and Motherwise: Working-class Women's Identity and Schooling.* London and New York: Routledge.

Mac An Ghaill, M. (1994). *The Making of Men.* Buckingham and Philadelphia: Open University Press.

Mikel Brown, L. (1998). *Raising their Voices: The Politics of Girls' Anger.* Cambridge, Mass.: Harvard University Press.

Mirza H. and Reay, D. (2000). Black Women Educators and the Third Space. In M. Arnot and J. Dilla bough (eds), *Challenging Democracy.* London: Routledge/Falmer.

Mishra, R. (1986). *The Welfare State and Society.* Brighton: Harvester Wheatsheaf.

Morley, L. and Rassool, N. (1999). *School Effectiveness: Fracturing the Discourse.* Brighton and London: Falmer Press.

Mortimore, P. (1998). *The Road to Improvement: Reflections on School Effectiveness.* The Netherlands: Swets and Zeitlinger Lisse.

Noden, P., West, A., David, M. and Edge, A. (1998). Choices and Destinations at Transfer to Secondary School in London. *Journal of Education Policy* Vol. 13, No. 2, 221–36.

O'Connor, J., Orloff, A. and Shaver, S. (1999). *States, Markets and Families: Gender, Liberalism and Social Policy in Australia, Canada, GB and USA.* Cambridge: Cambridge University Press.

Phoenix, A. (1991). *Young Mothers?* Cambridge: Polity Press.

Phoenix, A. (2002). Mapping Present Inequalities to Navigate Future Success: Racialisation and Education. *British Journal of the Sociology of Education* Vol. 23, No. 3.

Reay, D., Davies, J., Ball, S. J. and David, M. (2001). Choices of Degree or Degrees of Choice? Social Class, Race and the Higher Education Choice Process. *Sociology,* Vol. 35, No. 4, 855–74.

Ribbens-McCarthy, J. (2000). Maternal Mediations. Paper presented to ESRC seminar series on Parents and Schools at Bath Spa University College, October.

Shartrand, A. M., Weiss, H., Kreider, H and Lopez, M. E. (1997). *New Skills for New Schools: Preparing Teachers in Family Involvement.* Harvard Family Education Project.

Silver, H. (1994). *Good Schools, Effective Schools: Judgements and their Histories.* London: Cassell.

Slee, R., Weiner, G. and Tomlinson, S. (eds.) (1998). *School Effectiveness for Whom? Challenges to the School Effectiveness and School Improvement Movements*. London: Falmer Press.

Smit, F., van der Woolf, K. and Sleegers, P. (eds.) (2001). *Bridge to the Future*. Institute for Applied Social Sciences, University of Nijmegen, Nijmegen, The Netherlands.

Social Exclusion Unit (1999). *The Changing Welfare State: Opportunity for All: Tackling Poverty and Social Exclusion: First Annual Report*. London: The Stationery Office.

Standing, K. (1999). Lone Mothers and 'Parental Involvement': A Contradiction in Policy? *Journal of Social Policy*, Vol. 28, part 3, 479–517.

Tomlinson, S. (2001). *Education in a Post-welfare Society*. Buckingham: Open University Press.

Tsolidis, G. (2000). *Schooling, Diaspora and Gender*. Buckingham and Philadelphia: Open University Press.

Waggoner, K and Griffith, A. (1998). Parental Involvement in Education: Ideology and Experience. *Journal of a Just and Caring Education*, Vol. 4, No. 1, 65–78.

Walkerdine, V., Lucey, H. and Melody, J. (2001). *Growing up Girl: Psychosocial Explorations of Gender and Class*. London: Palgrave.

Weiss, H. (2000). The Effects of Work on Low Income Mothers' Involvement in their Children's Education at Home and at School. Paper presented at the final conference of ESRC Children 5–16 Research Programme Children: Making their future? 20–21 October London www.esrc.ac.uk/curprog.

West, A., Noden, P., Edge, A., David, M. and Davies, J. (1998). Choices and Expectations at the Primary and Secondary Stages in the State and Private Sectors. *Educational Studies* Vol. 24, No. 1, 45–60.

Whitehead, S. (1998). Disrupted Selves: Resistance and Identity Work in the Managerial Arena. *Gender and Education*, Vol. 10, No. 2, 199–215.

2
Turning it Around: Debating Approaches to Gender and North–South Learning

Helen Poulsen

Introduction: The (re-) emergence of North–South learning

This chapter is concerned with the gender implications of the emergence of 'North–South learning' as a new trend in international development theory and practice. North–South learning is understood as the focus on 'finding solutions for Northern poverty in the experience of the South' (Sweetman, 1997, p. 2): that is, turning around the 'usual process of advice giving' (Thekaekara and Thekaekara, 1994, p. 26) from 'North' to 'South'.[1] For example, participatory approaches to development and gender analysis are used increasingly in the 'North' as well as in the 'South' to address issues such as drug problems in Walsall (Greenwood, 2000). In particular, it focuses on why North–South learning has emerged as a strategy now, and situates the emergence of this tendency in the post-colonial social and political context at global, national and local levels.

This chapter is based on research carried out in 1999, which was based on case studies of three very different UK-based projects that draw on Southern approaches to development. First, the Full Circle Fund (FCF) is a Norwich-based micro-credit programme, adapted from the Grameen Bank model in Bangladesh. Second, the Oxford Development Education Centre (ODEC) has adapted REFLECT for community development work in Oxford. Third, Oxfam's UK Poverty Programme (UKPP), which draws on Oxfam's international experience.

This chapter takes a critical perspective on what is generally assumed to be a positive trend. It highlights, first, the risk that North–South universalises concepts, issues and problems around gender. This can be reinforced by collapsing of economic and cultural aspects of development, so that approaches and strategies are assumed to be objective, value-neutral and gender-blind. Second, North–South learning often uses participatory and community-focused strategies which may be rooted in distorted and romanticised perceptions of the community in the South. These approaches, given the failure of the state in the North to provide equitably, are very attractive. However, they risk importing hidden and conservative ideas about gender, and adding to the unpaid and unvalued burden of women's work.

I begin by looking at the increasing popularity of North–South learning. Then, I consider key literature and background information in the field of gender and development in North and South. A description of the study, including the background of three organisations on which case studies were based, is followed by a discussion of the main findings. The conclusion draws together the threads and aims to address some of the assumptions which underlie North–South learning.

The emergence of North–South learning

In recent years, there has been growing interest in examining common elements in the methods used by NGOs to tackle poverty in North and South (Rossiter, 1998, p. 1). Mayo (1997, p. 53) notes the increasing 'cross-fertilisation of ideas and approaches, to and fro between North and South'. North–South learning covers a wide range of projects, approaches and initiatives. In some cases, tools and methods developed in the South have been applied in the UK. For example, the Community Council for Berkshire used PRA in July 1997 to carry out an assessment of people's needs in Great Hollands housing estate in Bracknell (David and Craig, 1997). The theme of North–South learning has been taken up by the UK government, in particular the Department for International Development (DFID). According to a DFID paper, (Eyben, 1998, pp. 1–3), North–South learning is important because it will help to achieve international development targets, which requires a vision of global social policy to help 'regulate the global economy'.

Academic research, conferences and workshops have focused on comparing deprivation in North and South. For example, a workshop was held on 'Poverty and Social Exclusion in North and South' at the Institute of Development Studies (IDS), University of Sussex in April 1997. This workshop concluded that there was great scope for collaboration and recommended the development of joint North–South projects on specific themes (de Haan and Maxwell, 1998, p. 8). There have been increasing numbers of South to North study visits, in which practitioners and activists examine similar situations and organisations in order to share and exchange ideas. For example, in 1996, Sheela Patel of the Society for Promoting Areas Resources Centres (SPARC) in Bombay, India, visited council estates and tenant and community organisations in England and Scotland. In her report, Patel (1997) emphasised the need to mobilise members of communities, rather than professionals, to develop long-term solutions to the problems of poverty.

Articles on North–South learning have appeared in the UK media, but with quite varied opinions. Thekaekaras and Thekaekara note the hesitancy of the British media to accept the fact that there is poverty in the UK (1994, p. 21). An opinion piece in the *Daily Mail* similarly criticised Oxfam for bringing Stan Thekaekara from India to work with a community group in Matson, Gloucester, on the grounds that it was a waste of money since the UK is a rich country (Oxfam, 1998, p. 28). However, recently two rather more sympathetic articles have been published in the *Guardian*. In one, the Director of the Overseas Development Institute (ODI) suggests that the UK should look to the Third World for solutions to the problems of poverty (Maxwell, 1998). A number of international NGOs have turned their attention to the situation 'at home'. Based partly on the results of the Thekaekaras' visit, Oxfam started its UK Poverty Programme in 1995, with the justification that 15 per cent of British people live in poverty, but also that the gap between richest and poorest is one of the widest in the developed world. (Smith, 1998).

Significantly, one of the main areas or issues considered appropriate for North–South learning is gender. May (1997a, p. 6) suggests that 'patterns of female poverty and exclusion in the UK are consistent with international trends'. Consequently, as Rossiter (1998, p. 17) suggests, gender analysis tools 'could be applied to anti-poverty initiatives in the North'. David (David and Crars, 1997, p. 2) recognises gender analysis as one of the main areas of learning which are currently thought useful for anti-poverty work in the North. Eyben (1998, p. 5) suggests that 'perhaps the most common fault line for social exclusion is gender', and recounts how DFID's gender guidelines were 'enthusiastically seized upon by someone from the Highlands and Islands Development Authority who remarked that this was exactly the kind of thing they had been looking for' (Eyben, 1998, p. 5).

An analysis of these initiatives, projects and reports reveals a range of assumptions about North–South learning:

- That gender is a universally relevant concept, and approaches to gender issues are universally applicable.

- Because there are global similarities in the experience of poverty, that the causes of poverty are globally similar, and anti-poverty development strategies applicable across different contexts.
- North–South learning is a positive shift away from paternalistic models of development which deny the value of 'Southern' knowledge, towards an emphasis on participation and a focus on the community.

Critiques of approaches to gender

This section includes a brief review of key literature and set the global and UK national context for the emergence of North–South learning, situating it as a political question to do with gender, the postcolonial era and decline of the welfare state in the UK. Most agencies have gender policies (German and Randel 1998); gender has become 'not only a desirable attribute, but a development goal of agencies and policy makers' (Jackson and Pearson, 1998, p. 5). In the 1980s, the 'efficiency approach', now predominant in international aid agencies and national governments, gained currency in response to the world economic crisis. Gender policies were justified in terms of contributing to a more efficient and more effective development (Moser, 1993). However, this type of approach reinforced stereotypical representations of Third World women as 'ignorant, poor, uneducated, tradition-bound, domestic, family oriented, victimized'. Furthermore, third world women are not a unified, coherent group, an assumption that denies class, ethnic or racial differences between women (Mohanty, 1988, p. 71).

Empowerment requires the transformation of structures of subordination at all levels. That includes changes in 'law, civil codes, systems of property rights, control over women's bodies, labour codes and the social and legal institutions that underwrite male control and privilege' (Moser, 1993, p. 76). But with its goal of emancipation, governments and international aid agencies perceive empowerment as a threatening approach. Empowerment requires institutional transformation: development institutions and organisations are deeply gendered in their structures (Goetz, 1997, p. 2). Furthermore, the

mythical notion of community cohesion continues to permeate much participatory work, hiding a bias that favours the opinions and priorities of those with more power and the ability to voice themselves publicly. In particular, there is minimal consideration of gender issues and inadequate involvement of women. (Guijt and Kaul Shah, 1998, p. 1)

Critiques of the poverty alleviation agenda

Globalisation means that problems in North and South are seen as interconnected (Lewis, undated). Poverty alleviation has emerged as the main agenda only since 1973, when the World Bank first equated development and poverty alleviation (Culpeper, 1997), and 'for the first time in history, entire nations and countries came to be considered (and consider themselves) as poor, on the grounds that their overall income is insignificant in comparison with those now dominating the world economy. Consequently, national income was introduced as a new global measure for expressing the various stages of economic development' (Rahnema, 1992, p. 161). Anti-poverty strategies, universal, economistic and removed from context, hid other processes of political and cultural domination. (Rahnema, 1992, pp. 162–3). That is, the global poverty agenda legitimises the postwar division of the world into developed/ developing, North and South; obscuring continued political and cultural domination.

Furthermore, 'in development rhetoric, poverty shares the status of the veil, sati or genital mutilation in much of Western/ised feminist rhetoric; symbols of oppression, tradition or patriarchy, these are practices and forces to be eradicated' (Apffel-Marglin and Simons, 1994, p. 33). 'The combination of an instrumental interest in women as the means to the ends of poverty reduction, and the feminisation of poverty discourse has led to a damaging erosion of the differences between gender disadvantage and poverty' (Jackson, 1998, p. 46).

The rise and fall of the welfare state

The current period of late modernity is characterised by transformation of our day-to-day lives and social structures (Giddens, 1991). People in the North are living through a 'crisis of the beliefs and assumptions on which modern society had been founded', and of the 'historic structures of human relations' (Hobsbawm, 1994, p. 10). For Offe, this 'crisis of legitimacy' is the inevitable consequence of the inherent contradictions of the welfare state. That is, the fundamental conflict of interest between the objectives of the welfare state and the demands of private capital on which it depends (Offe, 1984a, p. 138). This leads to the inevitable failure of state function, which leads to the public questioning of state legitimacy, and political and economic crisis. This in turn leads to the emergence of new forms of political action, 'symptomatic of a growing uncertainty about the normative foundations of liberal democratic political systems' (Offe, 1984b, p. 269). The demands of this 'new political paradigm' in which he includes feminism, environmentalism and the peace movement are significantly non-economic. Offe speculates about whether such movements are based on a yearning for a return to a communal past (Offe, 1984b, p. 294).

In summary, although gender is on the development agenda, it is not enough and not always positive. 'Development' and discourses of poverty alleviation obscure complexity of continued economic, political and cultural domination. Furthermore, we are at a time in the North when welfare and our trust in the state are in decline.

The study

The study consisted of case studies of three organisations. 1), the Full Circle Fund (FCF) is a Norwich-based micro-credit for enterprise programme, adapted from the Grameen Bank model. The Grameen Bank is an NGO operating in Bangladesh since 1983, which starts from the assumption that the rural poor have the skills but not the capital to be productive. It therefore provides credit through a model based on group organisation and group collateral for lending (Holcombe, 1995, p. 38). 2), Oxford Development Education Centre (ODEC) has been experimenting with an interpretation of Freirian literacy in community development work with the African Caribbean Day Centre in Oxford. ODEC's approach is inspired by REFLECT (Regenerated Freirian Literacy through Empowering Community Techniques), developed by the UK-based NGO Action Aid since 1993. It draws on Freirian literacy and PRA techniques. Rather than using a primer, each literacy circle produces its own learning materials through analysing their own circumstances (Archer and Cottingham, 1996, p. 12). 3), Oxfam is an international relief, advocacy and development agency working in over 70 countries worldwide. It recently started a small programme in the UK, the UK Poverty Programme (UKPP) which draws on, and contributes to, international learning.

The case study data were analysed from the perspective of gender three different levels: global, national and local. The data were used to explore assumptions outlined in my introduction.

The politics of gender in the global context

Oxfam

Gender is an issue which is understood to justify Oxfam involvement in the UK, in that there are similarities in gender issues between the UK and Oxfam's international programme:

> The impact on women of the economic and social changes arising from structural adjustment programmes internationally has been well-documented. The UK experience suggests striking parallels, in particular on the changing roles for women and men, and on women's time. (May, 1997a, pp. 18–21)

However, a number of problems are implicit in this approach. First, a universal understanding of 'women', and 'women's time' is implied, and differences between women's situations across the world are concealed. Second, women and poverty are linked: '[p]overty in Britain, as elsewhere, has a female face' (Bronstein, 1998). Thus, gender is not addressed as an issue in itself; rather, it is merged with poverty, which can work to reinforce stereotypical representations of women as weak and helpless (Jackson, 1998, p. 46).

ODEC

While ODEC recognises that participatory education is not value-free or neutral, there is silence around the implications of approaches like REFLECT for gender: 'one of the things we're finding is that the tools can be used for anything . . . class and caste and gender . . . what is useful is this radical focus on transforming relationships' (interview, Alison Norris, ODEC). The problem with REFLECT as a framework is that it may be assumed to be gender-blind, that is, have unexplored gender biases. Second, as with other participatory methodologies, the issues that are raised tend to reflect the concerns of facilitators, so that if a facilitator is not gender aware, gender issues may be sidelined. A gender-aware facilitator would recognise, for example, that women as well as men are active in development, that they are constrained in different ways, as potential participants and beneficiaries in the development process; and that they may consequently have differing and sometimes conflicting needs, interests and priorities (May, 1997a, p. 17). However, it should be emphasised that REFLECT is one of a range of approaches that influence ODEC's approach to participatory education.

However, a holistic approach to gender is expressed: 'class and caste and gender... they're all oppressions, they're all interlinked and power relationships... you've got to look at all of it really' (interview, Alison Norris, ODEC). Gender issues have emerged as an important issue in some cases, however. For example, a group of single mothers in Oxford had to cope with sexual harassment in order to keep their jobs in nightclubs. Alison Norris links this with Nicaraguan women who had taken action against violent men. The problem with this is that gender issues are confined to limited issues including male violence and the domestic sphere, thus reinforcing the public/private divide. Further, the implication is that male violence is a global issue and that women in Nicaragua and UK, by implication, face the same problems. The challenge is how to create links through issues such as violence, without losing an awareness of the specific cultural, historical and political factors that contribute to it.

Full Circle Fund

Full Circle Fund is the only one out of the three projects that works exclusively with women. However, like ODEC it does not explicitly address poverty, although it is aimed at low-income women.

The concept of 'low income' used is based on the needs of local women. This recognises the need to refer to women's individual incomes 'because we cannot assume that women have access to their partners' or families income' (Full Circle Fund, 1998, p. 1). This includes women who are unemployed or unwaged, working part-time, in a low-paid job, facing redundancy or claiming state welfare benefits (Full Circle Fund, 1998).

FCF starts from a gender analysis of income, the market and the state. As a programme targeted at women, FCF's starting point is the recognition that women do not necessarily have access to the income of husbands, partners or other family members.

> [T]he thing with our participants is that they're just like you and I you know. They're just like you and I, who get divorced... I mean women are so close to poverty because of their status. (interview, Erika Watson, FCF)

Second, an understanding of the gendered nature of the market informs the project. 'All the government funding through Business Links and TECs[2] has been towards growth businesses' (interview, Erika Watson, FCF). Business start-up, therefore, is 'intrinsically gender-biased'.[3] The gendered understanding of state policies, in particular the benefits system, is explored in Part II.

However, a notable silence is apparent in terms of analysis of the international economy. As outlined in Chapter 4, this has been shown to have a significant impact on women's lives everywhere. Furthermore, the project does not directly address wider issues that are a prerequisite for empowerment, such as political participation. Having said this, however, FCF's project comes close to the empowerment approach described by Moser (1993, p. 77), where

> The very limited success of the equity approach to confront directly the nature of women's subordination through legislative changes has led the empowerment approach to avoid direct confrontation. It utilizes practical gender needs as the basis on which to build a secure support base, and a means through which strategic needs may be reached.

That is because it focuses on the 'practical gender need' of raising women's income: the project is at an early stage, and it remains to be seen what it may achieve in terms of more long term, strategic gains for women.

In summary, then, FCF is the only one of the three projects that explicitly defines its target criteria. While avoiding the use of the term poverty, it opts for narrow, income-based criteria, based on the needs of local women. Poverty is understood to be an entirely different issue in developing countries, thus reinforcing the North–South divide. The programme starts from a gendered understanding of income, the market and the state. However, there are noticeable silences in terms of the international context. I have suggested that its focus comes closest to Moser's concept of empowerment through practical gender needs. That is, it focuses on an income generation, and its explicit objectives are not necessarily transformatory.

North–South learning, policy and the state

In this section I explore the relationships and knowledges about gender and the state revealed by the three organisations. I will argue that the extent to which these projects challenge the way in which people relate to the state is limited, in particular the way in which women have traditionally been excluded from access to the state through the construction of gendered public/private spaces.

Analysis of project texts reveals very different perceptions and expect-ations of the UK state. For Oxfam, 'the British government has been failing in its obligations to the most vulnerable people in our society' (Oxfam, undated). This reveals a belief that the state should be responsible for 'care and protection' (Oxfam, 1998, p. 22). FCF's understanding starts from a gender analysis of UK policy and state institutions:

> the benefit system is actually very excluding rather than enabling ... it's really difficult to get a job when you're a single parent. Not just get a job, but be able to afford to have a job, because by the time ... you've paid your child care, travel costs ... it's just not worth it, you're better off with benefit. (interview, Erika Watson, FCF)

The benefits system, then, exacerbates the already tenuous position of women and their dependency on men or the state. The state, then, is gender-blind, if not discriminatory. In contrast, ODEC texts reveal an understanding of the state that is oppressive. For example, black children in Oxford are systematically discriminated against in the education system (interview, Alison Norris, ODEC). Perceptions of the state, then, vary from an understanding that the state is essentially benevolent, if imperfect, to an understanding that it is essentially discriminatory.

How do the projects envisage gendered dimensions of the state, and their role in addressing them? Oxfam's gender policy includes 'con-fronting the social and ideological barriers to women's participation' (May, 1997a, p. 76), but doesn't specifically address political barriers. Also 'promoting independent access for women to key resources, services and facilities' (May, 1997a, p. 76) is seen as important, but what about addressing the responsibilities of the state? For FCF, the structures of the state are recognised as inherently gendered, and gender legislation is seen as largely ineffective.

> gender is taken so seriously in the international arena, but locally you can't mention the word. I mean, we have doubts every so often about being a women's organisation because it really counts against us ... [Local funders] have real problems with us because they think we're not equal opps. (interview, Erika Watson, FCF)

For example, equal opportunities legislation is read selectively, does not necessarily protect women and may even discriminate against FCF as a women's organisation. It is suggested that 'cuts in public services and the welfare state have a significant impact on women, as the ones who bear the brunt of caring responsibilities' (Bronstein, 1998). However, not only cuts, but the very structure of those services and the welfare state itself that has been shown to disadvantage women. This highlights a key silence in all three projects in relation to gender: supporting women's political participation.

The new community in North–South learning

Critiques of the 'myth of community' from a feminist perspective suggest that, first, the concept of 'community' can conceal differences of class, race, and gender; second, it conceals internal dynamics that favour the opinions and priorities of those with more power and voice (Guijt and Kaul Shah, 1998, p. 1). Third, women tend to do a disproportionate amount of community work, which contributes to women's triple role[4] of domestic work, paid work and community work (May, 1997a, p. 27). This section will therefore explore in more depth understandings of the community in North and South that emerge from the three case studies, with a particular focus on the gender implications of those understandings.

Underlying this approach is the notion revealed by all three projects that UK society is in crisis, and communities are breaking down. Caroline Forbes of FCF suggests that 'when you're surviving in our culture you tend to survive by yourself...because we've lost so much of our sense of community' (interview, Caroline Forbes, FCF). Thus, British society is seen as undergoing a process of individualisation. At ODEC, the idea is expressed that it is hard to create links required for international learning because of 'apathy and internalised oppression' in the North (Norris and Maylin, 1999, p. 6). Similarly, Geraldine Terry of Oxfam observes that 'although basic services such as education are provided, there are problems of apathy, disaffection, and low self-esteem which prevent marginalised people from taking advantage of them' (Terry, 1998). Thus, an understanding is revealed that runs through all the projects that British communities, and wider society is in the process of breakdown and individualisation.

This image of breakdown and decay in Northern communities is a striking contrast to understandings revealed by the projects of 'community' in the South. For example, ODEC contrasts the response of women in Nicaragua and Oxford to abusive men:

> women in some of the *favelas* in Nicaragua had got together and gone and chucked out violent men...but for those women [in Oxford] it was really important to keep that job, and it kind of flared up and fizzled out again. (interview, Alison Norris, ODEC)

The implication is that in Nicaragua there is a stronger community spirit and sense of solidarity than in Oxford. Oxfam's annual report reveals an opposition between descriptions of the community in North and South. An estate in Gloucester is described as 'collapsing under the burden of unemployment, crime and poverty' (Oxfam, 1998, p. 28). Elsewhere in the document, however, 'people are doing what they can to rebuild their lives and communities' (Oxfam, 1998, p. 15) in Angola; in Bolivia 'community members have built reservoirs to conserve water' (Oxfam, 1998, p. 9), while in Azerbaijan Oxfam 'helped the community to build their own shower blocks and washing areas' (Oxfam, 1998, p. 23). The point is that when describing the UK, the emphasis is on poverty, crime and breakdown; when describing communities in the South, the emphasis is on rebuilding, creativity, and community strength. At FCF, a similar opposition is drawn:

> [The borrowing circle] really expands your network of personal recommendees, people who will recommend you . . . so, if you have a group of five and they're all out there making recommendations for you, which is probably what would have happened in the community, you know . . . going back to the difference between the national and the international. (interview, Erika Watson, FCF)

Thus, the perceived lack of 'networking' in the UK is contrasted to the international situation. An idealised perception of the Southern community as strong, healthy and creative, therefore, emerges from the texts. I would argue that the projects reveal a sense of community disintegration that is implicitly opposed to an idealised image of the Southern community, which is implicitly identified with some notion of the community in the past.

The community, then, is not a gender-neutral space: it can be exclusive for women and depends on women's work, thus adding to their already heavy burden. It is ironic, then, that all three organisations place a heavy emphasis on networking: in effect, building new communities. As described above, Oxfam's strategy of working through 'community networks' implies a risk that they are value-free and gender-neutral. Might not these 'new' communities then simply reinforce existing gender relations and structures of subordination? A key element of FCF's work is the establishment of lending circles. One obstacle is encouraging women to network: 'people who don't have many resources sometimes think networking is a talking shop, but networking is the most valuable resource in the service sector' (interview, Erika Watson, FCF). The implication is that networking is understood as a privilege of the rich. ODEC, too, expresses the objective of creating

> a living example of the world you want to see, really, in terms of... group learning, you don't have individual answers to things, reality is far too complicated for that, you create group understandings. (interview, Alison Norris, ODEC)

Thus a belief in a new form of 'collective' underlies her thinking. 'REFLECT and other participatory approaches help us to reclaim education as communal generation of the knowledge we need to shape our futures' (Norris, 1998). This highlights a need expressed by all three projects to build new forms of 'community'. However, it seems that this 'building' of new communities is based on a reconstitution of pre-capitalist community or a stereotypical notion of the Southern community, which has implications for gender. That is, the 'community' is based on the invisible work of women, and risks reinforcing their unseen, unvalued workload in new ways.

That the 'community' can be exclusive and isolating is, however, recognised as a problem in some texts. In Britain, 'the combination of employment, household, and community work means that women tend to be overworked and under-rewarded' (Bronstein, 1998). FCF similarly notes that one of the obstacles that women starting up in business face is isolation:

> what I really wanted was that support group of other people in the same position, because it's really lonely working for yourself, sitting looking at the blank wall all day waiting for the phone to ring. (interview, Erika Watson, FCF)

However, it seems to me that there is a silence surrounding the underlying reasons for this isolation. That is, the legislation around employment; state policies that reinforce women's dependency on men or the state, and cutting back of state provision which means that community work relies on women's unpaid work. However, this is not to say that community work does not have positive implications for women, in that it reduces feelings of isolation. Although everyone who becomes self-employed is isolated, structures such as sports clubs, pubs, colleagues from previous jobs, access to transport often mean that it is less of a problem for men.[5]

The politics of gender in North–South learning: conflict and silence

Analysis of the three projects revealed a number of gaps and silences in relation to gender. First, there is a risk of slipping into an assumption of universal, undifferentiated 'woman': in Mohanty's (1988, p. 65) words, an 'elision between "women" as a discursively constructed group and 'women' as material subjects of their own history'. Second, explicit links are made between women and poverty, which reinforces stereotypical images of women as weak and victimised. This resonates with Apffel-Marglin and Simons' (1994, p. 32) observation that 'the automatic equation of women with poverty justifies the development desire to transform all Third World women into "economically productive", autonomous, independent subjects'. Thus, the complexity of women's subordination remains unexplored, concealed by the economistic focus of 'poverty'. Third, the projects deal with a limited sphere of women's activities, confined to work and household. It is important that structures of subordination are transformed at all levels (Moser, 1993, p. 76). While the focus is on community and participation, it seems that the public/private divide, state structures and political decision-making processes remain unchallenged. Where political processes are addressed, as with FCF, this is done indirectly because of opposition and ignorance of the feminist agenda. This, it seems, is a major potential and indeed a challenge for North–South learning: put simply, how to combine the bottom-up traditions of the South with the top-down traditions of the North, for mutual benefit.

All three projects are using strategies that focus on communities, networking and creating links. Like Southern strategies, then, they focus on individual agency rather than structural change (Rossiter, 1998). Participatory, community-focused strategies, I suggested, are attractive now in the Northern context for a combination of reasons. First, analysis of the three projects shows that the 'community' in the North is understood to be in the process of breakdown and decay. Second, the 'community' in the South, in contrast, is understood to be vigorous, creative and strong. Third, the UK state is understood to be failing in its function as provider, or even actively discriminating against certain groups of people. All of these have created conditions in the UK where participatory methodologies, based on an ideology of self-help, initiative and community are very seductive.

There are, however, significant silences in the texts regarding the gender implications of networking and community building: my analysis suggests problems associated with the uncritical adoption of this approach. First, the 'myth of community' tends to hide internal differences and power dynamics (Guijt and Kaul Shah, 1998, p. 1). Second, community work is built on women's unpaid and unvalued work (May, 1997a, p. 21). The project documents point to the possibility that the reconstitution of pre-capitalist, or the formation of post-capitalist, forms of community could reinforce the burden of women's work, although this would need further research.

Furthermore, the extent to which the gendered dimension of the state and its institutions is recognised varies between the projects. There are silences in terms of tackling women's participation in the political sphere and engaging with policies and state institutions, a pre-requisite for the empowerment of women (Moser, 1993, p. 76). I would suggest that the move towards community-focused action supports Offe's (1984b, p. 269) suggestion that this is the inevitable consequence of a loss of trust, a 'crisis of legitimation' in the welfare state. Thus, rather than being a brave new development, North–South learning appears to be partly a reaction to a crisis of faith in the ability of the British state to provide. In the context of North–South learning this is reinforced and justified by a romanticised stereotype of the Southern community, on the one hand, and abstract, decontextualised concepts of poverty and gender on the other. Learning from the South, then, risks importing conservative and homogenising ideas about gender relations along with the tools, methods and approaches that are held up as being new and radical, unless a gender-aware approach is adopted. That is, unless critical attention is paid to the fundamental problem of how to make connections between the realm of abstract, universal ideas and local realities, and how to make explicit the differences between them.

Revisiting assumptions

An issue which emerged again and again throughout this study is the tension between false universalism and a paralysing relativism. This contradiction, and how to reconcile it, lies at the very heart of North–South learning, and all three projects are addressing it in different ways. I am faced with the challenge of drawing meaningful conclusions, while avoiding generalisations about their very different approaches. A second challenge concerns balancing a critical perspective with a recognition of the potential benefits of North–South learning generally, and the three case studies in particular. I hope to address these problems by returning to the three assumptions identified earlier about North–South learning and discuss whether texts from these specific projects either question, or reinforce those assumptions.

First, gender is a universally relevant concept and approaches to gender universally applicable. Project texts revealed divergent tendencies: on the one hand, a tendency to conceptualise 'woman' as a universally coherent category, thus denying the multiple nature of women's needs and the wide range of differences between women. This was reinforced by assumptions that development and anti-poverty strategies such as REFLECT and community development are gender-neutral. On the other hand, an opposite tendency to focus on narrow, localised interests was also revealed, thus denying the benefits of wider links between women and women's issues. The original assumption, then, is revealed as simplistic. North–South learning takes many different forms, but reconciliation of these universal and localised conceptualisations of woman and gender issues is a key concern.

Second, global similarities in the experience of poverty mean that causes and solutions are globally relevant. The project texts revealed widely divergent understandings of poverty. What is revealed, however, is the Western, individualistic logic underpinning global understandings of poverty, as abstracted and decontextualised. Thus, while recognising that problems in North and South are comparable on some level is key to North–South learning, framing these problems in terms of the concept of poverty is problematic. That is, it naturalises poverty as a universal referent, which ultimately serves to reinforce the North–South divide that such approaches seek to challenge. The above assumption then is based on an over-simplification of the concept of poverty, in particular the confusion of economic and cultural aspects, cause and effect of poverty. How the projects develop their own criteria of disadvantage, however defined, while keeping sight of global links is another key challenge for North–South learning.

Third, North–South learning represents a shift from paternalistic models of development to one that values Southern knowledge and participatory, bottom-up approaches. A feature common to all three projects is an emphasis on the (re-) building of networks and community participation. This is underpinned in part by a seductive stereotype of the 'community' in the South. This is constructed in opposition to a discourse of breakdown and decay in the UK, under-pinned by the rolling back of the state, and the increasing power of international markets, and the crisis of the welfare state. The implica-tions of this new community focus are far from clear: however, I would argue that in terms of gender they are problematic for three main reasons: 1), Community is often predicated on the unseen, unvalued work of women; 2), power dynamics of communities often disadvantage women; and 3), community focus denies individual difference. Thus, North–South learning is not necessarily beneficial for all groups, and may impact differently on men and women. The challenge, then, is how to learn with full gender awareness.

Past experiences of working in international development – often confusing and contradictory – have made North–South learning an important issue in a personal, practical and academic sense for me. I feel that I have gained a great deal of understanding of the politics of poverty, gender and development, in the UK and internationally. Previously, I had carried out research in the 'South' only; carrying out research in the UK, therefore, has been enlightening. I believe that the ease with which I gained access to people in Pakistan, for example, was based to some extent on the (often invisible) colonial privilege that still underpins development. It was far more difficult, here in the UK, to gain access to people. This observation was underlined by the fact that participants were able to comment on my analysis in a way that was only possible because we share the language of academic research. Thus, this research has enabled me to question and gain a better understanding of the roots of the North–South divide that has dictated the parameters of my experience in development so far.

Turning the question around

Learning has been occurring between countries now classified as 'North' and 'South' on a wide range of issues for centuries – art, music, science, sport, mathematics, to name but a few areas. What makes the development period extraordinary is that it has, perhaps for the first time in history, defined the countries of the 'South' as unequal partners in this exchange of knowledge, on the basis of a narrowly defined, Western-identified economic inequality. This implies that, in fact, my original question should be turned around: how has North–South learning in the field of development been suppressed to such an extent that now, at the end of the twentieth century, it appears to be a new idea? The answer, I feel, is in the power of development discourse: Foucault's 'regime of truth' (Foucault, 1980, p. 131) to which the three case studies offer the possibility of a radical alternative.

Notes

1 'North' generally refers to the industrial economies, and the 'South' to developing countries (Sweetman, 1997, p. 2). Thus 'South' has replaced labels like 'Third World' and 'developing' countries, which have been criticised for 'imposing an apparent uniformity on an extremely heterogeneous (culturally, politically and economically) group of countries' (Kabeer, 1994, p. xix). I recognise, then, that 'North' and 'South' are problematic constructs, perhaps best understood as metaphors (Eyben, 1998, p. 1). Where these terms are used, therefore, it is for want of a better alternative.

2 Training and Entreprise Councils (TECs) are a national network of agencies responsible for delivering and developing government training and entreprise programmes since 1990 (Callender, 1996, p. 45).

3 Business start-ups are labelled either 'lifestyle businesses': that is, one-person businesses with little capacity for growth, or 'growth businesses', defined as having the potential to generate jobs. Most women's businesses tend to be 'lifestyle businesses' because they face constraints in terms of capital and time. Capital often means property to put up as security; most property belongs to men, while women are constrained by family and other caring responsibilities (interview, Erika Watson, FCF).

4 Articulated by Moser (1993, p. 27).

5 I am grateful to Erika Watson for this observation.

References

Apffel-Marglin, F. and Simons, S. L. (1994). Feminist Orientalism and Development. In W. Harcourt (ed.) *Feminist Perspectives on Sustainable Development,* London: Zed, pp. 26–45.

Archer, D. and Cottingham, S. (1996). Action research report on REFLECT. ODA Education Papers No. 17. London: ODA.

Bronstein, A. (1998) Editorial. Links (online), 1998 (November), 6 paragraphs. Available: http://www.oxfam.org.uk/policy/gender/9811edit.htm(25 June 1999).

Callender, C. (1996). Women and Employment. In C. Hallett (ed.) *Women and Social Policy: An Introduction,* London: Prentice Hall and Harvester Wheatsheaf, pp. 31–51.

Chambers, R. (1992). Rural Appraisal: Rapid, Relaxed and Participatory. IDS Discussion paper 311. Brighton: Institute of Development Studies.

Culpeper, R. (1997). *The Multilateral Development Banks: Titans or Behemoths?* London: Intermediate Technology Publications.

David, R. and Craig, Y. (1997). 'Participation Begins at Home: Adapting Participatory Development Approaches from Southern Contexts'. *Gender and Development,* Vol. 5, No. 3, 35–44.

de Haan, A. and Maxwell, S. (1998). Poverty and Social Exclusion in North and South. *IDS Bulletin,* Vol. 29, No. 1, 1–9.

Eyben, R. (1998). Poverty and Social Exclusion: North–South Links. Talk, March. London: DFID.

Foucault, M. (1980). *Power/Knowledge: Selected Interviews and Other Writings 1972–1977.* New York: Harvester Wheatsheaf.

Full Circle Fund (1998). Full Circle Project Briefing, April. Norwich: Full Circle Fund.

German, T. and Randel, J. (1998). Approaches to Gender in Development Co-operation: At a Glance'. In T. German and J. Randel (eds.) *The Reality of Aid 1998/1999: An Independent Review of Poverty Reduction and Development Assistance,* London: Earthscan, pp. 234–42.

Giddens, A. (1991). *Modernity and Self-identity: Self and Society in the Late Modern Age.* Cambridge: Polity.

Goetz, A. M. (1997). Introduction: Getting Institutions Right for Women in Development. In A. M. Goetz (ed.), *Getting Institutions Right for Women in Development,* London: Zed, pp. 1–28.

Greenwood, L. (2000). PLA Notes 38: Participatory Processes in the North. London: IIED.

Guijt, I. and Kaul Shah, M. (1998). Waking up to Power, Conflict and Process. In I. Guijt and M. Kaul Shah (eds.), *The Myth of Community.* London: Intermediate Technology, pp. 1–23.

Hobsbawm, E. (1994). *Age of Extremes: The Short 20th Century.* London: Michael Joseph.

Holcombe, S. (1995). *Managing to Empower: The Grameen Bank's Experience of poverty Alleviation.* London: Zed.

Jackson, C. (1998). Rescuing Gender from the Poverty Trap. In C. Jackson and R. Pearson (eds.), *Feminist Visions of Development: Gender Analysis and Policy.* London: Routledge, pp. 39–64.

Jackson, C. and Pearson, R. (1998). Introduction: Interrogating Development: Feminism, Gender and Policy. In C. Jackson and R. Pearson (eds), *Feminist Visions of Development: Gender Analysis and Policy,* London: Routledge, pp. 1–16.

Kabeer, N. (1994). *Reversed Realities: Gender Hierarchies in Development Thought.* London: Verso.

Lewis, D. (undated). Bridging the Gap? The Parallel Universes of the Non-profit and Non-governmental Organisation Research Traditions and the Changing Context of Voluntary Action. CVO International Working Paper 1. London: Centre for Voluntary Organisation.

Maxwell, S. (1998). The Same Difference: Britain Should Look to the Third World in its Attempts to Tackle Social Exclusion Here. *Guardian,* 25 February.

May, N. (1997a). *Challenging Assumptions: Gender Considerations in Urban Regeneration in the United Kingdom.* A report to the Joseph Rowntree Foundation. Oxford: Oxfam and the Joseph Rowntree Foundation.

May, T. (1997b). *Social Research: Issues, Methods and Process.* (2nd edn). Buckingham: Open University Press.

Mayo, M. (1997). *Imagining Tomorrow: Adult Education for Transformation.* Leicester: NIACE.

Mohanty, C. T. (1988). Under Western Eyes: Gender Scholarship and Colonial Discourses'. *Feminist Review,* Vol. 30, 61–88.

Moser, C. (1993). *Gender Planning and Development: Theory, Practice and Training.* London: Routledge.

Norris, A. (1998). REFLECT in Oxford, England. PLA Notes, June, No. 32, 61–4.

Norris, A. and Maylin, P. (1999). *Global Alliances Meeting Report.* Oxford: ODEC.

Offe, C. (1984a). Legitimacy versus Efficiency. In J. Keane (ed.), *Contradictions of the Welfare State,* London: Hutchinson, pp. 130–46.

Offe, C. (1984b). Reflections on the Welfare State. In J. Keane (ed.), *Contradictions of the Welfare State,* London: Hutchinson, pp. 252–99.

Oxfam (1998). *Annual Report*. Oxford: Oxfam.

Oxfam (undated). *Oxfam and Poverty in Great Britain* (leaflet). Oxford: Oxfam.

Patel, S. (1997) *Slums of Bombay to the Housing Estates of Britain*. London: Centre for Innovation in Voluntary Action.

Rahnema, M. (1992). Poverty. In W. Sachs (ed.), *The Development Dictionary*, London: Zed, pp. 158–76.

Rossiter, J. (1998). *Poverty and the North–South Dimension: The Great Link Forward?* Oxford: Oxfam.

Smith, S. (1998). Why a British Poverty Programme for Oxfam? *Links*, November 4 paragraphs. http://www.oxfam.org.uk/policy/gender/9811gb.htm (25 June 1999).

Sweetman, C. (1997). Editorial. *Gender and Development*, Vol. 5, No. 3, 2–8.

Terry, G. (1998). In the North. *Links* (online), November, 11 paragraphs. Available: http://www.oxfam.org.uk/policy/gender/9811nort.htm (25 June 1999).

Thekaekara, S. and Thekaekara, M. (1994). *Across the Geographical Divide (A Report on the Visit of Stan and Mari Thekaekara to the UK in May 1994 to Look at Community Development and Urban Regeneration)*. London: Centre for Innovation in Voluntary Action.

3

Boys and Underachievement in the Canadian Context: No Proof for Panic

Kevin G. Davison, Trudy A. Lovell, Blye W. Frank and Ann B. Vibert

Introduction

Over the last fifteen years there has been an increase in scholarly work internationally in the area of boys, masculinities and schooling (Davison, 1996, 2000a, 2000b; Frank, 1987, 1990, 1993, 1994, 1997a and b; Epstein *et al.*, 1998; Kenway, 1995, 1998, 2000; Mac an Ghaill, 1994a, 1994b, 1996; Martino, 1994, 1995, 2000, forthcoming). This work, heavily influenced by feminist research on gender and education, has investigated, and often problematised, the complexities of the lives of boys in schools. It has focused on homophobia and heterosexism, bullying, sexual harassment, violence and underachievement. Over the last ten years in the United Kingdom and Australia there has been an outcry in the popular press about a crisis in the education of boys (Epstein *et al.*, 1998). Newspaper headlines have asked questions such as: 'Are Schools Failing our Boys?' 'What about the Boys?' and 'Do Boys Need More Male Teachers?'

Recently, British and Australian media frenzy over boys' under-achievement has been taken up by mainstream North American media. Two bestselling books (Kindlon and Thompson, 1999; Pollack, 1999) and many newspaper and magazine articles have assisted in the construction of the perception among some parents/guardians and educators that boys in school are being shortchanged. It was only a matter of time before this 'panic' was taken up by government organisations responsible for education in Canada.

In November 2000, the Department of Education and Culture for the Province of Nova Scotia issued a call for a background paper addressing the achievement of boys and girls in schools. The call requested a review of the available literature and an analysis of the existing statistical data, highlighting the gaps in the literature and the data, and proposing *practical* intervention strategies. The call recognised the importance of documenting the situation of historically marginalised boys in the Province of Nova Scotia, in particular, boys of African or First Nations heritage. As a research team with expertise in gender and schooling and experience in public schools, we were familiar with the 'panic' over boys and schooling. We felt well positioned to take up and critically examine data regarding boys and achievement in Canada, specifically in the context of the province of Nova Scotia. This chapter describes our experience in conducting the investigation and offers an analysis of the current situation in Canada in relation to the 'panic' over boys and achievement in schools.

The context

As a part of the research directive, we were required to interview several key staff within the Department of Education and Culture for the Province of Nova Scotia. We were particularly interested to know what motivated the Department to issue the call for the background paper. The responses indicated that the call arose from the growing public concern, reflected in the popular press, over the underachievement of boys. Some staff believed that, due to feminist initiatives, young women had made significant academic gains at the expense of boys, and they believed that there was a need to shift the focus to boys.

A common theme arising from the interviews was the *belief* that boys were underachieving and that their underachievement was not located in their behaviour, but in a variety of deficits within the educational system. These perceived deficits ranged from too few men teachers in elementary schools to a literacy curriculum that did not include the interests and experiences of boys. One official informed us that boys were required to read 'too many *silly, stupid* stories'. We were told that, in order to develop greater literacy levels, boys needed more 'transactional and *factual*' texts, as well as more texts that would appeal to them by depicting their experiences.

One of the Department's interests in the background paper was to generate a document that highlighted practical applications of boy-centred pedagogy. It became clear to us that the (under)achievement of girls was not a concern for those who initiated and funded the research. Further, we were told that the report was *not* to be an entirely theoretical paper, but a *prescriptive* document, which could be distributed to teachers without the need for extensive professional development for implementation.

The social geography

Because this background paper was commissioned by a Department of the government of Nova Scotia, the research was intended to focus on Nova Scotia specifically and only on Canada more generally. Therefore, it is important to describe those social and economic factors which may have an impact on boys and their achievement in this context.

Nova Scotia is a small province on the east coast of Canada with a population of almost one million people. At about 9 per cent, the unemployment rate is significantly higher than the Canadian average, and the province has a relatively greater rural population than many provinces in the country. In rural and small town areas of the province, unemployment is considerably higher than the provincial average, reaching 40 per cent in some of the more remote regions.

Located in the most economically depressed region of the country, the economy of Nova Scotia has historically depended upon now depleted resource-based industries. It is a region in which the population is decreasing and outmigration and low immigration rates are provincial concerns. Within this context, African Nova Scotians and members of the First Nations communities have suffered marginalisation, particularly within education.

Educational indicators

To our knowledge, comprehensive pan-Canadian research specifically regarding boys and underachievement has not been conducted. Nor has such research been conducted in the Province of Nova Scotia. There are, however, limited national and regional reports, specifically, *School Achievement Indicators Program* (SAIP) reports and *Education Indicators for Atlantic Canada*, which use gender comparisons to construct analyses regarding achievement levels in a variety of designated school subjects. These subjects include mathematics, sciences, reading and writing. While 'gender' achievement rates are reported, these data indicate that what is being referred to by this term is biological sex. Differences across race, ethnicity and socio-economic class are not taken into account within the analyses of the data provided by either assessment.

1. School Achievement Indicators program

Beginning in 1993, the *School Achievement Indicators Program* (SAIP) initiated the process of assessing the achievement of Canadian students aged thirteen and sixteen in a number of school subjects. The statistics in SAIP publications were collected and reported in a variety of ways, many of which used limited analytical focus. For example, SAIP compared student performance scores province by province, individual provinces versus the country as a whole, and gender as related to the whole country's student population. In addition to provincial and gender breakdowns, SAIP sorted students' performance into five achievement levels, with Level 1 being the lowest and Level 5 the highest.

Science assessments 1996 and 1999

The SAIP documents for science indicate that for both the *practical* and *written* tasks for thirteen and sixteen year olds in 1996 and 1999, there was no significant gender difference in measured achievement, with the exception of a 5 per cent difference in 1996 at Level 4 in favour of sixteen-year-old males. It is, however, significant to acknowledge that both boys and girls improved their performance at levels 3 to 5, between 1996 and 1999.

Reading and writing assessment 1994 and 1998

In 1994, 2.4 per cent of thirteen-year-old females scored at Level 5, the highest level of achievement measured in *reading*, while 0.6 per cent of thirteen-year-old males reached this level. Fourteen per cent more females than males reached Level 3. Clearly, thirteen-year-old males in 1994 did not score as well as females on the SAIP assessment in reading. In the 1998 SAIP *reading* section, the data for thirteen-year-olds show that fewer males and females scored at levels 3 to 5 compared to 1994 performances. For sixteen-year-old students in 1994, and again in 1998, females scored higher on the SAIP at most *reading* levels. The exception was at Level 3, which showed no significant difference. Males and females performed equally well at this level.

Writing assessment data for 1994 illustrate significant differences between scores for females and males for both age groups. Females scored at consistently higher levels, with the exceptions of Level 5 for thirteen year olds and Level 3 for sixteen year olds where differences are very small.

In terms of *writing* assessment performance of sixteen year olds in 1998, compared with 1994, more males and more females scored at levels 3 to 5. At levels 3 and 5 the increase was slightly greater for males than females, thus narrowing the perceived gap. Data shows that 45.5 per cent of males achieved at least Level 3, whereas 43.7 per cent of girls attained this level.

The SAIP documents for reading and writing in 1994 and 1998 do indeed indicate that male achievement, as measured by available assessment tools, in many cases, is statistically significantly lower than female achievement in both testing years. Therefore, current arguments that boys *across the board*, are falling farther behind are *not supported* when data are compared. In fact, in numerous cases, males are showing *improvement* at several levels, and some boys are doing very well.

Mathematics assessment 1993 and 1997

Mathematics assessments were divided into two areas: *content* and *problem-solving*. In the 1993 SAIP mathematics assessment, thirteen-year-old students participating in the *content* portion of the mathematics assessment demonstrated no significant difference, with the exception of slightly more girls than boys scoring at Level 3. By 1997 the results had changed, with more girls now registering at Level 1 (the lowest level) and more boys than girls scoring at Level 3. That is, boys' achievement in mathematics *content* improved since 1993.

For sixteen-year-old students the 1993 scores for the *content* portion showed more males than females scoring at Level 4, with other levels relatively equal for females and males. By the next round of assessment in 1997, there were more males than females in Levels 3, 4 and 5, and fewer males at level 1. In Levels 3 4 and 5 the gap had increased significantly *in favour of boys*.

In the *problem-solving* section of the 1993 assessment, thirteen-year-old females showed a slightly higher representation at Level 2 than did males. Ten per cent of males and only 4.6 per cent of females scored at Level 3 and over. By 1997, thirteen-year-old males at all levels had increased gains and fewer achieved Level 1 (the lowest level). Both males and females had shown improvement between 1993 and 1997; however, the increase was greater for males.

For sixteen year olds participating in the 1993 *problem-solving* portion of the assessment, 20 per cent of females achieved Level 3 and above, while 29 per cent of males were included in this category. By 1997, the per centage of males scoring at high levels had increased, with Level 5 showing positive gains and a larger gap in scores in favour of males.

From the statistical values in this section, it is clear that 'boys' are *not* falling behind in mathematics. These data illustrate that many boys are, in fact, pulling ahead in mathematics assessment scores.

Reflections on SAIP Results

When data provided by SAIP documents are compared, in some areas the achievement scores of boys and girls are different. The greatest difference between boys' and girls' achievement appeared, not surprisingly, in the area of reading and writing. Gender differences in reading and writing performance have historically been a focus of concern for at least three hundred years (Cohen, 1998); the weaker performance of boys relative to girls on literacy assessments is neither new nor more marked than in the past. What are not visible in light of the perceived deficit of boys in reading and writing are the differences in achievement among boys. For example, it is clear that in all areas assessed *some* girls and *some* boys do very well at mathematics, science, reading and writing; *which* boys (and *which* girls) are struggling not provided by the assessment data. A further limitation of the various SAIP reports is that they provide no data comparing boys' and girls' achievements at the provincial level.

Available statistics did not allow us to draw definitive conclusions regarding the achievement of boys in relation to girls in Nova Scotia. Further, the available statistics did not allow comparisons of boys' performance to other boys over time, possibly a better measure of how boys are achieving in Canadian schools. Currently available statistical records fall short of the information needed to address the issues of gender and achievement in Canadian and Nova Scotian schools.

2. Graduation rates/dropout rates

For the years 1990 to 1995 girls in Nova Scotia graduated at a higher rate than boys. For example, in 1990–91 60 per cent of male students graduated while 73 per cent of females graduated. By 1995 there was relatively steady growth in the rate of graduation for both groups, with boys having a completion rate of 70 per cent and girls 78 per cent. These statistics indicate that there was a notable increase in the graduation rate of boys relative to girls over this period. According to these statistics, boys are remaining in school longer than they have in the past (Atlantic Provinces Education Foundation, 1996). Clearly, growing concern in the popular press about retention rates of boys is misplaced.

One reason for this shift in retention rates for both boys and girls may be located in the rate of growth in the provincial economy during this period (Atlantic Provinces Economic Council, 2000). When the economy is performing well and there are more available jobs, more students may choose to enter the workforce rather than continue with their education. However, when there are fewer jobs available more students may choose to remain in school (Atlantic Provinces Education Foundation, 1996, p. 16).

Additionally, in many developed countries, gender analyses of labour force data indicate that 'young men with poor literacy and numeracy skills may well find relatively well-paid work in labouring and skilled manual work' (Gilbert and Gilbert, 1998, p. 12). The difference in rates may be related to the availability of types of paid employment thought to be more appropriate for males. While it is widely reported that there are few to no jobs available for undereducated workers, regional industrial changes may provide opportunities for work in unskilled labour. Closer examination of the gendered dynamics of job placement for post-school employment indicates that girls who graduate from high school with strong literacy skills are less likely to get full-time employment than boys who do not graduate and who have weak literacy skills (Kenway, 2000).

Another important factor in the dropout rate of the Nova Scotia high school population relates to family dynamics. Family Literacy Association of Nova Scotia reports that: 'Children of parents who are unemployed and have not completed high school are five times more likely to drop out of school than children of employed parents' (Family Literacy Association of Nova Scotia: 1999, p. 9). Overall dropout rates, then, are likely to be connected to the state of the economy in a variety of ways and, in general, are strongly deflected by socio-economic class factors. Given these phenomena, the continuing silence of regional and national academic assessment reports on issues of education and class is at best curious.

3. Quality of school life

According to the *Education Indicators for Atlantic Canada* (Atlantic Provinces Education Foundation (1996), a survey of grade eight students in this region concluded that

> girls are overwhelmingly more positive about all aspects of their school life than boys. Girls also responded more positively than boys on self-esteem related items. Comparisons show the percentage of positive responses to items by females to be an average of nine percentage points higher than that of males. (p. 44)

The most striking feature of this comment is the difference between girls' and boys' responses to the survey item 'school is a place where I like to be'. Seventy per cent of girls responded in the affirmative whereas only 54 per cent of boys responded in the same way. Further, two items surveying the social context indicated that not all boys feel safe at school. For example, 65 per cent of boys compared with 73 per cent of girls reported that they feel safe from personal harm. Clearly, 35 per cent of boys did not feel safe at school. In a related item, more boys (57 per cent) than girls (53 per cent) reported that students picked on each other all the time.

These statistics, while limited in scope, suggested that social problems in the lives of boys at school need to be examined in order to address issues of underachievement.

4. Social aspects of schooling

In discussions of boys' educational achievement it is important to acknowledge the impact of social aspects of schooling. These social aspects may contribute in significant ways to boys' underachievement in schools. Research indicates that the way boys engage with 'traditional' and acceptable notions of masculinity has an impact on day-to-day activities in schools. For example, 'Eighty per cent of administrators' and teachers' time which is devoted to managing boys' behaviour is time lost to curriculum leadership, organising supportive school environments, community liaison and parent support' (Gilbert and Gilbert, 1998, p. 14).

Bullying, harassment and other acts of social terrorism have received increasing attention in the popular press (Hazler, 1996; Pemberton and Cullbert, 2001). Acts of violence and harassment have been documented as beginning at the pre-school level (Skelton, 1997; Yelland, 1998) and continuing into adulthood (Cunnison, 1989). Bullying, once thought of as a natural part of childhood, is now being examined as a serious crisis for students and their schools. Experts in the area recognise that the dynamics are complex. In these acts of harassment, the roles of victims and bullies are fluid and shifting; victims often become the aggressors, and vice versa (Hazler, 1996). Bullying as a gendered practice may prevent students 'from learning and from taking any positive nourishment from school life' (Salisbury and Jackson, 1996, p. 112). Kenway maintains 'harassing behaviour has a demonstrably negative impact on the quality of boys' and girls' experiences of school and their educational directions and performances' (Milligan *et al.* and Collins *et al.*, cited in Kenway, 2000, p. 99). In Nova Scotia, educators have begun to address the issue of violence in schools by implementing The League of Peaceful Schools (Adams, 1994) and the Healthy Relationships program (Men For Change, 1994). In addition, a number of school boards are beginning to develop and adopt various anti-bullying programmes. Boys who do not fit the image of 'acceptable' masculinity can find themselves isolated and labelled even at primary level. Boys who are called 'sissy' know all too well that they have to adapt their behaviour in order to bring it in line with dominant masculinity. This usually means expunging anything that can be seen as girl-like (Lees, 1986; Rofes, 1995; Epstein *et al.*, 1998a). Participation in the school process itself could be considered as being 'girlish' and therefore dangerous. In particular, strong performance in reading and writing, activities gendered in favour of girls and the primary location of boys' underachievement, threatens 'acceptable' masculinities. 'If a commitment to schoolwork is characteristic of girls, and if to be masculine requires being different from girls, then boys' commitment to schoolwork becomes a challenge to their masculinity' (Gilbert and Gilbert, 1998, p. 140). Similarly, a staff member of the Nova Scotia Department of Education and Culture noted that, in her experience, boys who did well in school were singled out for ridicule and exclusion by classmates.

We may be able to conclude that masculinity is related to other oppositional behaviours. For example, 'to be seen to commit to schoolwork for its own sake would be seen . . . as acquiescing to school authority, as taking on the values of the school, as going over to the other side. For most of them [boys] it would also risk being seen as effeminate' (Gilbert and Gilbert, 1998, p. 143). Race and class dimensions add to the complexity; as one student said, 'if you get higher than, say, about 65%, then you're perceived as or accused of trying to be white. I think it's sad that in order to be Black, you have to be stupid or you have to not do your school work or just sit there at the back of the classroom' (Frank 1997a, p. 21). These beliefs about the consequences of full engagement with schooling and associated white values were corroborated by African Nova Scotian and First Nations (Mi'kmaq) educators at the Nova Scotia Department of Education and Culture.

The underachievement of boys in schools may be more closely related to the intersections of socio-economic class, race and gender then to gender alone. Therefore, if underachievement is tied to class (International Adult Literacy Survey, 1997, p. 21), examining the growth of poverty in Canada and Nova Scotia may shed greater light on why some boys are underachieving. 'In 1997 the number of poor children [in Nova Scotia] was estimated to be 48,000, this being an increase of 41% since 1989. The rate of child poverty in Nova Scotia is 22.4%, the second highest in Canada' (Campaign 2000, 2000). This striking rise in poverty in Nova Scotia, particularly combined with the history of marginalised groups in resisting dominant schooling (Willis, 1977; Kunjufu, 1986; Mac an Ghaill, 1988), may contribute more to the underachievement of boys than curriculum content, the lack of male teachers in elementary schools or pedagogies that may appear to advantage girls.

Having examined the available literature and statistics on boys and schooling, we reported to the provincial Department of Education and Culture that there is little evidence to support the perception of a pan-Canadian crisis regarding boys' underachievement in schools. If we wish to examine achievement levels across social differences, the major gaps in the available data need to be addressed.

Conclusion

> When the Ministry of Education calls and asks for help with any emancipatory project, hang up immediately. (Sexed Tetes Collective, 1993)

In the process of carrying out the government contracted research on which this chapter is based, we discovered that the media 'panic' which inspired the research itself was misplaced and unfounded. There were very little statistical data available in Canada, or in Nova Scotia specifically, examining gender differences in academic achievement in public schools. The data that were available (SAIP) did not indicate that boys were falling significantly behind girls; in fact, these data suggest that boys' academic achievement levels actually improved during the 1990s. The one area in which there were notable differences in girls' and boys' achievement scores was, unsurprisingly, on the reading and writing assessments.

Research on boys and schooling consistently highlights the importance of considering the social construction of masculinity as it informs educational practices and outcomes (Willis, 1977; Frank, 1987, 1990, 1993, 1994, 1999; Connell, 1989, 1995; Mac an Ghaill, 1994a,1994b, 1996; Martino, 1994, 1995, 2000, forthcoming; Kenway, 1995, 1998, 2000; Davison, 1996, 2000a, 2000b; Alloway and Gilbert, 1997a, 1997b; Salisbury and Jackson, 1997; Epstein *et al.*, 1998; Gilbert and Gilbert, 1998;), yet the popular press and media apparently continue to insist on misleading interpretations of scant data. This contradiction between ten years of scholarly research on boys and schooling and the 'panic' in the media may be attributed to several factors.

To begin with, concern over the academic underachievement of boys is not new. Similar concerns have been raised at various points in history (Cohen, 1998). None the less, late twentieth-century communications and media technologies have enabled an extraordinarily speedy information distribution which, simultaneously, constrains complexity. Popular media are therefore limited in their ability to examine the complexities of issues such as boys and schooling or to take up such issues in the kind of detail required for a more than cursory analysis. Furthermore, the 'panic' over boys' underachievement appears to have risen out of a response to earlier feminist gains aimed at girls and young women in schools. This backlash against feminist analysis may in effect act to disadvantage boys by ignoring the abundant international research on gender and schooling and reverting to traditional and restrictive binary comparisons between girls and boys in school. In addition to documenting contradictions and gaps in the literature and data on the Canadian context, our report argued for more careful sociological analyses of and research on boys and schooling, and for more comprehensive professional development on gender and education as two means of approaching questions of differences in boys' and girls' academic achievement.

The response of officials to the preliminary background paper we submitted to the Department of Education and Culture was mixed. Some felt that the analysis did not sufficiently support media claims (with which they concurred) about boys' underachievement. Others, including particularly African Nova Scotian and First Nations staff, understood and supported the analysis offered in the paper. However, as we write this chapter it remains unclear in what manner or to what extent the recommendations for practice we offered will be taken up or implemented. Presently it would appear that, because the background paper we compiled did not meet prior expectations or support prior assumptions on the part of key officials in the Nova Scotia Department of Education and Culture, it may have a considerably limited impact on future educational decisions made by the Province.

References

Adams, H. (1994). *Peace in the Classroom: Practical Lessons in Living for Elementary-Age Children*, Winnipeg: Peguis Publishers Limited.

Alloway, N. and Gilbert, P. (eds.) (1997a). *Boys and Literacy: Professional Development Units*, Carlton, Australia: Curriculum Corporation.

Alloway, N. and Gilbert, P. (1997b). Everything is Dangerous: Working with the 'Boys and Literacy' Agenda. *English in Australia*, Vol. 119, No. 20, 35–45.

Askew, S. and Ross, C. (1988). *Boys Don't Cry*, Milton Keynes: Open University Press.

Atlantic Provinces Economic Council (2000). *Atlantic Report*, Vol. 35, No. 3.

Atlantic Provinces Education Foundation (1996). *Education Indicators for Atlantic Canada Report*, Halifax, Nova Scotia.

Campaign 2000: 2000 URL: www.campaign2000.ca/.

Cohen, M. (1998). 'A Habit of Healthy Idleness': Boys' Underachievement in Historical Perspective. In D. Epstein, J. Elwood, V. Hey and J. Maw (eds.) *Failing Boys? Issues in Gender and Achievement*. Buckingham: Open University Press.

Connell, R. (1989). Cool Guys, Swots and Wimps: The Interplay of Masculinity and Education. *Oxford Review of Education*, Vol. 15, No. 3, 291–303.

Connell, R. (1995). *Masculinities*, Berkeley: University of California Press.

Council of Ministers of Education Canada (1993). *School Achievement Indicators Program Report on Mathematics Assessment*, Council of Ministers of Education, Toronto.

Council of Ministers of Education Canada (1994). *School Achievement Indicators Program Report on Reading and Writing Assessment*, Council of Ministers of Education, Toronto.

Council of Ministers of Education Canada (1996). *School Achievement Indicators Program Report on Science Assessment*, Council of Ministers of Education, Toronto.

Council of Ministers of Education Canada (1997). *School Achievement Indicators Program Report on Mathematics Assessment*, Council of Ministers of Education, Toronto.

Council of Ministers of Education Canada (1998). *School Achievement Indicators Program Report on Reading and Writing Assessment*, Council of Ministers of Education, Toronto.

Council of Ministers of Education Canada (1999). *School Achievement Indicators Program Report on Science Assessment*, Council of Ministers of Education, Toronto.

Cunnison, S. (1989). Gender Joking in the Staffroom. In S. Acker (ed.), *Teachers, Gender and Careers*, London: The Falmer Press.

Davison, K. G. (1996). Manly Expectations: Memories of Masculinities in School. Unpublished Master's thesis, Simon Fraser University, Burnaby, British Columbia, Canada.

Davison, K. G. (2000b). Boys Bodies in School: Physical Education, *The Journal of Men's Studies*, Vol. 8, No. 2, 255–66.

Davison, K. G. (2000a). Masculinities, Sexualities and the Student Body: 'Sorting' Gender Identities in School. In C. James (ed.) *Experiencing Difference*, Halifax: Fernwood Press, pp. 44–52.

Epstein, D., Elwood, J., Hey, V. and Maw, J. (eds.) (1998). *Failing Boys? Issues in Gender and Achievement*, Buckingham: Open University Press.

Family Literacy Association of Nova Scotia (1999). Pamphlet on Family Literacy.

Frank, B. (1987). Hegemonic Heterosexual Masculinity, *Studies in Political Economy*, Autumn 159–70.

Frank, B. (1990). Everyday Masculinities. Unpublished doctoral dissertation, Dalhousie University, Halifax, Nova Scotia, Canada.

Frank, B. (1993). Straight/Strait Jackets for Masculinity: Educating for 'Real Men', *Atlantis*, Vol. 18, Nos. 1 and 2, Fall/Spring, 47–59.

Frank, B. (1994). Queer Selves/Queer in Schools: Young men and Sexualities. In S. Prentice (ed.), *Sex in Schools: Canadian Education and Sexual regulation*, Toronto: Our Schools/Our Selves Education Foundation.

Frank, B. (1997a). External Review of Cole Harbour District High School. Unpublished report for the Halifax Regional School Board, Halifax, Nova Scotia, Canada.

Frank, B. (1997b). Masculinity Meets Postmodernism: Theorizing the 'Manmade' Man, *Canadian Folklore Canadien*, Vol. 19, No. 1, 15–33.

Frank, B. (1999). External Review of Digby High School. Unpublished report for the Southwest regional School Board, Nova Scotia, Canada.

Frank, B. and Davison, K. (eds.) (forthcoming). *Masculinities and Schooling: International Practices and Perspectives*, Halifax: Fernwood Press.

Gilbert, R. and Gilbert P. (1998). *Masculinity Goes to School*, London: Routledge.

Hazler, R. (1996). *Breaking the Cycle of Violence: Interventions for Bullying and Victimization*, London: Taylor and Francis.

International Adult Literacy Survey (1997). *Literacy of Canadian Youth*, September.

Kenway, J. (2000). Factors Influencing the Educational Performance of Males and Females in School and their Initial Destinations after Leaving School, Deakin University, University of South Australia.

Kenway, J. (1998). *Answering Back: Girls, Boys and Feminism in Schools*, London: Routledge.

Kenway, J. (1995). Masculinities in Schools: Under Siege, on the Defensive and under Reconstruction, *Discourse: Studies in the Cultural Politics of Education*, Vol 16, No. 1, 59–79.

Kenway, J. and Fitzclarence, L. (1997). Masculinity, Violence and Schooling: Challenging 'poisonous pedagogies', *Gender and Education*, Vol. 9, No. 1, 117–33.

Kindlon, D. and Thompson, M. (1999). *Raising Cain: Protecting the Emotional Life of Boys*, New York: Ballantine Books.

Kunjufu, J. (1986). *Countering the Conspiracy to Destroy Black Boys*, Vol. II. Chicago: African American Images.

Lees, S. (1986). *Losing out: Sexuality and Adolescent Girls*, London: Hutchison.

Mac an Ghaill, M. (ed.) (1996). *Understanding Masculinities: Social Relations and Cultural Arenas*, Buckingham: Open University Press.

Mac an Ghaill, M. (1994a). The Making of Black, English Masculinities. In H. Brod and M. Kaufman (eds.), *Theorizing Masculinities*, Thousand Oaks: Sage, pp. 183–99.

Mac an Ghaill, M. (1988). *Young, Gifted and Black: Student–Teacher Relations in the Schooling of Black Youth*, Milton Keynes: Open University Press.

Mac and Ghaill, M. (1994b). *The Making of Men: Masculinities, Sexualities and Schooling*, Buckingham: Open University Press.

Martino, W. (1994). Masculinity and Learning: Exploring Boys' Underachievement and Under-representation in Subject English, *Interpretations*, Special Edition: *Boys in English*, Vol. 27, No. 2, 22–47.

Martino, W. (1995). Deconstructing Masculinity in the English Classroom: A Site for Reconstituting Gendered Subjectivity, *Gender and Education*, Vol. 7, No. 2, 205–20.

Martino, W. (2000). Policing Masculinities: Investigating the Role of Homophobia and Heteronormativity in the Lives of Adolescent School boys, *The Journal of Men's Studies*, Vol. 8, No. 2, 213–36.

Martino, W. (forthcoming). 'Dangerous Pedagogies': Exploring Issues of Sexuality and Masculinity in Male Teacher Candidates' Lives. In B. Frank and K. Davison (eds), *Masculinities and Schooling: International Practices and Perspectives*, Halifax: Fernwood Press.

Men for Change (1994). *Healthy Relationships: A Violence-prevention Curriculum*, Men for Change: Halifax.

Pemberton, K. and Cullbert, L. (2001). Teen Suicides from Bullying a Worrying Trend, *The Vancouver Sun*, 11 January, p. A1.

Pollack, W. (1999). *Real Boys: Rescuing Our Sons from the Myth of Boyhood*, New York: Henry Holt and Company.

Rofes, E. (1995). Making our Schools Safe for Sissies. In: G. Unks (ed.), *The Gay Teen: Education, Practice and Theory for Lesbian, Gay and Bisexual Adolescents*, New York: Routledge, pp. 79–84.

Salisbury, J. and Jackson, D. (1996). *Challenging Macho Values: Practical Ways of Working with Adolescent Boys*, London: The Falmer Press.

Sexed Tetes Collective (1993). Gender Equity/Gender Treachery, *Border/Lines*, pp. 46–54.

Sketton, C. (1997). Primary Boys and Hegemonic Masculinities. *British Journal of Sociology of Education*, Vol. 18, No. 3: 349–69.

Willis, P. (1977). *Learning to Labour: How Working-class Kids Get Working-class Jobs*, New York: Columbia University Press.

Yelland, N. (ed.) (1998). *Gender in Early Childhood*, London: Routledge. Routledge and Kegan Paul.

Part II
Macro Policies and Micro Effects

4
Gender Equity Policy and Education: Reporting on/from Canada

Linda Eyre, Trudy A. Lovell and Carrol Ann Smith

Introduction

Research that reveals how specific local practices connect to global trends continues to be important in feminist work in education. An understanding of the influence of historical, social, economic and political contexts is especially important in gender equity policy research as this is often a contested and hostile terrain (Gelb and Hart, 1999; Ozga, 2000). Also, through regional and national comparisons we can see how education policy is influenced by social movements and larger institutional structures and processes. When we see similar gender equity activity – or the lack of it – across provinces, states, territories, countries and continents, we know that education is no longer – if it ever was – merely a local matter. There is more going on.

This chapter presents some preliminary findings of a study of gender equity policy and elementary (primary) and secondary public (state) education in Canada, since the 1970s.[1] The research is part of a larger comparative study of gender equity policy and public education in the US and in Australia (Marshall *et al.*, 1999; Gaskell and Taylor, 2001). Because public education in Canada is a provincial responsibility, it is necessary to look at education policy province by province, territory by territory. In this chapter, we focus specifically on gender equity and education policy in Nova Scotia.[2] We also make some connections to the findings of the national study, and raise some pivotal methodological issues brought to our attention through our recent work in the Northwest Territories.

The research is grounded in feminist/critical policy analysis (Marshall, 1997). This approach contributes to policy research by bringing forward a gender dimension. It reveals how gender equity policy differs from mainstream policy because it challenges white, male privilege, and it is often undermined, distorted, appropriated or co-opted by dominant groups. Feminist/critical policy analysis looks at policy-making from the point of view of those inside organisations and those at the margins. It employs narrative analysis – gleaning insider stories to understand how women's activism has shaped education policy and how, in turn, the women's movement has been shaped by institutional structures.

We take 1970 as a starting point for this work. In 1970, the Canadian government established a Royal Commission on the Status of Women. The Commission's 300-page report addressed substantive inequalities for women in six key categories[3] and put forward a plan of action to secure women's 'equal participation in educational and economic opportunities' (O'Neil and Sutherland, 1997, p. 203). Although the party membership were supportive of the recommendations, the report did not lead to the changes hoped, especially with regards to abortion, day care and the rights of Aboriginal women (Young, 2000). However, the Liberal government's efforts to appease the emerging feminist movement led to a range of activity, including the establishment of the position of Minister Responsible for the Status of Women, and a Secretary of State Women's Program. It created an advisory body, the Canadian Advisory Council on the Status of Women, and supported the National Action Committee on the Status of Women (NAC), as well as provincial Status of Women groups. In the 1980s women's rights were specifically recognised in the Charter of Rights and Freedoms. Liberal and Conservative governments have since made a public commitment to women's equality at three United Nations world conferences: the federal and provincial governments and the territories adopted the Convention on the Elimination of all Forms of Discrimination Against Women (1982), Nairobi Forward-looking Strategies for the Advancement of Women (1985), and the Beijing Platform for Action (1995).

If these promises still stand, it would be reasonable to expect improvements in attention to the situation of women in Canada. But in the 1990s the government disbanded the position of Minister Responsible for the Status of Women and replaced it with a Secretary of State who reports to the Minister of Canadian Heritage. It shut down the Canadian Advisory Council on the Status of Women, and reduced funding for NAC and provincial women's organisations. In the provinces, whatever the political stripe, social and economic equality has taken a back seat to privatisation, deregulation, downsizing and cuts to social services and education. All of which, and more, led Young to conclude that 'relations between feminist organizations and all three political parties had soured considerably by 1993' (2000, p. 162).

Throughout all of this, individuals and groups in the women's movement across the country have struggled to keep gender equity on the education policy agenda. Yet little is known about their work. In this study we look specifically at the gender equity work in public education of key individuals in teachers' associations/unions, Departments/Ministries of Education and school districts/boards. We look at how women's issues and feminist discourses have been taken up since the 1970s in different historical, economic, social and political contexts. We look at the shared values and the struggles, how the linkages among the different groups have been strengthened and weakened; and how they came together in the 1970s and fell apart in the late 1980s and 1990s.

Our work is based on the assumption that policy-making is a process involving struggle and negotiation between players inside and outside of the state, and competing discourses of feminism (Taylor *et al.*, 1997; Ozga, 2000). We want to make the work of women in this process visible – women whose knowledge and contribution is often unrecognized. At the same time, we want to problematise the category 'woman' (Bannerji, 1997). Who are the women, inside and on the margins, who have played a role in shaping gender equity policy in public education, and who are the women who have been excluded from this work? Another way to think of this is, whose gender issues have made it to the policy table, whose have not, and why? To this end, we held in-depth interviews with key players working inside provincial governments, school boards and teachers' unions, and with women working individually or in groups to force change in the governing bodies. We spoke to people who were involved with policy-making in public education in the 1970s, 1980s and 1990s; and those involved today. Some individuals we already knew, others were suggested to us by interviewees or professional contacts. We used a combination of foreshadowing questions and a life history approach in order to leave room for lines of thought that we had not considered. The interviews were taped and transcribed. We scrutinised official records of government debates on women's issues, and analysed the texts of education policy documents, minutes of meetings, resource materials, publications, and press releases. We analysed these texts and the interview transcripts for clues about how gender equity issues were framed and taken up across the decades. We looked for examples of state control, as well as instances of resistance and agency. We looked for patterns, commonalities and differences over time.

Here we present a snapshot of gender equity and education policy-making in Nova Scotia. We look at the work of insiders and individuals working on the outside of the Nova Scotia Teachers' Union, the Nova Scotia Department of Education and selected school boards as these were the main sites of policy-making in public education since 1970 in the province. We explore what Fraser names as 'the tacit norms and implicit assumptions that are constitutive of [government] practices' (1989, p. 146), and what Ng identifies as the systemic relations of power that are 'taken for granted and not ordinarily open to interrogation' (1993, p. 191).

Nova Scotia

Canada is a large landmass, with a relatively small population density. The ten provinces and three territories have very different historical, social, economic and political histories which shape decisions that are made around education. Nova Scotia is part of Atlantic Canada – a region with an Aboriginal, Black and European history – which Morton (2000) argues is often overlooked or treated in a stereotypical or token fashion in studies of Canada. Social inequities are often ignored 'in an effort to cling to the illusory postcard image of Atlantic Canada with its crashing waves, rolling hills, green fields and forests, clean air and happy "folk"' (Kelly, 1990). Or the 'region's dominant narrative of economic underdevelopment and political marginalization' (Morton, 2000, p. 119) predominates.

The social and cultural history of the province complicates the story in terms of gender. Recent changes in federal and provincial politics have had a major impact on education, health and social services in the province. The region has an average income below the national average, has suffered losses to its fishery and mining industries, and has one of the lowest social assistance rates in the country. Yet, as Morton explains, women in the Atlantic region have a history of resistance to colonialism, capitalism and gender inequality; community ties, especially in rural areas, have been 'both empowering and restrictive for women' (2000, p. 122). And, as Turpel-Lafond reminds us, prior to the arrival of Europeans, Aboriginal women did not have 'a cultural or social history of disentitlement ... from political or productive life' (1997, p. 69).

Research on gender equity activity and education in the region is limited. Our archival investigation of the work of community based women's groups in the province since the 1970s revealed that many groups with a range of feminist perspectives have existed in the province, but few have attended to education issues, and most groups have been short-lived due primarily to a lack of economic resources and volunteer 'burnout'. The Nova Scotia Advisory Council on the Status of Women, formed in 1977, is still in existence, but other than advising government on women's issues it has little power. We were drawn, therefore to look to the Nova Scotia Teachers' Union, the Nova Scotia Department of Education, and local school boards for gender equity activity in education since 1970. We have organised the qualitative information into three periods which roughly correspond to the three decades researched.

The Nova Scotia Teachers' Union

The Nova Scotia Teachers' Union (NSTU) serves as both the representative of Nova Scotia teachers in collective bargaining and as a professional association. It was formed in 1895 in response to a paper presented by Margaret Fulton, a teacher from the tiny village of Central Economy. Regrettably, the importance of Miss Fulton's contribution did not ensure an organisation sensitive to gender issues. Of a total of 41 NSTU presidents since 1921 only four have been women, in a profession dominated in numbers by women. Today, only four out of 22 members of the provincial executive are women and only three out of 11 professional staff. One woman active in the Union said that today 'the Union is more sexist than the [government]'. Another talked about how, if gender equity issues are adopted by the Union, it is because no one could possibly object to them. We heard much about the 'old boys' club', of silencing women during meetings and of tokenism. One woman took a generous view when she said, 'the Union always takes a gentle approach to gender equity'.

1970s: 'The Committee on the Committee on the Committee'

In the 1970s women members attempted to seek change in the conditions for women teachers in the province. Their focus was primarily on discrimination against married women teachers, and increasing the number of women in leadership positions. But their efforts were blocked in a variety of ways. For example, in 1975, a group of seven women members attempted to initiate a Status of Women committee. The executive approved the concept in principle, but the name and the composition of the proposed committee caused so much consternation that the matter was tabled for further consideration. When, four months later, the executive finally struck a committee to examine the proposal, this new committee recommended that the committee on the committee become the committee, and that this committee be ongoing! Fearing that the consideration of women's issues separate from those of men might be divisive, the executive determined that the name of the committee was to contain no reference to women, and amended the proposal to ensure that the committee would serve both women *and* men. Furthermore, the committee was to include the man who helped put forth the strange amendment. Delaying tactics such as this proved debilitating and frustrating for women members. It wasn't until 1979 that a standing committee empowered to study and make recommendations on a variety of issues pertaining to women came in to existence. The women had achieved a voice, but was anybody listening?

1980s: 'Is anybody listening?'

The early 1980s saw a lot of union activity around gender equity due to the energy generated by the Status of Women committee and the brief appointment to the executive staff of Past President Florence Wall, who subsequently became Chair of the Nova Scotia Advisory Council on the Status of Women. In 1980, the NSTU submitted guidelines on sex-role stereotyping in curriculum to the Nova Scotia Department of Education, and in 1982 the Status of Women Committee tabled recommendations concerning pensions. Liberal feminist activity took hold, but recommendations that struck more closely at the heart of institutionalised sexism were not supported. The Women in Education Committee, as it became known, was not accorded any power.

But having a woman in a position of leadership did make a difference. During the last four years of the decade when Karen Willis Duerdon was NSTU president, gender equity was frequently on the agenda. More women were on the provincial executive than ever before, or since. And in 1988, the Nova Scotia Department of Education, the Nova Scotia School Boards Association and the NSTU, jointly issued an Affirmative Action statement which advised school boards to adopt 'policies and procedures which ensure that women who are qualified and prepared are *given the same careful consideration as men for positions in educational administration'*. This weak interpretation of the concept of affirmative action led to a Letter of Understanding about Affirmative Action which was appended to the next agreement between the NSTU and the government. But Duerdon expressed doubt that the agreement was ever effective even when it became part of the contract.

1990s: 'The big chill'

Despite the continuing efforts of the Women in Education committee, attention to gender equity diminished in the 1990s. After 1992 when the government froze teachers' salaries, attention to gender issues and education competed with fiscal policies. As one woman told us, the executive 'didn't act on their resolutions because there were always more important issues at hand... [gender equity] was never a high priority in terms of money or time'. The Women in Education committee was also seen as threatening to male leadership in the Union. An insider told us that when the committee brought in powerful feminist speakers, such as Heather Jane Robinson and Sylvia Gold, 'it caused a lot of fear'. Indeed, the Committee did not have the support of all women. One interviewee said:

> There is this kind of reluctance to affiliate... with [women's groups] because they don't see it as career enhancing – it would seem to be one of those raving feminist kinds of things. And there were those who still felt that having a *Women* in Education Committee discriminated against men. They are still lobbying to change the name and the focus of the committee to this day.

The struggle to have gender equity taken seriously by the male leadership of the NSTU has lasted 30 years. At the 1998 council, delegates directed the Women in Education Committee to conduct a survey designed to 'determine how best to ensure that women and other under-represented groups are adequately represented on the provincial executive and other leadership positions in the Union'. Based on the survey, the Committee presented eight comprehensive recommendations aimed at addressing the barriers to women in the Union. The recommendations have been 'accepted by the Union for consideration', but to date no action has been taken. A similar directive was given to a group of management consultants in 1970, and nothing happened.

2000: 'A masculinist culture prevails'

Over the years, a few key women have worked extremely hard to advance the cause of gender equity against heavy inertia in NSTU. Although since its inception four women have served as president, the Union has been and still is informed by masculinist beliefs and values. We heard again and again how men continue to dominate Union politics and continue to hire and encourage people who support initiatives they are comfortable with.

The current situation for women in education in the province is telling. In 1998 only 39.5 per cent of administrative positions were held by women, most of these being in elementary schools, while 65.6 per cent of teachers were women. And while Union attention to gender equity has dwindled, a new phenomenon has surfaced. The NSTU publication *The Teacher* and the Executive Minutes abound with discourses about 'child poverty' and 'violence in schools' – both assuredly feminist issues – but presented from a liberal, individualistic perspective as if they have nothing to do with gender or feminism. The perception is that direct reference to gender equity or women's issues is politically dangerous.

Meanwhile, the advances achieved are in danger of being lost. In 2000, for the first time, the executive of the NSTU hired a staff person to take responsibility for equity. The person they chose is neither a woman nor a member of a minority, but rather a male past-president! One person said:

> I find it very hard that in the year 2000, 16 out 17 executive directors of Canadian teacher organizations are male – out of [teacher] populations that are female up to 60 per cent and higher. What does a union reward? What does a union perceive as a strength? I think we have some major issues around that.

We do indeed.

The Nova Scotia Department of Education

In the 1970s, the starting point of our research, the Nova Scotia government was comprised almost entirely of men, and women's issues rarely made it to the legislative assembly. The following incident should give a sense of the prevailing discourses of the political powers of the time. In 1977 a lengthy final debate ensued on *Bill 102: The Statute Law Respecting Women*. Speeches in favour of the bill were eclipsed by sexist comments from the floor, ranging from biological discourses about women's weakness, to women wanting it 'both ways' when it came to pay equity and family maintenance support. A perspective that was reiterated, with vehemence, when time came to advance equal pay for work of equal value legislation into practice. A senior departmental administrator said:

> There was a tremendous amount of discussion with men, who used to posit the spectre of financial chaos for business and the economy

generally, if we ever got so extreme and rash as to get into equal pay for work of equal value. That would bankrupt us and it would bankrupt the government.

Such comments were made by men who felt no risk in having their words recorded for public release. Financial prosperity maintained at the blatant expense of women was not seen as problematic then – or now – pay equity continues to be an issue for women in Canada. Passage of the *Law Respecting Women,* led to some gender equity activity in various government departments, including the Department of Education.

1970s: 'May we strongly suggest?'

In the late 1970s, Department of Education officials (all men) began to address the discrepancy in the ratio of women in leadership roles at the school level and within boards, relative to the number of women teachers in the province. In describing the situation at the time, a senior bureaucrat said:

> There was not a woman principal of a high school in all of Nova Scotia. If there were one, it would have been a small, rural high school that nobody really thought about. There were no women inspectors of schools. There wasn't a single woman superintendent on any Board in the province and there were 60 some Boards then. When I first joined the department we had a meeting of the deputy minister's directors, and the only woman present was the head of the regional library which was part of the department at that time. She was part of the department all right but, it was a peripheral connection and, of course, by that time it was generally accepted that a librarianship was a reasonable place for a woman. But, she was the only woman present in the room.

Women became pregnant and left because that was the policy of the time; some Boards were also still in the habit of firing women teachers who married.

In an effort to rectify this situation, the minister issued a directive on hiring practices to school boards in the province. Directives were mere *suggestions*, rather than official policy. We were told that this approach was based on the belief that there was a greater likelihood of compliance if there was an appearance of choice. A senior bureaucrat noted that even this approach faced opposition.

Our reading of the public records showed that whenever male privilege within the ranks of administrators was threatened, arguments about female *deficit* by merit of reproductive capacity were trotted out, repeatedly. A senior official told us that misogynistic comments, behind closed doors, were also common in the Department, though rarely committed to paper. No doubt, in the expectation that because they were uttered in a room full of men, their words were safe. (Which does, of course, raise the question about how the men who now appear dismayed responded at the time – a question we might have asked but didn't; interviewing 'up' raises its own problems about power and intimidation, staying in the interview or being shown out the door!) Nevertheless, it is important to remember that such comments came from men who were in a position to make decisions about employment and professional advancement of women in education in the province at that time.

1980s: 'Fixing the girls'

In the 1980s the enrolment of girls in mathematics and science was seen as key to ensuring that girls would have equal access to the higher-paying, higher-status, post-school work opportunities, an approach closely aligned with the forms of liberal feminism available at that time. The Department developed promotional materials for schools in an attempt to create a climate which would encourage more young women to become interested in sciences and mathematics. But funding for gender equity initiatives tended to be sparse and typically one-off grants which carried no guarantees of renewal. And although some textbooks at the time were reworked in a token effort to reflect First Nations and African Nova Scotia history, gender inclusion issues were dealt with in a tertiary way, as an afterthought.

Department efforts were also directed at opening up industrial arts (IA) courses to girls. In an article in *Education Nova Scotia*, a publication of the Department of Education, the author noted that there were new opportunities opening up for girls in non-traditional fields where feminine traits of *appreciation of colour* and *patience with frustrating tasks* would put them at an advantage for employment! Clearly, the author did not understand the issues. Curiously, the pressure to open up home economics to boys did not come from the Department; it was left to teachers at the local district and school level.

Interest in having girls engage in non-traditional training programmes in vocational schools (now known as community colleges) arose in the late 1970s, and it was in this sector that directives were seen to be more powerful, as that system was more closely linked to government control. A Department official said:

> In the late seventies if you saw young women [in vocational schools] you knew that they were going to either the [Certified Nursing Assistant] class or the hairdressing salon. We made very significant efforts and initiatives across the vocational schools to open up... non-traditional courses for women. In a few cases establishing a quota and saying, we are going to ensure that... x per cent of the class is women, and that sort of thing. We had some flexibility with the community college system that of course, we didn't have with the public school system, because the province ran the community college system. We had a greater degree of control there.

But the 'control' the government had in the community college system did not challenge patriarchal thinking about the value of women's traditional work. Girls' 'problems' would be rectified by getting more young women to seek training in traditionally male work areas. The effectiveness of advocating for gender equity through passive directives rather than proactive policy was captured by a senior official when he summed up his experience with a note of irony:

> Throughout Nova Scotia, after we were all through sending our letters and making our speeches... and having it known that the Minister and the Deputy and everyone else was all fired up to do something about this, the net result was about zero. Hard to believe, isn't it?

We don't think so.

1990s: Shifting priorities: 'What about the boys?'

There was little official gender equity activity in the Department in the 1990s. One senior bureaucrat told us that attention to women issues in education could no longer be justified due to the rise in women's economic circumstances and the prevailing belief that gender equity was no longer an issue in the workplace. He pointed out that women were equally represented in medical and law schools and other forms of higher education, this being a result of hard work, on the part of able women who worked towards these goals. Such individualistic arguments continue today. Instead, the Department has recently turned its attention to boys and the currently high-profile notion that boys are falling behind in school, especially in the area of literacy. Unlike the 'fix the girls' response of the 1970s and 1980s, the boys are fine, but the system is deemed inadequate, a practice that has historically been the case when male students are thought to be demonstrating lower achievement levels than girls (Cohen, 1998). To that end there is a renewed call to 'masculinise' the curriculum.

And impossible tasks

Recently, the Department incorporated gender-related work into a broader framework. A woman has been hired as 'multi-cultural' director for student services with responsibility for issues of race, gender, sexuality, culture and class. The vast scope of the task suggests that this is a token gesture by the Department. It is unclear how this appointment will affect future gender equity work in the province.

Nova Scotia School Boards

While gender equity activity in the Department has been token at best, it is probably in the individual school boards that women working inside and outside the bureaucracy have had most influence,[4] albeit against great odds. In the interests of space, an example of recent activity around sexual harassment might suffice.

In the early 1990s, in the aftermath of the Anita Hill case in the US (Morrison, 1992), several school boards across the province became aware that there was a need to be seen to be concerned about sexual harassment. In at least one board this concern was motivated by secretaries who brought forward complaints of sexual harassment against their employers. In this case the board formed a committee of administrators, teachers, parents, staff, custodians and students to draft a policy. But a women administrator involved in the work spoke to us of the resistance of some people within the group to name the issues directly and sidestep the work of the committee. She said that it became clear that several of these individuals were not present of their own accord, but had been encouraged to get involved 'to make sure the women didn't go too far'. In another board, a teacher involved in the process told us that he found himself presenting the document to a committee of the board, while two male board members sat behind him and ridiculed his presentation. At the end of the presentation one of the men came to the table and extolled the virtues of the policy 'without a hint of dishonesty showing on his face'. As Smith (1990) says, people are more likely to transgress against those who are less likely to be able to provide them with real consequences for their behaviour.

A feminist administrator with one board described the efforts of women and some men in her district to develop a sexual harassment policy:

> I cannot remember a policy being developed by the Board that meant so much volunteer work...It was only because of the passion of the people involved that it ever got off the ground...I think they thought we would go away once the group got running, but we didn't...We worked with next-to-nothing...we bought our own binders and put packages together at my dining room table...and then took them around to the schools.

Once policy was drafted, in some boards taking more than a year to achieve, it was clear that implementation was not high on the list of priorities. Money to get policy disseminated was in short supply, often obtained through individuals carefully approaching board members who were known to support the process, and having them persuade the powers or those 'who imagined themselves to be' to fund the work. Even then, we heard that the funds were much like an allowance, doled out in tiny sums to well-behaved children. It would appear that the policy documents received little direct implementation and were more often used as resource guides only.

Over the years, the same women often worked across the system, influencing Union, Department, board and school-based activity. This is somewhat in contrast to the idea of 'women building alliances and coalitions...[bringing] women together from unions, parties, and community groups' (Briskin, 1999, p. 147). We wondered if this is where place matters. As one woman told us 'these same women were involved with everything'. They were also willing to risk being ostracised by speaking out about gender issues – and many were. These are the same women who spoke to us about feeling exhausted by the outright resistance and isolation they had experienced over the years. They are ready to relay the work to new people with fresh ideas and untapped energy, but find that few people are interested or willing to continue the work.

For some, the lack of current attention to gender issues at the local level may also have to do with the perception that gender equity has been achieved. One woman said:

People think [gender equity] has been dealt with...You can see some women around, you can see some visible minorities, so we've dealt with it. We've done all we need to do.

As well as the current political climate:

All the things associated with globalisation – competitiveness, standards – all those things make people focus inward, they focus very much on the individual...So the larger issues of equity...are no longer important...Now you must meet these standards, you are going to get tested...It's at war with the larger questions of equity and societal responsibility.

And its masculinist culture:

I think it's the shifting kind of political climate in terms of expectations and the kinds of directives that are coming up to us from government that have made it a much more masculinist kind of work. You know – produce the report! Get the finances in order! Be a good manager! Make sure you get all this stuff done! Make the most of less!

Still, for other women, the turn away from gender equity activity in the 1990s had to do with the intensification of teachers' work:

It's plain exhaustion! I think people have gotten busier and busier so that these groups that were advocating and sustaining some of the work in the eighties are just exhausted because their work is becoming so much more intense that people simply do not have the energy or the time to commit to it.

They also pointed to the reality that younger teachers without permanent contracts are hesitant to align themselves with anything controversial. Feminism and gender equity activity were articulated as high risk in terms of future job security in the twenty-first century.

Making connections

Our findings in Nova Scotia reflect a pattern evident in other provinces. The 1970s and 1980s were a time of gender equity activity in education when connections were being forged among the women's movement, the teachers' unions, Departments/Ministries of Education and school boards. The major issues addressed reflected feminist discourse of the time: increasing the number of girls in mathematics, science and technology; conditions for women teachers; and more women in administrative positions. Whether provincial governments and unions took gender equity seriously, they could not be seen to be avoiding gender issues.

But in the last decade, provincial economic 'restructuring' agendas have resulted in diminished attention to issues of social justice (Bashevkin, 1998). The work of women in education committees in unions across the country has taken a back seat to concerns about budgets cuts, teachers' salaries and working conditions. In Departments/ Ministries of Education, if gender equity is addressed at all, boys are now seen as the new educationally disadvantaged. Women's issues and education have been undermined and distorted through neo-conservative discourses of individualism and humanism. Public narratives, such as 'school violence', 'child poverty', 'literacy', 'life-long learning', predominate. Even 'anti-discrimination' and 'social justice' are being interpreted from a liberal individualistic perspective. And gender equity has been added to the portfolio of individuals responsible for a broad range of equity issues, including racism, homophobia, culture, disability, religion and language. The effect has been to neutralise and undermine gender equity work. A move seemingly supported by the unions. A more critical and sophisticated understanding of gender equity is absent. As Bashevkin says, 'the curious situation in which [supposedly] activist social movements defend passive government policies seems more and more inconsistent' (Bashevkin, 1998, p. 245).

Equality and social justice in education is seriously threatened under the new state formations. In Ontario, Premier Harris's conservative agenda has had a major impact on gender equity policy in education in that province, and threatens to drift across the country. Moves to deregulate the power of the unions, dissolve the women teachers' association (the main site of gender equity activity in the province) and, more recently, give financial rewards to parents who send their children to private schools, work against social equality. And people who once worked on equity issues in government saw their roles reassigned. As Henry (2001) says, under market-led systems, schools are not rewarded for their attention to equity, but for discipline policies and exam results.

For some of the women we have spoken with there was a sense of achievement; for others it was battles lost; and for still others, a bewilderment in how to proceed in the shift to the marketisation and privatisation of education and erosion of gains already achieved. In her analysis of social movements, Gaskell describes what happened in

British Columbia in this way: 'The women's movement came together, came apart, was involved with educational institutions, and lost its relationship to them... social movements challenge institutional politics; institutional politics supports, incorporates, and ultimately defeats social movements' (2001, p. 14).

A turning point

I (Linda) interrupt this text with a word about recent interviews with women in the Northwest Territories.[5] As a white woman, I arrived in Yellowknife grounded in white feminism. I left with more questions about the appropriateness of the research questions and my assumptions about the usefulness of using gender equity as a starting point. Staring me in the face were, as Henry succinctly states, 'the politics of equality and difference, dilemmas of who can speak for whom, and the complex interlayering of culturally, historically and geographically specific factors' (2001, p. 98). I returned with a sense of shame about my limited white, privileged feminist worldview. For the Aboriginal women with whom we spoke, healing fragile communities was a priority; gender equity and schooling was a non-issue.

In retrospect, why would women in Aboriginal communities give priority to education issues when education is a colonising practice?[6] The qualitative information that we gathered (stole?) in the Northwest Territories has yet to be analysed thoroughly, but it has certainly raised important questions about the activity of the women's movement in Canada that we need to revisit in the provinces as well. We now need to consider more closely whose voices have been absent from the gender equity debates, and why? Why, for example, did the community-based women's groups in Nova Scotia pay little attention to the school system? As Morton (2000, p. 119) states, there is an 'uneasy relationship between gender and region' that deserves closer scrutiny. Research is a reflexive process (Lather, 1991). As Fellman eloquently points out 'every insight is inhabited by its own blindness' (in Kelly 1997: 56). And, as McLeod (1998, p. 431) says: 'We need to understand feminist interventions in education and other social domains – as both emancipatory and disciplining'. But, at the same time, we must not let our concerns paralyse our actions.

The work continues

In the current conservative climate and neoliberal agenda, if we can't move on policy – our work can still expose the contradictions in what policy makers say and do. As Lorde says:

Whether we speak or not the machine will crush us to bits-and we will also be afraid. Your silence will not protect you. (in Ferguson, 1984, p. 2)

Holding governments accountable means bringing a critical feminist analysis to the dominant discourses of the state, no matter how hostile the response. It requires subjecting all education initiatives and reforms to feminist scrutiny. In our interviews we heard about the slide back to masculinised administrative units and the increasingly feminised and casualised teaching workforce (Blackmore, 1999); women burned out; no longer vigilant. Concern about a masculinist culture in the teachers unions and departments of education is evident across the country. Part of the answer lies in having more women in positions of power. But as Blackmore reminds us, '"not any woman will do"... when social justice is a basic tenet of a feminist practice of educational leadership' (1999, p. 221). A critical feminist mass is necessary for any substantive change to take place.

Change also involves exposing the limitations of supposedly gender neutral policies and equity initiatives in education that individualise the issues, ignore difference, and avoid the material conditions of women's lives. It means exposing the contradictions and paradoxes of government equity initiatives (Coulter, 1996; McAdie, 1998; Eyre, 1999) and other reform policies and programmes. It means publicly asking who is being accountable for the development or enforcing of gender equity policy in education with the shift to new forms of governance while promoting, as Henry says, more 'sophisticated understandings' of gender issues 'to change the way equity matters are framed' (2001, p. 90). It may also mean beginning with place (Kelly, 1990); while running the risk of reifying boundaries, unless we begin here we are always looking elsewhere for models or answers which absent the contexts in which specific regions are located.

It also means subjecting the women's movement to scrutiny. Whose women's movement is it? Which women? What are the issues that must be addressed to further the education of all women? Which strategies are appropriate for addressing goals yet to be achieved? Although many (mostly white) women that we interviewed spoke enthusiastically about the accomplishments of the 1970s and 1980s, our point is not to argue for the continuance of white, liberal, middle-class feminism. As Carty points out 'White women played an instrumental role in maintaining racist relations of rule put in place by their men, the colonial administrators' (1999, p. 38). Perhaps it is these questions that are also holding back feminist initiatives in the schools, and may be the movement's greatest challenge yet. There is talk about the end of feminism by prominent feminists and anti-feminists. Our own work may also leave that impression. But scholars such as Bashevkin (1998) and Young (2000), young feminists such as Mitchell, Rundle and Karaian (2001), and activist groups like the 'Guerrilla Girls', beg to differ. The women who organised and participated in the World March of Women, and challenged the Summit of the Americas, as well as the many women who participate in community activism, including on-line discussion groups, offer hope. The movement continues, but further work is needed to explore how new forms of activism can both limit and offer possibilities for feminist work in schools. In the meantime, feminists in education need our ongoing support – with or without the emperor's blessing.

Notes

1 The project entitled 'A Study of Gender Equity Policy and Education in Six Canadian Provinces and the Northwest Territories' was funded by the Social Sciences and Humanities Research Council of Canada, with Linda Eyre as principal investigator and Jane Gaskill as co-investigator.
2 This work was carried out by Heather Goulding, Trudy Lovell and Carrol Ann Smith.
3 The categories addressed in the Report were: women in the Canadian economy; education; women and the family; taxation and child care allowance; immigration and citizenship; and criminal law and women offenders.
4 Although School Boards are subject to government education policies, they can also develop their own policies and directives. Our investigation of activity at the Board level continues, but is complicated by the amalgamation of Boards over the years, and most recently into seven regional boards. There is also a danger of focusing on the urban Boards and missing activity in the rural areas.
5 This work was carried out by Linda Eyre, Jane Gaskill and Elizabelth Blaney.
6 Thanks to Ann Vibert for making this point.

References

Bannerji, H. (1997). Geography Lessons: On Being an Insider/Outsider to the Canadian Nation. In L. Roman and L. Eyre (eds.), *Dangerous Territories: Struggles for Difference and Equality in Education*. New York: Routledge.
Bashevkin, S. (1998). *Women on the Defensive: Living through Conservative Times*. Toronto: University of Toronto Press.
Blackmore, J. (1999). *Troubling Women: Feminism, Leadership and Educational Change*, Buckingham: Open University Press.

Briskin, L. (1999). Unions and Women's Organizing in Canada and Sweden. In L. Briskin, and M. Eliasson (eds.), *Women's Organizing and Public Policy in Canada and Sweden*. Montreal: McGill-Queen's University Press.

Carty, L. (1999). The Discourse of Empire and the Social Construction of Gender. In E. Dua and A. Robertson (eds.), *Scratching the Surface: Canadian Anti-Racist Feminist Thought*. Toronto: Women's Press.

Cohen, M. (1998). 'A Habit of Healthy Idleness': Boys Underachievement in Historical Perspective. In D. Epstein, J. Elwood, V. Hey and J. Maw (eds.), *Failing Boys: Issues in Gender and Achievement*. Buckingham: Open University Press.

Coulter, R. P. (1996). Gender Equity and Schooling: Linking Research and Policy, *Canadian Journal of Education*, Vol. 21, No. 4, 433–52.

Eyre, L. (1999). After Beijing: Women and 'Education and Training' in New Brunswick. *Atlantis*, Vol. 24, No. 1, fall/winter.

Ferguson, K. (1984). *The Feminist Case against Bureaucracy*, Temple Philadelphia: University Press.

Fraser, N. (1989). *Unruly Practices: Power, Discourse and Gender in Contemporary Social Theory*. Minneapolis: University of Minnesota Press.

Gaskell, J. (2001). B. C. Schools and the Women's Movement: Social Movements and Institutional Change in the 1970s, Unpublished paper.

Gaskell, J. and Taylor, S. (2001). The Women's Movement in Canadian and Australian Education: From Liberation and Sexism to Boys and Social Justice. Unpublished paper.

Gelb, J. and Hart, V. (1999). Feminist Politics in a Hostile Environment: Obstacles and Opportunities. In M. Giugni, D. McAdam and C. Tilley (eds), *How Social Movements Matter*. Minneapolis, MN: University of Minnesota Press.

Henry, M. (2001). Globalisation and the Politics of Accountability: Issues and Dilemmas for Gender Equity in Education. *Gender and Education*, Vol. 13, No. 1, 87–100.

Kelly, U. A. (1990). On the Edge of the Eastern Ocean: Teaching, Marginality and Voice. In D. Henley and J. Young (eds), *Canadian Perspectives on Critical Pedagogy*, The Canadian Critical Pedagogy Network, Canada.

Kelly, U. A. (1997). *Schooling Desire: Literacy, Cultural Politics, and Pedagogy*. New York: Routledge.

Lather, P. (1991). *Getting Smart: Feminist Research and Pedagogy With/In the Postmodern*. New York: Routledge.

Marshall, C. (Ed.) (1997). *Feminist Critical Policy Analysis: A Perspective from Secondary Schooling*, Vol. 1. London: Falmer Press.

Marshall, C., Taylor, S. and Gaskell, J. (1999). Teacher Unions and Gender Equity Policy: Building Social Capital in Three Countries. Unpublished paper.

McAdie, P. (1998). The Abandonment of the Pursuit of Equity, *Canadian Woman Studies/Les Cahiers de la Femme*, Vol. 17, No. 4, winter, 6–14.

McLeod, J. (1998). The Promise of Freedom and the Regulation of Gender – Feminist Pedagogy in the 1970s, *Gender and Education*, Vol. 10, No. 4, 431–45.

Mitchell, A., Rundle, L. B. and Karaian, L. (2001). *Turbo Chicks: Talking Young Feminisms*, Toronto: Sumach Press.

Morrison, T. (ed.) (1992). *Race-ing Justice, Engendering Power: Essays on Anita Hill, Clarence Thomas, and the Construction of Social Reality.* New York: Random House.

Morton, S. (2000). Gender, Place, and Region: Thoughts on the State of Women in Atlantic Canadian History. *Atlantis*, Vol. 25, No. 1, fall/winter, 119–28.

Ng, R. (1993). 'A woman out of control': Deconstructing Sexism and Racism in the University, *Canadian Journal of Education*, Vol. 18, No. 3, 189–205.

O'Neil, M. and Sutherland, S. (1997). The Machinery of Women's Policy: Implementing the RCSW. In A. Carter and S. Rodgers (eds.), *Women and the Canadian State/Les Femmes et L'Etat Canadien.* Montreal: McGill-Queen's University Press.

Ozga, J. (2000). *Policy Research in Educational Settings: Contested Terrain.* Buckingham: Open University Press.

Smith, D. E. (1990). *Texts, Facts, and Femininity: Exploring the Relations of Ruling.* London: Routledge.

Taylor, S., Rizvi, F., Lingard, B. and Henry, M. (1997). *Educational Policy and the Politics of Change.* London: Routledge

Turpel-Lafond, M. E. (1997). Patriarchy and Paternalism: The Legacy of Canadian First Nations Women. In A. Carter and S. Rodgers (eds.), *Women and the Canadian State/Les Femmes et L'Etat Canadien.* Montreal: McGill-Queen's University Press.

Young, L. (2000). *Feminists and Party Politics.* Vancouver: UBC Press.

5
Genderspace: Learning Online and the Implications of Gender

Katherine Hanson, Sundra Flansburg and Marianne Castano

Introduction

Throughout history, the social construct of gender has carried stereotypes expressed through the use of language and other social practices in face-to-face interactions and in written text. Today, the easy availability of computers has presented another medium of expression and with it, another context with gender considerations and implications. While considerable research focused on the issues surrounding the effects of gender in classrooms, information on how gender affects online learning is scarce. Very few new online learning technologies address the emerging issues of gender and safety in online classrooms (Machanic, 1998). The availability of computer-mediated communication (CMC) tools has paved the way for online education and learning. The US Department of Education statistics suggest that approximately 20 million students will be enrolled in college in the United States by the year 2010 (Cardenas, 1998), and many other countries are experiencing similar interest and growth in this new form of distance education. Online education based on CMC is one of the ways academic institutions are addressing the rise in student enrolment and related costs (Blum, 1999), as well as a resource for professional development for busy teachers. A 1994 study by American Demographics showed that women are about equally as likely as men to use home computers for educational purposes. Women are also more likely than men to be a major target market for CMC-based higher education.

The potential and benefits of online education have been heralded. However, many issues surrounding technology and gender including the opportunity to learn anywhere at any time have surfaced and concerns specific to online technologies have emerged. In this essay we describe some of the particular areas of online technology and gender that we are currently exploring in our research and practice, including gender issues related to technology design, online communication and expectations and learning online. As we approach these areas, underlying the discussion is our conviction that gender exists alongside and overlapping other personal and social identities like race, ethnicity, social class, ability, and so on. We first provide a summary of current research on gender in online communications in general, then link this to a discussion of gender and online learning. This framework outlines the beginning point for our research on gender equity in online learning, a research project supported by a grant from the National Science Foundation.

Review of the research

Two main theories address the interpretation of online communications from a gender perspective. The first argues that online communication provides a more equal playing field for women and people of colour because, as opposed to face-to-face situations, gender, race and ethnicity, and other personal/social identities, can be hidden. For example, women are better able to participate and complete thoughts online than in face-to-face interactions where they tend to be cut off or interrupted more often (Turkle, 1995; Shapiro, 1997). We (1993) found that in online interactions most men tend to deal with the content of what women say instead of dismissing it as coming from a woman, as they tend to do in face-to-face situations. Further, a characteristic of online communication is its lack of easy social contextualisation (Mahoney and Knupfer, 1997). Because CMC instructional tools are predominantly text-based, certain identifying characteristics of online participants are not necessarily known or easily assumed. The notion of a gender-blind participation online is more likely to ensue, should the participants choose consciously to conceal gender-identified characteristics or patterns.

The second theory maintains that online interaction is a reflection of real world conversation, where gender and race patterns exist (King, 2000). Participants in fact continue to 'do gender' or 'do race' often without knowing it. Both female and male participants tend to use conversational and interpersonal patterns that could be identified as 'female' and 'male' (Deaux and LaFrance, 1998; Ferris, 1996). For instance, in contrast to the first theory, men are seen as introducing more new topics and often ignoring topics introduced by women. At the same time, participants tend to disclose more personal information whether consciously or not (Castano, 1996), including their gender, as they 'adapt into the stream of language and textual behaviours messages that might otherwise be nonverbal' (Walther *et al.*, 1994, p. 65). In other words, this approach acknowledges that in current society gender is much more than a visual appearance. Because of strong socialisation that frames much of our everyday actions, gender identities become known even when not overtly stated.

Online communications and anonymity

Asynchronous CMC and Gender Online communication is either asynchronous (such as email) or synchronous (such as Internet Relay Chats). Literature on CMC suggests that a majority of online communication, including the delivery of online learning and corollary activities, is asynchronous (e.g. Blum, 1999). With this feature comes the notion of anonymity, in that very little personal information about the other person is known unless that person chooses to disclose such information (Castano, 1996). The use of pseudonyms adds to one's anonymity. With this perception of anonymity, participants can easily assume a different gender identity or shield their identity and gender. However, while services are available on the Internet so one can use pseudonyms or create new and multiple email addresses (Barlow, 1996; Grossman, 1997), only a certain number of CMC venues offer this capability, especially in distance education settings. Even when a certain level of anonymity is available, one's gender is still often visible in CMC as demonstrated by a participant's discourse style, which the individual may not be consciously aware of or not able to change easily (Blum, 1999). Such information does not depend on visual or auditory channels of communication; text alone is adequate. For instance, research on US-based gender patterns finds that men's language tends to have strong assertions; is self-promoting and authoritative; includes presuppositions and rhetorical questions; seeks to challenge others; and is either humorous or sarcastic. Women's language, on the other hand, tends to have attenuated assertions; includes apologies, explicit justifications and questions; is more personal; and usually seeks to provide support to others (Herring, 1993). At the same time, participants from different racial/ethnic groups may use different communication styles from white women. If, for example, the majority of participants in a discussion are white and middle class, they will often unconsciously frame a conversation that essentially marginalises or silences participants from other racial/ethnic groups. This is true for both face-to-face and online interactions, resonating with

King's (2000) and Ferris's (1996) assertion that online communication usually mirrors that of face-to-face communication.

One facet of online communication that receives considerable attention is the development of virtual communities. To have a feeling of community, we need to feel like we belong (Watson, 1997); to have our own private and safe space (Borg, 1996; Dyson, 1998; Horn, 1998); and to feel like we are known to the members of the community and know its members (Dyson, 1998; Horn, 1998). Because online communication in mixed settings tends to be male-controlled and often silences women (Blum, 1999; Herring, 2000), many women-centred or women-only online groups exist (Balka, 1993; Camp, 1996), while men-only groups are rare (Herring, 2000).

The conventional masculine valuing of agonism and the conventional feminine valuing of social harmony can lead to conflicting experiences online: the contentiousness of messages from males tends to discourage women from participating. On the other hand, women's concern with politeness tends to be perceived as a waste of time by men (Herring, 1996) or even censorship (Grossman, 1997). Women are more likely to thank, appreciate and apologise, and get upset by violations of politeness (Smith *et al.*, 1997). However, men tend to be more aggressive, and online aggression tends to win over less aggressive behaviour (Herring, 2000). Flaming, or the 'practice of trading angry and often ad hominem remarks on any given topic' (Turkle, 1995, p. 217), is often tolerated and even enjoyed by men (Herring, 1994). Such online behaviour may affect online learning. Since online learning settings usually include asynchronous discussions where students post their messages in a discussion forum for everyone to read and respond to, the gender differences found in asynchronous modes of communication could very well transfer to online learning. Additionally, as racial bias is a recognised component of onsite education, and can be assumed also to play out in online forums, there are parallel implications for the development of online learning environments.

Learning styles and communication patterns

In a study conducted by Blum (1999) with US undergraduate students on asynchronous-based instruction, it was found that female online students tended to exhibit learning styles similar to face-to-face ones, preferring to learn in a connected manner. Online female students tend to place emphasis on relationships, are empathic in nature and would rather learn in an environment where cooperation is embodied more than competition. However, male students preferred to learn in a separate manner. This study also found that female online students used cooperation as a learning tool. They tended to ask more questions and ask for help from other students on such things as homework. They also preferred learning from other students rather than going through formal channels of information. Online male learning styles had elements of a controlling nature. Male messages had a tone of certainty and were often arrogant and assertive. Similar to face-to-face environments, males tended to dominate the learning environment. Gender differences were also found in online communication patterns, some of which were similar to face-to-face communication patterns. For example, female messages consisted of words of a more 'elegant' nature, such as 'acquire' while men used 'get'. The overall tone of female messages was less 'rough' in nature. They used fewer insults, less slang and almost no derogatory remarks. Males also tended to communicate in a more impersonal manner, while females used a more personal style (Blum, 2000).

Findings from Blum's study suggest that higher education students who were learning via CMC-based distance education prefer to learn the same way as they do in a face-to-face setting. Their communication also reflects patterns seen in face-to-face discussions. Racial/ethnic differences were not addressed in this study. Since the majority of US female undergraduates are white, however, we could assume that these generalisations hold for a white population or mainstream culture but may not represent the communication patterns and learning-structure preferences of other women. Similar research needs to determine if adults in professional development settings or participants in informal online learning environments have similar patterns.

Courseware design

Gender and technology design has received little attention until now, apart from some excellent studies on game design and gender. Research still needs to be conducted on the implications of gender and race on the design of courseware and course design. In the educational setting, we know that many training and other educational materials are written by males (Mahoney and Knupfer, 1997). An extensive review of Web-based page design documents revealed that the topics of gender representation in language and general page design were not addressed (Mahoney and Knupfer, 1997). The fact that materials and tools are designed primarily by males or females is not in itself an indication of gender bias, but it does indicate a probability that what is designed reflects a gendered and raced way of thinking or basic approach to use.

Gender and diversity

Missing from most of the research on gender and online technologies is a recognition that gender does not exist in isolation from race, ethnicity, social class, and other identities. By failing to consider how these 'intersections' affect and define gender, much of the literature may ascribe middle-class, Caucasian patterns to all interactions or expectations online, when in fact there are significant differences among women or among men. In addition, given the current environment and power structure surrounding online technologies, what is termed a male pattern is very likely a white, middle-class male pattern. Similarly, the female pattern generally described is very likely to be a white, middle-class pattern. A more complex understanding of gender and diversity should be integrated into mainstream research initiatives if the promise of the virtual world is to be achieved.

The limits and possibilities of new technologies

Our practice-based experience with online technologies and settings has led us to begin the exploration of how technology as a tool both reflects and challenges current societal assumptions. We begin with understanding that there is no one, all-encompassing online experience. The context of an interaction, be it on an 'open' listserv or a 'closed' discussion within an extended online course, will, to a large extent, define how participants approach and conduct themselves online, as well as what they take from the experience. It is difficult to speak of a generic online course or online communication style, in part because so many different contexts provoke so many different experiences, and in part because experiences can be so different according, for instance, to the person's gender, social class, race or ethnicity, or comfort level with new technologies. With this in mind, however, we seek to raise a number of questions that future research can help answer.

Gender and technology design

Research questions about the gender/technology relationship were initially concerned with girls' and women's technology avoidance and the lack of women in computer science and technology. Significant research focused on the relationship between girls' interest and engagement with computers as a harbinger for their later move to technology careers. Looking especially at the design of computer games and the public perception that computers were seen as 'male', much of this research focused on the redesign of games to get girls interested in technology. Others, such as Brunner (1999) and Spender (1995), looked into the paradigms that frame the ways that women and men perceive computers and technology and their role within the lives of individual women and men. Similarly, Spender and others raised issues about the discourse in maths, science and technology, especially the use of male metaphors and interaction patterns that were often competitive and individualistic-as opposed to the collegial style attributed to more women. With the emergence of online learning as a means to expand access to learning, similar questions need to be asked about the use of technology as a tool for expanding skills and knowledge, but also about the role of the underlying technology and the construction and content of courses. This parallels earlier examinations of the hidden curriculum of the classrooms, of the socialisation process and the transmittal of power through social structures, and the outcomes for marginalised groups.

Current technology discourse continues for the most part to talk about the obvious inequities of access. Boys are the ones who play with the technology – and these are mostly white boys, who grow up into adults who own software companies. They are part of the *Triumph of the Nerds* that Robert X captured in his 1996 film. Few African Americans or Latinos are visible in this world, and almost no females. Issues of access and outcomes, however, may be missing a deeper issue, raised in Postman's *Technopoly* (1993). The very design of the computer systems – the platform, the software, the construction of the environment – may in fact be replicating the very power and access inequities that they were said to diminish. The tools we create replicate the mindset, metaphors, maps, expectations and assumptions that the creators carry, either consciously or unconsciously. For example, the study of textbooks can show how changing perspectives and values shift the content and perspectives passed on to the reader. Earlier in the last century, history texts portrayed a 'Western Expansion' into the American Frontier, populated by warlike tribes and buffalo. The presence of women in US experiences – even when they were significant contributors to science, politics, or the World War II industrial efforts – went unnoticed. White historians framed the questions and context to form their own experience and for the most part there was one accepted perspective. They thus promulgated the white mainstream male perspective of the world; even women and people of colour often accepted this as the proper perspective or discourse. Clearly things have changed and these underlying assumptions are routinely challenged, but underlying assumptions influenced by gender, race, ethnicity and class continue to frame our education paradigm.

Technology and all its uses – computer games, composition, net searches and, of course, online learning – similarly carry some of the perspectives of those who develop them. And, as Postman (1993) suggests, if the primary developers are white male engineers who value traditional linear thinking, then the technology carries that as a structure – and users unconsciously fit themselves into that mode. The continued use of this linear structure can then force users to adopt that way of thinking and communicating until it becomes second nature. The nonlinear, synergistic thinkers, the people who think 'outside the box', may be being converted to linear thinkers, who now create from that perspective and who replicate it in their new work. Postman's caution that we will have a nation or generation who cannot create except with a computer, who cannot conceive of different ways of seeing, has implications for the development of technology-based education. For example, if we develop one way of educating (a standardised version of online learning) what will happen to the collective energy and creativity that many forms of seeing, thinking, communicating offer?

What implications does this have for the replication of existing power structures? Until challenged as part of the Civil Rights and women's movement, assumptions about who controlled power – who was powerful – reinforced a male-dominated system in which white middle-class males were the arbiters and purveyors of power. Whether it was representing God as an elderly white European male with flowing locks and blue eyes, presenting father as the head of family and the important 'breadwinner' or maintaining the privilege of whiteness for both men and women, the society was designed to maintain that power system and most people accepted it without question. It was what they knew, what they experienced, what they sustained – and, of course, what they passed on to their children. As a society still in flux, the questions about power, about women's roles and about the marginalisation of African Americans, Latinos, Indians and anyone else who doesn't fit the mainstream model are addressed less and less often. But the power of these issues continues, the marginalisation persists – and the system may be supported by a new tool: the computer. At the same time, the technology harnessed within the computer has the potential to empower, to provide resources to individuals and groups who have never before had easy access, to create new services and jobs, or to expand one's worldview and friendships across continents. Integral to this liberating perspective is the assumption that the technology is a neutral presence. Examining both the liberating potential and the underlying assumptions/hidden curriculum of the technology can help to expand both the paradigm guiding technology development and the opportunities for empowerment.

In research on men and women's conversations, Tannen (1990) and others (e.g. Lakoff, 2000) have pointed out the different ways in which we communicate, often talking past one another. Multicultural studies, diversity initiatives, intercultural understanding and anthropology and sociology continue to point out the complexity of human communication – different ways of talking, different listening styles, different ways of interacting, which all impact on both the speaker and the listener. This leads to another set of questions. For example, what does one make of interactions that are silent because of hearing deficits, or ones in which one or more of the participants are not sighted? What happens when individuals do not speak the same language or have the same set of references in which to ground their conversation? What happens if one person assumes the power role and the other does or does not recognise that? All these issues come together with new complexity in the environment of online learning. And we are only beginning to understand this complexity or to examine it.

For example, how will the mind map of the designer influence the design of the technology itself? It may be difficult to imagine another structure, look or arrangement of features for a computer or for the coding script that makes it work. The computer as we know it grew out of a set of parameters and was created by a line of men and women who, over time, adhered to those parameters. The keyboard and look of the current computers mimic earlier typewriters, which were designed to reflect certain assumptions and meet certain needs, but there is no reason why the equipment might not be organised in a far different way. But we borrow from what we know to create something new. In the process, we pass on a framework that may no longer apply, but which has power none the less. But what are the implications of the very design of the computer and of the coding that supports it?

We can begin some of this exploration by asking different questions. For example, in this virtual world of online learning, how does the computer and its structure mitigate conversation? Does conversation become more stilted, more casual and less precise? Does it become more open or intimate? Do some individuals feel more comfortable touching the equipment, experimenting with the Internet, with e-mails? Do we assume a level of intimacy with individuals we have never met because it may feel as if there are no boundaries?

If the platform is constructed from an assumption that the designer or the course facilitator is the powerful source, how does this impact the

discussions among individuals who use it? Does this assumption lock out new ways of using or designing the environment or even the courses themselves?

Does the computer-assisted learning environment – ranging from computer drills to Internet searches to online courses – create a new set of entitled learners, those who are comfortable in this new environment because it mirrors their own? Are there one or more 'learning styles' or ways in which individuals process information that represent the original developers and 'call out' to similar learners. If this is the case, the computer-assisted learning environment will be more welcoming and productive for some, unwelcoming for others and a potential mechanism to train individuals in one modality of thought.

How does the worldview of those who create the content for online courses affect the experience and outcomes of the participants? As we have found in classroom interactions, teacher–student relationships, curriculum and the other aspects of the face-to-face classroom, this plays a strong and invisible role – at least until the student drops out, gets a good or bad grade, or ceases to respond. While research has focused on versions of these questions in terms of the school and university, little has been done to uncover the unconscious patterns of thought and behaviour that guide the development and interactions in online classes. Such questions also call for an examination of the research on outcomes of online learning – does this environment work better for some? Who is attracted to the online course, how do they interact, are there new patterns of discourse emerging and who benefits, all remain solid research and practice questions.

Online interactions and communications

The way that communication and interactions occur online has interested many, and is, of course, integral to how and what people learn in online settings. In the early years of more widespread Internet use, as we saw above, there was a belief among some that by making face-to-face encounters obsolete, the Internet would free people from the expectations and limitations imposed on them in this hierarchical society based on gender, race, class and other identities. For instance, it was thought that if one could not 'see' that someone was an African American woman, then that woman would not feel the constraints she would participating in a face-to-face interaction and whomever she interacted with online would/could not use stereotypes or biases in framing exchanges with her. Indeed, this online utopia would help us create a medium in which people would define themselves based on how and what they chose to share with others, rather than be defined by others based on preconceived notions related to gender, race, class and other identities.

This early belief has, of course, proved to be overly simplistic. People who are raised in a society that dictates behaviours and values based on gender, race and class will often communicate this information in a multitude of unconscious ways in the types of interactions they become involved with and the ways they approach them. And even more importantly, the same people who are cued to structure their worldview based on knowing these aspects of the person(s) with whom they are interacting will relentlessly look for clues and make assumptions about a person's identity, even when they can't be sure.

Another issue that has arisen in our practice is that this supposed 'anonymity' is not the desired goal of many people online, and there may be tendencies related to this based on gender. Certainly, experiences with different degrees of anonymity on the Internet have reaped interesting results. There is an impression among a number of online 'practitioners' that people tend to be less aggressive or overt with negative behaviours towards each other when anonymity is lessened, at least to some degree. This is not surprising when we consider the multitude of studies in different settings that show that if people feel a high degree of anonymity, they will tend to do things (often negative behaviours) that they would not do if their identity was or could be known. Because of this, many online discussion formats, and especially those that cater to women, now require participants to provide a real name and some kind of contact information at least to the administrator, even if this is not accessible to the other participants.

The desire for anonymity also seems to be related to gender and to the types of environment used. For instance, in a 'closed' discussion that is considered safe to women, many tend to find anonymity uncomfortable, while in an 'open', public discussion where audience composition is unknown, anonymity is often preferred. As in other areas of women's lives, online interactions are fraught with the possibility of harassment and other types of violence. This makes the issue of anonymity central to discussions around online environments, while at the same time one that many women find difficult. For example, in one of our online courses we ask participants in evaluations about the positive and negative aspects of taking a course online. A portion of these teachers, who are primarily middle-class, Caucasian women, but who also include some women of colour, have repeatedly expressed their discomfort with never being able to see their classmates. These women want to 'know' the other participants in the same way they would in an in-person setting.

While discomfort with the level of anonymity online is probably very related to gender, it may also be related to the types of people who become teachers in the US. It is certainly an area that is crucial to investigate further. How do we guarantee safety online, which tends to be done now by increasing anonymity or (en)closing a group, while at the same time making the environment welcoming to all kinds of people?

There also appears to be a group dynamic that works either to keep people from revealing personal data or to encourage it. In one of the first activities in our online course for maths and science teachers, the participants are asked to introduce themselves and reflect on their earliest experiences with maths and science. If one of the first participants to do this activity reveals her or his race or other related information (gender is almost always known since a class list with names is given to each participant), the other participants tend to do this as well. This appears to be more common when there are people of colour in the group who take the lead on speaking about race and ethnicity.

Another component of online interactions and communications is the opportunity it provides for gender 'swapping' and other types of identity play. Though little has been researched on this aspect of gender roles online, it is generally accepted that this occurs on a regular basis. Jazwinski (2001) points out that more males than females tend to 'gender-bend', assuming a female identity, whole more females tend to mask their gender. Researchers like Danet (1998) view it from the perspective of the potential online technology offers, interpreting the possibility as a liberating aspect of online communication. Others (Bruckman, 1993; Herring, 1998) have looked at the actual practice, finding that females tend to try to assume androgynous names and behaviours in order to avoid sexual aggression or attention, and males tend to assume female names and behaviours in order to attract this attention. Our experience has also found males assuming female identities and extreme stereotypical behaviours in order to enter primarily female-centred conversations on discussions lists. We have seen examples of women being accused of male dominance because their communication style is more confrontational or aggressive than stereotypical female patterns. Since communication styles and interactions vary hugely by culture, language and social class, much of what is now discussed as gender patterns are not – they represent white, middle-class, Euro-American styles. With this recognition as a starting point, many questions arise. For example, if we understand gender as a concept that is defined also by race, class, location and other factors, will what we now see as gender patterns in online communication remain the same? To what extent is our current understanding based on white, middle-class patterns? If we are striving to create and support an online discussion environment that is empowering to a diverse group of people, how do we approach this differently? Is ensuring that designers, facilitators and others who now control the online environment are representative of diverse populations enough? Put another way, how do those of us who are not a part of the mainstream online environment creatively approach and challenge the existing structures and transform them?

Expectations and learning online

The third area that we are exploring concerns expectations and learning online. While there is little existing research around this area that uses a gender perspective, our practice is raising interesting issues. For example, when we asked our online course participants why they enrolled in an online course, many mentioned aspects specific to this new format, like the ability to access the course regardless of the hour or day, and regardless of where they are located geographically. These benefits work for many of these participants, though there is an inherent tension when those with busy schedules enrol in an online course because of the schedule flexibility, to find that this work simply turns into a 'third shift' in their day and is still difficult to manage.

As could be expected, participants tend to base their expectations on their prior experiences with face-to-face courses. For instance, many of the dissatisfactions or frustrations voiced by participants are phrased in terms of its differences to face-to-face experiences. A group of participants in each course report their frustration with never having a face-to-face encounter, or never getting to 'know' the other participants in face-to-face interactions. This expectation shows participants comparing their online experiences with a traditional classroom in which one can interact with others in person. This kind of feedback has led us to begin to explore in more depth the kinds of conscious and unconscious expectations participants bring to their online experience, and how in an online course we can both work with these expectations and challenge them. Since expectations are integral to participants' satisfaction or dissatisfaction with their course experience, as well as to the learning that takes place, this is an important area for research and practice. For instance, if some participants speak of a lack of community or sense of group online, how do we work to improve group connection while at the same time challenging participants to recognise how online communities can be different, but nevertheless legitimate? How can we draw from the best of what these new technologies offer to create new expectations about connection?

This reflection has also led us to reframe the way that we have traditionally approached some aspects of our research. Underlying many of the questions asked about online courses is the assumption that they should be compared with traditional, in-person courses. To some extent this is true, but it may also limit our ability to exploit the full potential of this different medium. If our goal were to make the online course experience as near as possible to a face-to-face course situation, it would be easy to underutilise or miss some of the aspects of online courses available only through this new medium. So rather than ask if an online course 'as good as' a traditional course, we ask how we can fully utilise the potential of this technology to make this as good a course as possible, make it a different experience not possible in a face-to-face setting.

In closing

Common to all three of the areas outlined above is the belief that when using and researching technologies we must do so contextually, and not see the 'tools' in isolation of their creators and users. It is vital not just to look at what is there, but also to ask who is designing and producing the technology, and how are their questions, interests, and agendas are reflected. What is being reproduced consciously and unconsciously? We must challenge both the technologies and the products created from them to better meet a diversity of needs and interests rather than require a range of learners to mold themselves to fit a narrow vision of the possibilities. One of the most difficult tasks to undertake is to imagine what is not there, not represented, in other words what could be; it is also a vital task.

References

American Demographics (1994). American Demographics Business Reports: Markets, *American Demographics*, 16(12).

Bailey, S. M. and Campbell, P. B. (1999). *The Gender Wars in Education*, February http://www.camDbell-kibler.corn/Gender Wars.htm

Balka, E. (1993). Women's access to online discussions about feminism. *Electronic Journal of Communication* 3(1). h!!Q://W\\lw.cios.orgj\V\,w/eic/v3nI93.htm

Barlow, J. P. (1996). A declaration of the independence of cyberspace. http://ww\v.eff.or ub/Censorshi/lntemet censorship bills/barlow_0296.declaration.

Blum, K. D. (1999). Gender differences in asynchronous learning in higher education: learning styles, participation barriers and communication patters. *Journal of Asynchronous Learning Networks*, Vol. 3, No.1, May.

Borg, A. (1996). 'Why Systers?' In Chemy, L. and Weise, E. (eds.), *Wired_women: Gender and New Realities in Cyberspace*. Seattle: Seal Press.

Bruckman, A. S. (1993). Gender Swapping on the Internet. *Proceedings of INET93*. Reston VA: The Internet Society.

Brunner, C. (1999). *The New Media Literacy Handbook: An Educator's Guide to Bringing New Media into the Classroom*. New York: Anchor Books.

Camp, L. J. (1996). We Are Geeks, and We Are Not Guys: The Systers Mailing List. In L. Chemy and E. R. Weise (eds.), *Wired-Women: Gender and New Realities in Cyberspace*, Seattle: Seal Press, pp. 114–25.

Campbell, P. B. and Hoey, L. (2000). *Equity Means All: Rethinking the Role of Special Programs in Science and Math Education*. http://www.wcer.wisc.edu/nise/News Activities/Forums/Cam bell a er.htm

Cardenas, K. (1998). Distance Learning. *Academe*, May–June.

Castano, M. (1996). A Comparison of Face-to-Face and Computer-mediated Communication in a Cross-cultural Setting. Qualifying paper in partial fulfilment of doctoral studies. Harvard University, Cambridge, MA.

Danet, B. (1998) Text as Mask: Gender, Play and Performance on the Internet. In S. Jones (ed.), *Cybersociety 2.0: Revisiting Computer-mediated Communication*, Newburg Park: Sage, pp. 129–58.

Deaux, K. and LaFrance, M. (1998). Gender, in D. T. Gilbert, S. T. Fiske and G. Lindzey (eds.), *The Handbook of Social Psychology*, Vol. 1. Boston: McGraw Hill, pp. 788–827.

Dyson, E. (1998). *Release 2.1*. New York: Broadway Books.

Ferris, S. P. (1996). Women On-line: Cultural and Relational Aspects of Women's Communication in On-line Discussion Groups. *Interpersonal Computing and Technology*, Vol. 4(3–4), October 29–40.

Gilligan, C., Lyons, N. P. and Hammer, T. J. (1990). *Making Connections: The Relational Worlds of Adolescent Girls at Emma Willard School*. Cambridge, MA: Harvard University Press.

Gilligan, C. (1993). *In a Different Voice*. Cambridge, MA: Harvard University Press.

Gray, J. (1992). *Men Are From Mars, Women Are From Venus*. New York: HarperCollins.

Grossman, W. M. (1997). *Net.wars*. New York: NYU Press. httQ://W\vw. nyuQress.nyu. edu/netwars.html.

Herring, S. C. (1993). *Gender and Democracy in Computer-mediated Communication*. h!!Q://www.cios.orgLgetfile/HERRING V3N293.

Herring, S. C. (1994). Politeness in Computer Culture: Why Women Thank and Men Flame. In M. Bucholtz, A. Liang and L. Sutton (eds.), *Cultural Performances: Proceedings of the Third Berkeley Women and Language Conference*, Berkeley: Berkeley Women and Language Group, pp. 278–94.

Herring, S. C. (1996). Posting in a Different Voice: Gender and Ethics in Computer-mediated Communication. In C. Ess (ed.), *Philosophical Perspectives on Computer-Mediated Communication*, Albany, NY: SUNY Press, pp. 115–45.

Herring, S. C. (2000). Gender differences in CMC: Findings and implications. *The CPSR Newsletter* 18(1) Winter.http:/www.csr.orublicationslnewsletterslissuesl2000l Winter2000/herrin.

Horn, S. (1998). *Cyberville*. New York: Warner Books.

IDC (1998). *Worldwide and U.S. IT Education and Training Markets, 1998–2003*. Framingham, MA: International Data Corporation.

Jazwinski, C. H. (2001). Gender Identities on the World Wide Web. In C. R. Wolfe (ed.) *Learning and Teaching on the Worldwide Web*. San Diego and London: Academic Press.

King, L. J. (2000). Gender Issues in Online Communities. *The CPSR Newsletter*, Vol. 18, No. 1, Winter.

Knupfer, N. N. and Rust, W. J. (1997). Technology, Mass Media, Society and Gender. In *Proceedings of Selected Research and Development Presentations at the 1997 National Convention of the Association for Educational Communications and Technology* (19th, Alburquerque, NM, 14–18 February). ERIC Document ED409844.

Knupfer, N. N. and Clark, B. I. (1996). Hypermedia as a Separate Medium: Challenges for Designer and Evaluators. In *Proceedings of Selected Research and Development Presentations at the 1996 National Convention of the Association for Educational Communications and Technology* (18th, Indianapolis, IN, 1996). ERIC Document ED 397805.

Lakoff, R. T. (2000). *The Language War*. Baskelaye: Univerisity of California Press.

Machanic, M. (1998) *Safety in On-line Learning Environments*. Electric Edge. Fall.

Mahoney, J. E. and Knupfer, N. N. (1997). Language, Gender and Cyberspace: Pulling the Old Stereotypes into New Territory. In *Proceedings of Selected Research and Development Presentations at the 1997 National Convention of the Association for Educational Communications and Technology* (19th, Alburquerque, NM, 14–18 February). ERIC Document 409852.

Mangione, M. (1995). Understanding the Critics of Educational Technology: Gender Inequities and Computers, 1983–1993. In *Proceedings of the 1995 Annual National Convention of the Association for Educational Communications and Technology (AECT)* (17th, Anaheim, CA, 1995).

Postman, N. (1993). *Technopoly: The Surrender of Culture to Technology*. New York: Vintage Books.

Shapiro, A. L. (1997). *The Control Revolution*. New York: Century Foundation.

Smith, C. B., McLaughlin, M. L. and Osborne, K. K. (1997). Conduct Controls on Usenet. *Journal of Computer-mediated Communication*, Vol. 2, No. 4. h: 1 *Iwww.ascusc.or.cmclvol2lissue4lsmith.html*

Spender, D. (1995). *Nattering on the Net: Women, Power and Cyberspace*. North Melbourne, Australia: Spinifex Press.

Tannen, D. (1990). *You Just Don't Understand*. New York: William Morrow.

Turkle, S. (1995). *Life on the Screen: Identity in the Age of the Internet*. New York: Simon and Schuster.

Walther, J. B., Anderson, J. F. and Park, D. W. (1994). Interpersonal Effects in Computer-mediated Interaction. A Meta-analysis of Social and Anti-social Communication. *Communications Research*, Vol. 21, No. 4, 460–87.

Watson, N. (1997). Why We Argue about Virtual Community: A Case Study of the phish.net Fan Community. In S. Jones (ed.), *Virtual Culture: Identity and Communication in Cybersociety*. London: Sage.

We, Gladys (1993). Cross-Gender Communication in Cyberspace. Unpublished graduate research paper for Simon Fraser University available from author: email: we@sfu.ca.

6
Inside Leadership Circles and the Managerial Quagmire: Key Influences on Women Administrators' Mobility and Opportunity in US Higher Education

Mary Ann Danowitz Sagaria and Melissa A. Rychener

Introduction

The appointment of Ruth Simmons in 1994 as president of Smith College was hailed as a landmark event in US higher education because she was the first African American president of a Seven Sisters College. Seven years later, her 2001 appointment as the first woman president of Brown University and the first person of colour[1] to head an elite Ivy League institution was another marker event in higher education in the United States. The status of women administrators has changed greatly in the past 25 years, but most attention has been directed to the extraordinary accomplishments of women presidents such as Dr Simmons. The experiences of the majority of women administrators, the landscapes of their institutions and the context of higher education have garnered little attention. Understanding changes in the representation of women administrators and current contexts associated with mobility and opportunity is critical for understanding the status of women administrators in American universities in the twenty-first century. In this chapter we present a current account of women administrators' status in relationship to their mobility and opportunity and the current characteristics and dynamics of higher education institutions.

The situation of women administrators

Between 1976 and 1997, within a loosely configured system of 3,885 American institutions, women increased their share of executive, administrative and managerial positions from 26 per cent or 26,929 (US Department of Health, Education and Welfare 1977–78) to 45.9 per cent or 69,432 (US Department of Education 2001). Within this administrative cohort women increased their presence within the leadership circle of college and university presidencies and chancelleries. The percentage of women in these chief executive roles changed from 9.5 per cent or 204 in 1986 to 19.3 per cent or 459 in 1998 (Ross and Green, 2000). The encouraging news from these data is that the number of women is increasing and more of them are obtaining senior leadership positions and wielding greater influence in chief executive roles.

Presidents and chancellors

The appointment of women college presidents attracts a great deal of attention, because women in these roles have considerable institutional salience and broad social significance. Thus, these appointments represent potential opportunities for institutions both to enhance external relations and send a powerful message about their commitment to diversity and equity. At the same time, news coverage of these appointments illustrates the tendency of the media to define these higher education leaders differently from their male counterparts. Reports focusing on gender, race and class, including aspects of their appearance, personality, dress and background, diminish the professional and scholarly accomplishments of women presidents. For example, in 1994 when Judith Roden was appointed the first woman president of the University of Pennsylvania, the *New York Times* reported this remarkable event in the Home Section, which focuses on lifestyle matters. The paper described her 'pert manner and bouncy determination' and her 'designer clothes' alongside her academic achievements (Glazer-Raymo, 1999). Seven years later, the headline in *New York Times* reporting Ruth Simmons' appointment as president of Brown University was 'Proud Daughter of a Janitor Reaches an Academic Peak'. The article described her academic and professional accomplishments, but devoted equal attention to her personal life and tastes. It noted she 'wears dark St. John knit suits and doesn't own a pair of jeans, and has been followed around department stores by clerks who seem convinced she is about to shoplift something – an experience not unlike those recounted by countless other black and Hispanic Americans' (Steinberg, 2000). Such commentary about a president's dress or personal life is rare in describing the appointments male presidents. The uneven coverage reinforces the view that women in a man's domain surpass conventional standards of excellence. However, their personal lives continue to be bound by conventional notions of femininity and ethnicity, and it is appropriate to evaluate their lives based on those conventions.

The number of women presidents has been increasing, but their gains differ greatly by type of institution. Women are least likely to be chief executive officers of the more influential, selective, complex and prestigious institutions. For example, a woman president leads only one of the top twenty research universities. However, across the spectrum of institutions the percentage of presidencies held by women increased in all types of institutions between 1986 and 1998. According to the American Council on Education's 2000 study of higher education's presidents (Ross and Green 2000), gains were made from 4 per cent to 13.2 per cent in doctoral-granting institutions, from 10 per cent to 18.7 per cent in master's granting institutions, from 7.9 per cent to 22.4 per cent in two year colleges, and from 6.6 per cent to 14.8 per cent in specialised institutions.

Women and men presidents have both similar and different demographic characteristics. They have held similar prior positions including chief academic officer, senior executive and chief executive officer. Women have served less time – on average, 5.6 years in their presidential posts – while, on average, men have served 7.3 years. Women are slightly more likely (84.6 per cent) than men (79.4 per cent) to have earned a doctoral degree. They are about the same average age (women 56.4 years and men 57.9 years). They are both likely to be white (women 86.2 per cent and men 89.3 per cent).

The more striking differences between women and men presidents are in their personal lives. Women are more likely (18.8 per cent) than men (4.0 per cent) to have been outside the employment market for personal/family reasons. Women and men differ most significantly in their marital status. Most (90 per cent) men presidents are currently married while slightly more than half (57 per cent) of the women presidents are married. Furthermore, women presidents are more likely to be serving without the support of a partner, even if they are married. Some 74 per cent of the spouses of women had paid employment while 50 per cent of the spouses of men had paid employment (Ross and Green, 2000). Thus, within the leadership circles in American higher education, women and men achieving presidencies have somewhat similar professional and academic accomplishments. Yet, inferences from these and related data suggest that some women and men presidents differ in enacting professional/social responsibilities, in their home activities, companionship and their sexual orientation – all of which may influence their role and perceptions of their role of presi-dent. Alongside the movement of more women into college and univer-sity presidencies, the reality remains that prevalent organisational conditions confine the majority of women administrators to the administrative quagmire, lower-level managerial positions. It is to these conditions that we now turn.

Women administrators' mobility and opportunity

Job changes, opportunity structures, networks, and sponsoring and mentoring govern domains of mobility and opportunity. The first of these, job changes, tend to take place differently for women than for men, and internal mobility is the most significant form of career advancement for women. In higher education white women and people of colour are more likely than white men to build their careers in one organisation (Johnsrud and Rosser, 2000; Sagaria and Johnsrud, 1991; Sagaria and Moore, 1983). In fact, most women tend to build their careers in one or two institutions (Moore and Twombly, 1991). Therefore, career systems in an organisation are especially important for women.

Each career system has opportunity structures within its formal organisational charts and personnel policies that may give preference to internal candidates through informal norms about loyalty and certain political persuasions that reinforce dominant cultural norms (Sagaria and Dickens, 1990). Unfortunately, there is little systematic inform-ation about opportunity structures because they must be studied and understood within a particular organisation. None the less, relevant generalisations can be drawn. For example, data on the effect of broad banding positions (categorisations of wide groups of diverse positions requiring related skills) and patterns of hiring preferences for internal candidates are available on campuses. Information about opportunity structures is usually embedded in university women's commissions' reports (Allan, 2000), affirmative action and equal opportunity audits, and offices of human resources studies that are seldom well publicized or widely distributed. On some campuses these practices have unanticipated consequences of disadvantaging women's career advancement (Sagaria and Johnsrud, 1987) because people tend to hire individuals like themselves (Kanter 1977; Sagaria, 2002) or engage in homophily (Ibarra, 1997). For example, policies and practices estab-lished at a research university to promote white women and people of colour through internal promotion actually had the reverse effect

(Sagaria and Johnsrud, 1987, 1991). According to a group of women provosts (chief academic officers) the conditions that counter these tendencies are the presence of individuals within the institution, who are diverse in terms of gender, race and ethnicity and the willingness of senior administrative leaders to take risks with hiring decisions (Lively, 2000).

Networks, sponsors and mentors also significantly influence administrative mobility. Contact networks and social and ascribed status contribute to hiring into administrative positions requiring high levels of discretion (Pfeffer, 1977; Harvey, 1999) such as deanships (Lindsay, 1997) and vice-presidencies. Networks are also becoming increasingly important, with the trend of colleges and universities utilising private search firms or head-hunters to assist in the hiring of senior administrators. Before 1985, less than 16 per cent of colleges and universities hiring presidents used search firms, but between 1995 and 1998, search firms participated in almost half of the presidential searches reported to the American Council on Education (Ross and Green, 2000). These search firms tend to rely on referrals and informal networks to identify and recommend candidates, rather than firsthand information from administrators and staff in the hiring institution. This may be more of a liability for white women and men and women of colour seeking to change jobs than for white men, because the former are likely to have different networks than the latter, who make most administrative hiring decisions (Lindsay, 1997; Sagaria, in press). Within administrative searches in a research university, chairs of search committees were reluctant to accept information as factual or complete unless they knew the reference or informant. Consequently, they effectively limited the range of information they were willing to consider valid, such as information from references provided by women candidates who were unknown to search committee members (Sagaria, in press). Networks are also important to gain insights into the culture of an organisational unit or university. This is especially so for mobility across institutional boundaries. The majority of new deans at doctoral granting universities were hired from other universities and they were invited to apply for their position or were informed about the vacant post by a search committee member or someone inside the hiring university. In other words, they did not learn about the position vacancy through advertisements in newspapers or other published sources, despite legal expectations that all universities advertise in order to recruit women and people of colour (Sagaria, 1986).

Two forms of networks, created and inherited, influence mobility. Created networks are those intentionally formed to exchange information and provide support. For example, in 1999 five of the eleven[2] female chief academic offices of the American Association of Universities (the association of 61 selective research universities) met, for the first time, to establish a foundation to influence policies and decisions.

Women have rarely had access to inherited networks, those into which one is born or enters through educational lineage, to open opportunities in the more prestigious institutions. These inherited educational networks are especially important because they facilitate movement for women with personal characteristics that are not typically associated with the administrative leadership role they hold. Ruth Simmons' appointments as president of Smith College and then Brown University followed other accomplishments from Ivy League institutions including earning a PhD and serving as a department chair and provost. Likewise, Donna Browder Evans' appointment as dean of the College of Education at Ohio State University in 2000 marked the appointment of the second woman and the first African American to this post. She came to that research university's deanship after holding several deanships at regional universities. Prior to those appointments, however, she had earned a baccalaureate and two graduate degrees at the Ohio State University.

A mentor's tutoring and advocacy can also be an asset for administrative mobility and opportunity. Women in senior administrative positions, such as chief academic officer, report that university presidents serve as sponsors, advocates and provide job skill coaching for subsequent positions (Lively, 2000). Others, such as Alberta Arthur, former president of Chatham College, attributed her ascent from director of admissions at Harvard University to becoming a college president to her mentor being in a meeting where he advocated for her to fill the post at Chatham. However, some findings indicate that because men and women have separate networks, women do not have access to as many mentoring opportunities as men (Brass, 1985; Ibarra, 1992) and that differences between women's and men's networks can limit women professionally in and outside of higher education (Sagaria, 2002). For example, in a newspaper publishing company with an even gender balance, women and men had separate, segregated networks. Because men dominated senior management positions, women as a group had less influence than men (Brass, 1985). The exception to this was women in evenly balanced gender workgroups who were perceived by management to be as influential as men. Thus, when women are the numerical minority in an institution, they are even less likely to have access to male management networks (Kanter, 1977; Brass, 1985).

Women in senior leadership positions, however, tend not to rely solely on formal institutional leaders' mentoring. For example, women in corporate and government settings perceived by management as having potential for senior leadership roles are more likely to seek out other women for instrumental or career-related advice and mentoring than women who are not perceived to have high potential (Scott, 1996; Ibarra, 1997). Although these networks may differ from men's in that they span different organisational levels and divisions, for women to be successful these informal ties are as important to their career success as men's more ready access to an institutional mentor.

Women receive more promotions than men, largely because more job changes occur within the lower-ranking positions in which women predominate. Recent research from the private sector (Lyness and Judiesch, 1999) corroborates findings about women in higher education (Sagaria, 1988). Both studies indicate women are slightly less likely than men to receive promotions at higher levels, regardless of level or gender composition of the job, and women are more likely to attain their positions due to internal promotions than to hiring. These phenomena may, in part, be occurring because women have fewer contacts in other organisations and because women are less likely to be recommended by search firms (Lyness and Judiesch, 1999). However, upper-level positions are more likely to be filled by external hires, which can have negative implications for women's access to institutional decision-making and likelihood of being sponsored or mentored by more influential persons (Lyness and Judiesch, 1999).

Characteristics and dynamics of higher education

Organisational conditions, such as the growth of administrative positions or bureaucratic accretion (Gumport and Pusser, 1995; Massy and Zemsky, 1997), the emphases on efficiency and economic centrality, the development of a mid-level quagmire, and decreased social equality (Fischman and Stromquist, 2000) have had tangible consequences for the mobility and opportunity for the vast majority of women administrators. Administrative mobility opportunities increased in tandem with the exponential growth of administrative positions beginning in the mid-1960s (Leslie and Rhoades, 1995; Sagaria and Johnsrud, 1987). This organisational growth occurred in all higher education sectors, but especially at the research universities. Institutional support positions in the University of California system increased by 104 per cent between

1966 and 1991, nearly two and a half times faster than instructional positions (Gumport and Pusser, 1995). As a group, non-academic and non-teaching professionals have been the fastest growing job category in higher education; especially in the areas of institutional advancement, technology and minority student services (Grassmuck, 1991). Some American universities, like their British counterparts, have appointed a majority of women to administrative positions (Leonard, 1998) with many of the appointments made to fill newly created staff positions at the lower salary levels.

The economic downturn of 2001, after nearly three decades of unpredictable funding fluctuations (from major revenue sources such as inflation recession, operating costs increasing faster than inflation; (Gumport, 1997) is contributing to sharply declining revenues in higher education institutions. In order to reduce costs to respond to lower revenues, some college and universities are reducing staff (Jacobson, 2001; Kellogg, 2001; Van Der Werf, 2001). Using traditional models, these reductions result in disproportionately large losses of women and people of colour (Butterfield and Wolfe, 1993). All indications are that institutional solutions to reduce personnel costs tend to begin with reductions in support staff and administrative assistants, those positions within the managerial quagmire that are most likely to be held by women. Based on recent case law, the courts are unlikely to rule that targeting layoffs to ensure gender and racial representation is justified (DeMitchell, 1998). Therefore, downsizing is likely to inhibit further the career mobility of women and people of colour and also cause some to lose their jobs.

Technical rationality is driving midlevel managers' mobility

During the 1990s an increased emphasis on efficiency (Fischman and Stromquist, 2000), economic centrality and academic capitalism (Slaughter and Leslie, 1997), led to the growth of the managerial sector at middle and lower levels. At the same time, as universities attempted to reduce expenditures and increase revenues and returns from employees (Massy and Zemsky, 1997; Leonard, 1998) there has been an exponential increase in the number of women in the lower-level positions oriented towards accountability, external relations and client services.

Institutions recruit for lower and mid-level posts within their local geographic area

Furthermore, there is a tendency to promote women from one job to another because they are often known to be trustworthy employees and such appointments give the illusion of equal opportunity or affirmative action (Sagaria, 1988). As Pritchard and Deem (1999) observed in colleges in England, increasingly women are drawn into subordinate management positions because they previously have been 'outsiders' and in these newly created positions they are being called on to subvert resistance to management practices and challenge bureau-professional inefficiencies. Prichard and Deem's (1999) observations aptly describe practices in the United States. For instance at the Ohio State University, a new dean of a college with 130 faculty members (academic staff) and 83 managerial staff changed a cabinet staffing arrangement of direct supervision from six academic staff and one mid-level manager to five academic staff and six middle managers (of whom four are women). While it is too early to know the consequences of this organisational reconfiguration on the careers of these middle managers, currently their positions principally deal with managerial control, including finances and personnel, external relations, efficiency and client services. The women managers have had either the majority of, or their entire careers at the same university.

The prominence of technology is changing the way higher education functions
Technology is changing the nature of teaching, times and locations of instruction, the use of information (Levine, 2000), the ownership of intellectual property, the substance and form of research, and university management and decision-making. During the 1990s, universities' single greatest area of administrative and financial investment was in technology. The pattern is anticipated to be similar for the 2000 decade. For example, the California State University, comprised of 23 campuses, is planning to pay between $240 and $270 million in three years (Gallick, 1998) in a private partnership to finance educational technology. While much attention has been directed to virtual classrooms, capital expenditures and communication systems, minimal attention has been directed to the increase in both the actual numbers of technology-related positions and the importance of the chief information officer. The new and increasingly powerful position of chief information officer is held by a man at three-quarters of colleges and universities (College and University Personnel Association, 2000). To the extent that women are absent from this technological revolution, their entry and possibilities for mobility in higher education are eclipsing. In 1984 women earned 37 per cent of the bachelors' degrees in computer science and computer engineering. But, in 1999, women earned less than 20 per cent of those degrees (Olsen, 2000). Because the

BA is the typical credential for mid-level administrative positions, with the master's degree becoming increasingly sought (Johnsrud and Rosser, 2000), women may have less access and influence in one of the more salient domains of higher education in the future.

Decreased social equity

Two forces are profoundly diminishing the commitment to diversifying administrative and professorial cohorts. The first is the rollback of affirmative action. The decision of the University of California in 1995 to end the use of sex and race in hiring and admissions marked a watershed that was followed by further legislative attacks on affirmative action. Decisions of this kind and of the current Bush administration's dismantling of affirmative action have removed legal inducements for colleges and universities to diversify their administrators, staff and faculty.

The second force is the privileging of economically central and entrepreneurial activities. Without regard for equity issues, university resources are being directed to male-dominated academic fields such as engineering, computer science and the physical and natural sciences. Additionally, auxiliary services, such as athletics, are growing in staff and resources. There is an increasingly common practice in these academic and non-academic areas to fill appointments such as directors of research or athletics without regard to equity. Instead, units undertake targeted searches with 'a licence to hunt for a particular person' as a way of achieving excellence. This especially seems to be the case in prestige areas such as research centers and academic administrative units associated with the sciences, engineering and business, which are gaining increasing importance in universities and where women constitute a small minority among administrators and faculty. In contrast, areas such as nursing, education and social work, which are female-dominated, are more likely to be diminishing in importance and experiencing declining resources (Slaughter, 1993) and reductions in administrative positions. Taken together, these forces are likely to diminish significantly opportunities for women within academic organisational sub-units, where the largest numbers of women have been educated and hold positions.

Conclusion

It is important to celebrate the advancement of women as insiders in key leadership positions and to see them as indicators of equality.

Alongside this, scholars and practitioners must look realistically and ask probing questions about the meaning of the numerical gains of women in administrative positions. In many cases women are in an administrative quagmire doing very instrumental work (Prichard and Deem, 1999). They are part of a loosely structured system where career paths are not defined (Sagaria and Dickens, 1990), but are idiosyncratic and confusing (Kanter, 1987). The interpersonal dimension of careers – networks, mentoring and sponsorship may become increasingly important to offset the changing characteristics and dynamics of higher education institutions that may thwart advancement gains and mobility opportunities for women. Most importantly, we scholars committed to equality should engage more fully in uncovering the underside of academic organisations and women administrators' career experiences in order to advocate for and develop institutional strategies to challenge unintended consequences of organisational decisions and practices. Alongside that, we should unpack the cultural biases embedded in our organisational structures of efficiency and market shaping practices which marginalise women and promote particular values that further their desire for leadership (Blackmore, 1999). We should also provide leadership and information to increase the awareness of women and men within both administrative leadership circles and the administrative quagmire about potentially opportunity enhancing and inhibiting organisational conditions so that individuals at lower management levels can make more informed decisions about their work. Lastly, we should translate our academic discourses to practical public outlets to reach those about whom we write.

Notes

1 In this chapter, people of colour are defined as born or naturalised American citizens who identified racially or ethnically with one or more of the racially and underrepresented groups in the United States. Typically, this would include people of African, Latino/Hispanic, Asian and Native American descent.
2 In 2000 women held the post of provost, chief academic officer, at 11 of the 61 universities in the American Association of Universities (AAU). Top research universities such as AAU institutions have been the slowest to hire women as presidents and provosts.

References

Allan, E. (2000). Constructing Women's Status: Policy Discourse of University Women's Commission Reports. Unpublished Dissertation, The Ohio State University, Columbus, Ohio.

Blackmore, J. (1999). *Troubling Women: Feminism, Leadership and Educational Change.* Buckingham: Open University Press.

Butterfield, B. and Wolfe, S. (1993). Downsizing without Discriminating against Minorities and Women. *CUPA Journal*, Summer, 23–7.

Brass, D. J. (1985). Men's and Women's Networks: A Study of Interaction Patterns and Influence in an Organization. *Academy of Management Journal*, Vol. 28, No. 2: 327–43.

College and University Professional Association (2000). *2000–01 Administrative Compensation Survey.* Washington D.C.: CUPA-HR.

DeMetchell, T. A. (1998). Race, a Relevant Factor? Our Fractured View of Affirmative Action: *Piscataway Township Board of Education V. Taxman. International Journal of Educational Reform*, Vol. 7, No. 2, 72–9.

Fischman, G. and Stromquist, N. (2000). Globalization and Higher Education in Developing Countries. In John C. Smart (ed.) *Higher Education: Handbook of Theory and Research, Vol. XV*, New York: Agathon Press, pp. 501–21.

Gallick, S. (1998). *Technology in Higher Education: Opportunities and Threats.* Faculty Association for the University of California-Los Angeles. ERIC Document 415 929.

Glazer-Raymo, J. (1999). *Shattering the Myths: Women in Academe.* Baltimore, MD: Johns Hopkins University Press.

Grassmuck, K. (1991). Throughout '80s, Colleges Hired More Non-teaching Staff than Other Employees. *Chronicle of Higher Education*, Vol. 37, A22.

Gumport, P. (1997). Public Universities as Academic Workplaces. *Daedalus*, Vol. 26, No. 4, 113–36.

Gumport, P. and Pusser, B. (1995). A Case of Bureaucratic Accretion: Context and Consequences. *Journal of Higher Education*, Vol. 66, No. 5, 493–520.

Harvey, W. B. (1999). *Grass Roots and Glass Ceilings: African American Administrators in Predominantly White Colleges and Universities.* Albany, NY: SUNY Press.

Ibarra, H. (1992). Homophily and Differential Returns: Sex Differences in Network Structure and Access in an Advertising Firm. *Administrative Science Quarterly*, Vol. 37, 442–7.

Ibarra, H. (1997). Paving an Alternative Route: Gender Differences in Managerial Networks. *Social Psychology Quarterly*, Vol. 61, 191–202.

Jacobson, J. (2001). Minnesota University Plans More Staff Cutbacks. *Chronicle of Higher Education.* 8 June.

Johnsrud, L. K. and Rosser, V. J. (2000). *Understanding the Work and Career Paths of Midlevel Administrators.* San Francisco: Jossey-Bass.

Kanter, R. M. (1977). *Men and Women of the Corporation.* New York: Basic Books.

Kanter, R. M. (1987). The New Managerial Work. *Harvard Business Review*, November–December, 85–90.

Kellogg, A. (2001). The University of Northern Iowa Eliminates 146 Adjunct Positions. *Chronicle of Higher Education.* 23 November.

Leonard, P. (1998). Gendering Change? Management, Masculinity and the Dynamics of Incorporation. *Gender and Education*, Vol. 10, 171–84.

Leslie, L. and Rhoades, G. (1995). Rising Administrative Costs: Seeking Explanations. *Journal of Higher Education*, Vol. 66, No. 2, 187–212.

Levine, A. (2000). *Higher Education at a Crossroads.* Occasional Papers from the Center for Higher Education Policy Analysis, Los Angeles, CA: University of

Southern California, http://www.usc.edu/dept/chepa/projectspapers_pastpapers.html.

Lindsay, B. (1997). Surviving the Middle Passage: The Absent Legacy of African American Women Education Deans? In L. A. Castenell and J. M. Tarule (eds.), *The Minority Voice in Educational Reform: An Analysis by Minority and Women College of Education Deans*. Greenwich, CT: Ablex Publishing Group.

Lively, K. (2000). Women in Charge. *The Chronicle of Higher Education*, Vol. 14, A33–A35.

Lyness, K. S. and Judiesch, M. K. (1999). Are Women more likely to be Hired or Promoted into Management Positions? *Journal of Vocational Behaviour*, Vol. 54, No. 1, 158–73.

Massy, W. F. and Zemsky, R. (1997). A Utility Model for Teaching Load Decisions in Academic Departments. *Economics of Education Review*, Vol. 16, No. 4, 49–365.

Moore, K. M. and Twombly, S. (eds.) (1991). *Administrative Careers and the Marketplace*. San Francisco: Jossey-Bass

Olsen, F. (2000). Institute for Women and Technology Works to Bridge the Other Digital Divide. *The Chronicle of Higher Education*, Vol. 46, A47.

Pfeffer, J. (1977). Toward an Examination of Stratification in Organizations. *Administrative Science Quarterly*, Vol. 22, 553–67.

Prichard, C. and Deem, R. (1999). Wo-managing Further Education: Gender and the Construction of the Manager in the Corporate Colleges of England. *Gender and Education*, Vol. 11, No. 3, 323–42.

Ross, M. and Green, M. F. (2000). *The American College President: 2000 edition*. Washington, D.C.: American Council on Education.

Sagaria, M. A. D. (1986). Deanship Selection: Connections *and* Consequences. Paper presented at the meeting of the American Educational Research Association, San Francisco.

Sagaria, M. A. D. (1988). Administrative Mobility and Gender: Patterns and Processes in Higher Education. *Journal of Higher Education*, Vol. 59, No. 3, 305–26.

Sagaria, M. A. D. (2002). An Exploratory Model of Filtering in Administrative Searches: Toward Counter Hegemonic Discourses. *Journal of Higher Education*, 73(6): 677–710.

Sagaria, M. A. D. and Dickens, C. (1990). Thriving at Home: Developing a Career as an Insider. *New Directions for Higher Education*, Vol. 18, No. 4, 19–28.

Sagaria, M. A. D. and Johnsrud, L. K. M. (1987). *Many are Candidates but Few Compete: The Impact of Internal Position Change of Administrative and Professional Staff on White Women and Minorities*. Columbus, OH: The Ohio State University.

Sagaria, M. A. D. and Johnsrud, Linda K. (1991). Administrative Promotion: The Structuring of Opportunity Within a University. *The Review of Higher Education*, Vol. 15, No. 2, 191–211.

Sagaria, M. A. D. and Moore, Kathryn M. (1983). Job Change and Age: The Experience of Administrators in Colleges and Universities. *Sociological Spectrum* Vol. 3, 353–70.

Scott, D. B. (1996). Shattering the Instrumental-Expressive Myth: The Power of Women's Networks in Corporate-Government Affairs. *Gender and Society*, Vol. 10, No. 3, 232–47.

Slaughter, S. (1993). Retrenchment in the 1980s: The Politics of Prestige and Gender. *Journal of Higher Education*, Vol. 64, No. 3, 250–82.

Slaughter, S. and Leslie, L. (1997) in J. Smyth, (ed.) *Academic Work: The Changing Labour Process in Higher Education*. Bristol, PA: Society for Research into Higher Education and Open University Press.

Steinberg, J. (2000). *The New York Times*. 11 November.

US Department of Education (2001). *Digest of Education Statistics*. Washington, D.C.: National Centre for Education Statistics.

US Department of Health, Education and Welfare, National Centre for Education Statistics. (1997–98). *Numbers of Employees in Institutions of Higher Education, Fall 1976*. Washington, D.C.: Department of Health, Education and Welfare, National Centre for Education Statistics.

Van Der Werf, M. (2001). Golden Gate Plans Major Cuts. *Chronicle of Higher Education*. 20 April.

Part III
Politicising Educational Identities

7
Feet of Class and Relations of Power
Jacky Brine

Introduction

This chapter explores the consciousness of class that underpins my research interest in education policy. It focuses on what I know about relations of class, how I came to know it, and the present relationship between that knowledge and my research interest in policy. The first section explores the relationship between my educational biography and its policy context, focusing primarily on the construction of class, gender and learner identities within a secondary modern school of the early 1960s. Less immediately obvious was the construction and assumption of 'whiteness' and unproblematised 'Britishness'. In this chapter, I highlight the understanding that identities are framed by their time and place; had I been born in 1984 rather than 1948, in France or Canada rather than England, into a middle-class rather than a working-class family, black rather than white, my biography would be very different. This is not simply due to the obvious differences in experience or privilege, but due also to the particularities of the education policies that operated at that time and place. In the second section I consider the relationship between my auto/biography and my interest in policy research.

There is, at the centre of my research into educational policy, an interest in the extent to which the choices we make, the agency we exert, are framed by the policies of a particular time and place, which are themselves of course further framed by contemporary economic and social realities. That is, as Wright-Mills has said, 'to grasp history and biography and the relations between the two in society' (1970, p. 12). I now take this approach to my educational biography, so that I might illustrate it and relate it to the policy and the economic and social context of the time.

There are many biographical and analytical accounts (see, for instance, Mahony and Zmroczek, 1997) of the conflicts of identity experienced by English postwar, generally white, working-class children who found themselves at grammar school, alongside middle-class children. By comparison, there have been few firsthand accounts of the cultural habitus of the secondary modern school (Bourdieu, 1990), of schooling's consolidation of a white working class identity; the working classes, of all ethnicities, generally remain those that are written about, rarely themselves the writers.

> Until the age of 26, when I began my first degree, I was uncomplicatedly and unconsciously working-class and, by the age of 29, as my learner identity changed, so I was assumed by others to be middle-class. It was as if my pre-university years were dismissed, wasted, erased. Yet this is not so. I look at my world with the consciousness of the many explicit and implicit ways in which class privilege and oppression are maintained, especially through the policies and practices of compulsory education.

The title of this chapter draws on the observation made by Pat Mahony and Christine Zmroczek (1997, p. 4) that:

> Class experience is deeply rooted, retained and carried through life rather than left behind (or below). In this sense it is more like a foot which carries us forward than a footprint which marks a past presence.

In reality these working-class feet have taken me through a stone-walled maze into the arbours of the middle-classes. They ground me in my consciousness of class and the power relations that surround it, my understanding of the world – in Freirean terms, my critical reading of the world, 'a world [seen] not as a static reality, but as a reality in process, in transformation' (Freire, 1972, p. 56).

There are many ways of defining social class (Crompton, 1998), the most common being that related to occupation or the possession of economic, social and cultural capital (Bourdieu, 1997). Beyond such structural definitions are constructions of identity and consciousness. Identity differs from consciousness in that identity is how we perceive ourselves, whereas consciousness is how we perceive our world – that is, a politicised understanding of class. How, then, are class identities constructed, and what role does education play in such construction? Kuhn has written that 'class is something beneath your clothes, under your skin, in your reflexes, in your psyche, at the very core of your being' (Kuhn 1995, p. 98). Whereas identity may change, this deep, internalised knowledge of class may become the basis of politicised consciousness. For example, as an established academic, I am not, by any structural definition, working-class, but I am marginal in both, and although, as hooks (1994) has argued, this can be beneficial, it can also be slippery and even painful. Despite such an ambiguous identity, my consciousness of class is one lens through which I consistently view the world, and here I look specifically at the English education policy of the 1950s and early 1960s, a period in which policy was based on an extremely clear understanding of class.

Narrative, auto/biography and history

The developing feminist interest in narrative and auto/biography appears as a reworking of the earlier feminist creed that the personal is political. Goodson (2000) details the way in which, from its original status as the ultimate sociological method, to its fall from grace as first the quantitative and then the ethnomethodological approaches took over, to its current postmodern return to grace – its lack of representativeness and subjective nature are now its greatest strength (Munro, 1998). This move towards life history seems to contradict Hammersley's (2000) observation of the discernible trend towards quantitative research, research that will have greater impact on policy-making and practice than previously. 'Evidence-based' and 'transparently accountable' quantitative methods are privileged over and above qualitative. Auto/biography, however, illuminates the lived reality not fully evident in quantitative studies.

In writing this chapter I initially questioned its broader relevance and interest: Was it self-indulgent? This may in part be so, but it is also more than this for it is sited in a particular time and place that constructs a unique framework for experience and construction of identity as have been discussed by Harvey (1989), Weiner (1994) and Swindells (1995). Goodson (2000) writes that the first stage of this type of research, the life story, is distinguished from the second stage, the life history, by other data that contextualise it within its time and place.

In this chapter I focus on one particular aspect of my identity – my learner identity, most specifically that of a white, working-class girl who failed her Year 6 11-plus examination. This identity is not, of course, separate from my other identities; it shifts and fragments across discourses, practices and positions (Hall, 1990). This learner identity, like others, was, and is, always in the process of change, framed by the time, place, power relations and other identities of the self at the time referred to, and subsequently further framed by the time, place, power relations and other identities of this particular time of reflection on it. The construction of identity is, then; 'a dynamic process grounded in biography and history, subjected to description and reflection, and constantly presented to and negotiated with other people' (Walker, 2000, p. 8).

This focus on the researcher's own 'intellectual auto/biography' can increase our understandings of what we do and why we do it. In doing so there is, of course, the danger of self-indulgence, the vulnerability of disclosure (Walsh, 1997), and, as in all accounts of oral history, the fallibility of memory (Marcus, 1995). Then again there is the question of selectivity, silence and subjectivity. I choose the tale to tell, selecting what to disclose and what not, what to emphasise and what to erase – even from within this specific focus on my educational biography. I may, as Goodson (2000) warns, be attempting a false cohesiveness in my tale. Others would make different selections and tell it differently; it is contrived, written in a style that will I hope engage feelings, imagination and intellect. At the same time it is speckled with references and other trappings of the academic chapter, it is not just my personal story; it is, most importantly, the story of an individual framed by the specificity of a particular education policy. I approach this chapter as a sociologist, whose basic belief is that society, as it is constructed, benefits some to the detriment of others. I view my biography, my actions as elements of wider figurations, networks of dependencies, wherein I wish to compare my private experience with the fate of others. That is,

> to see the *social* in the *individual*, the *general* in the *particular*, to show how [my] individual biography intertwines with a shared *history* of a time, place and class; to ask questions that make evident things into puzzles, to defamiliarise the familiarity of my biography. (Bauman, 1990, p. 10)

The sociological premise of making the familiar strange is then, in this chapter, applied to my own life. Such an approach has been new to me; questions of truth, selectivity and self-indulgence have gone alongside pain and anger as I discovered the blatant class interest evident in the policy of the time.

I am concerned that my tale should not be seen in any way as a validation of individual meritocracy, for

While we bring with us insider knowledge of class inequalities, at the same time the academic from a working-class background represents a justification of right-wing rhetoric. (Reay, 1997, p. 20)

In drawing on my insider knowledge of 1960s English secondary modern education, the point is not that my life panned out in a way that led to my return to education, but that for the vast majority of working-class people, both white and black, their days of compulsory schooling are all the formal education they will ever receive. Despite rhetoric, excuses, blame and numerous changes in policy and practice, the continued failure to critically educate and creatively stimulate is, as evidenced by adult literacy rates, I suggest, little short of criminal, and, at the very least, morally indefensible. Nor do I wish to romanticise or glamorise in any way the life of being working-class, nor to pathologise or victimise.

Auto/biography and policy

I was born in 1948 into postwar England, a time of rationing and utilitarianism, of bombsites only partly obscured by advertising hoardings, and the regular testing of air-raid sirens. It was also a time of hope – hope for peace, for plenty, for health, education and opportunity. My extended family hovered on the borders of the skilled and unskilled working class. Both my grandfathers worked in the public sector, one for the water board, the other for the refuse service. Uncles worked as machinists in the local factories and aunts, who had worked in the ammunitions factory, now worked in the cigarette factories, shops or offices. In 1948 my father was a conscripted Royal Marine; my mother had worked in the office of a large bookshop. My maternal grandmother, with whom I lived until the age of ten, 'took washing in' for other people. I was surrounded by hard-working adults.

In the September following my fifth birthday in 1953 I started at the local infants school. Located in a solid lower-middle/skilled working-class area of pre-war housing, this was a Victorian building with small windows, classrooms coming off the central hall and none of the colourful playground fixtures or art that are found today. The classes were large and we spent most of the time sitting at our desks. I did not like school, and once, shamed by the teacher for not being able to read, I left in tears and ran home, wanting never to return. At the age of seven, I went up to the junior school and somehow learnt to read. I had no understanding of how important school or learning was; it was just somewhere

I had to go, and my memories of this first school are chiefly of the play-ground, a small space covered in tarmac and segregated into girls' and boys' areas.

English education of the 1950s and early 1960s was framed by the 1944 Education Act. It was based on the inter-war understandings of an ethnically homogeneous, classed society, rather than the emergent postwar challenge, and as such, it reinforced the status quo. The Act raised the school leaving age to 15 and introduced the tripartite system of grammar, secondary modern and technical schools, entry to which was decided by the 11-plus examination. This system reflected the structured hierarchical labour market of the postwar Fordist economy. At the top were the owners (of shares, capital, land and production), educated through the English public (fee-paying) or private school system – the future leaders, decision-makers and politicians. Next were the grammar school-educated managers for industry and the public services of the new welfare state. Then, educated through the technical schools, there were the craftsmen, engineers and mechanics necessary for postwar production. Finally, there was the secondary modern-educated mass that would populate the pre-technological factories and offices, the numerous and necessary cogs within an economy heavily dependent on labour for the recently formed organisations of the welfare state, the nationalised industries and all stages of industrial production.

The 11-plus was based on the presumed objectivity of psychometric 'intelligence' testing – the IQ. Cyril Burt argued that each child had particular innate and unalterable intelligence that could be measured objectively.

> Intellectual ability...is inherited, or at least innate, not due to teaching or training; it is intellectual, not emotional or moral, and remains uninfluenced by industry or zeal. (Burt, 1953, quoted in Simon, 1999, p. 175)

The 11-plus *seemed* to show a direct relationship between low class and low intelligence. As intelligence was innate, there was little that education could do to improve it. Therefore, the schooling of those children who failed the exam did not try to increase their knowledge but to mould their character for both the labour and domestic markets. Two months into Year 6 my grandmother died and I returned to live with my parents on a large, new, peripheral council (public housing) estate – and I joined a new junior school. After an assessment that I do

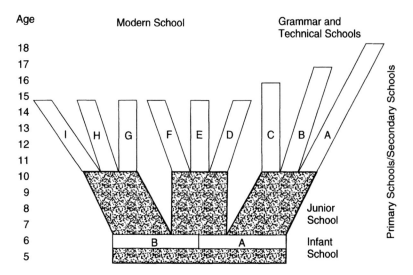

Figure 1 The Streamed system of education

not remember, I was placed in the second stream of a three-stream final year. In the top stream my younger brother and sister both spent a great deal of time, especially in Year 5 and 6, preparing for the exam, whereas we in the B stream never practised and I wasn't at all aware of it, or its significance for my future. My early inability to read, however, was to have very long-lasting consequences.

An unattributed writer of 1953 commented that a child placed in the A, B or C category at the age of six or seven is almost certain to remain in it as s/he grows older (Simon, 1999). Figure 1 shows that by Year 2, children were streamed, meaning that whereas those in the A stream were on track for grammar school, those in the B stream stood no chance at all. Years 3 to 6 reinforced the streaming, ensuring that only those in the A stream would go to a grammar or technical school – a maximum of 25 per cent; the remaining 75 per cent would, like me, go to a secondary modern. It is interesting to note here that despite the rhetoric of 'secondary education for all' and 'opportunity' there were at that time, fewer grammar schools than before the war – hence the need for early and sustained selection.

The policy process is, of course, complex and messy, and, despite its long-lasting prevalence, not all educationalists or politicians accepted the inevitability of psychometric-based schooling, and even as I entered primary school (five years before I sat the exam), some academics and politicians criticised it. There were some that believed coaching could increase IQ by an average 14 points. Simon (1953) argued that the 11-plus effectively reinforced class difference. In 1955 the 11-plus became a pre-election issue, and the Conservative minister suggested increasing the number of grammar places and providing greater flexibility for movement at age 13 or 15, arguing that 'the 11-plus is [too] early to show your paces if you come from a bad or dumb home' (Simon, 1999). Further significant criticisms were produced in 1957 by a committee of leading psychologists, and in 1958 by the National Foundation for Educational Research (NFER). The NFER report concluded that at least 10 per cent of children in any age group would be wrongly allocated.

However, despite such debate, the suggested changes did not materialise and, in 1958, unprepared and unwittingly, I sat the 11-plus, failed and went to a secondary modern school.

Critiques of the 11-plus have questioned their objectivity (Howe, 1997; Gillborn *et al.*, 2001) and have argued that there is no such thing as a test that measures innate ability, but that all tests measure knowledge and skills that have been explicitly learnt; thus B and C stream children stood very little chance. The power of the 11-plus lies in its cloak of meritocracy and equality of opportunity. The central concept of ability was framed by an emergent discourse of fairness, objectivity and equality; all children were given an 'equal' chance, and those who 'failed' were seen as being without academic ability and would thereafter be appropriately and differently educated.

Prefabricated, with large windows and several storeys high, the new secondary modern had gender-segregated playgrounds and a very large sports field, a couple of tennis courts and a small swimming pool. Most significantly, this secondary modern had grammar streams 'attached'.

When I entered the school in 1959 there were 1,595,559 children in secondary modern schools, compared with 641,044 in grammar schools and 99,224 in technical schools (Simon, 1999, Table 5a). Although in the 1960s there were nearly 4,000 secondary modern schools in England and Wales, this was one of the very few new ones. Most schools were solely secondary modern and most were badly maintained and very poorly resourced – the old elementary schools simply renamed (McCulloch, 1998). A few English local authorities implemented the 1944 Act through a mixture of grammar schools and bilateral schools, either technical-modern or, as in the case of my city, ten grammar-modern schools, such as mine. Yet despite what might have seemed like an early version of comprehensive schooling, there was in fact (in my school at least) an impermeable divide between the modern and the grammar. Furthermore, there was a hierarchy of status that existed even amongst the grammar schools, and a grammar of this type, whilst effectively separate from the secondary modern, would be very low status:

> Streamed throughout, classes ran from c to e, with a final f, remedial class; the Grammar school attachment was a and b. I was placed in class e. The following year I was in class d and by Year 9, continually at the top of class c (the top of the Secondary Modern school). But I could go no further. I had hit what I have elsewhere referred to as the concrete cellar of class. (Brine, 1999)

Dent, the editor of the *Times Education Supplement* at the time, identified five types of secondary modern school: the elementary, the higher elementary, the (inferior) academic, the specialist and the vocational (McCulloch, 1998). My school fitted most closely to the inferior academic. Dent remarked that in schools such as these, academic subjects were taught in much the same way, although to a less advanced level, as in grammar schools. When compared with the other types of secondary modern this may be so, but there was no comparison to be made with grammar schools themselves. Nevertheless, this lower academic ethos, coupled with the grammar stream, meant that the teachers and the other facilities were arguably better than in other secondary modern schools.

This highly restricted curriculum was deliberate government policy and both reflected and constructed class relations. For example, a key policy document of the time, the Norwood Report (Board of Education, 1943), devoted only half a page to the secondary school curriculum, yet 100 pages to that of the grammar schools, believing the secondary moderns to be beyond their scope. Furthermore, local authorities and individual schools were given enormous freedom to 'experiment' with the curriculum, provided they did not try to 'imitate' the grammar schools, for they were, as stressed by one of the main Chief Education Officers of the time, to be as distinctive from grammar schools as possible (McCulloch, 1998). The subsequent influential Newsom Committee (Ministry of Education, 1963) continued this approach to the modern curriculum. Although discussions ranged over the degree of restriction, the basic premise that the secondary modern curriculum should be restricted was not contested. The aim was 'alertness of mind' rather than an understanding of the world.

The curriculum of the modern school was very different from that of the grammar. For example, at the age of 14 I was able to drop maths.

We were excluded from gaining any kind of critical understanding of our world: geography was physical, history was always the 'cave men' and 'the Romans', science was basic biology; languages, literature and, subsequently, maths were non-existent. Homework was definitely not for us. My experience of secondary education was one in which I experienced a consolidation of both class- and learner-identity where each reinforced the stagnation of the other.

The Newsom Committee considered the place of English within the curriculum and advised teachers not to 'think of the weaker boys and girls as living in a kind of nature reserve, debarred by lack of ability from the great things of our civilisation, since that way lies apartheid' (quoted in McCulloch, 1998, p. 124). Even though here the Committee warns against such an attitude, the choice of language is indicative of the pathologisation of the predominately white working classes. The recommendation of the Committee was for a functional English and a similarly restricted mathematics; in 1962 an HMI suggested a restricted syllabus that would concentrate solely on the basic need to add, subtract, multiply and carry out simple division of numbers and money. Moreover, as McCulloch (1998) has pointed out, the curriculum was based on a particular classed perception of the social characteristics of the pupils.

Furthermore, the curriculum constructed a gendered identity of class; one that would 'educate' girls for their 'future vocation of home-making and the nurture of children' and thus the curriculum should emphasise 'home-making and how to grow into women' (MoE, 1948, quoted in McCulloch, 1998, p. 121). In their submissions to the Newsom Committee of the late 1950s/early 1960s the National Association of Head Teachers and the Association of Teachers of Domestic Science argued strongly for the centrality of domestic subjects within the curriculum – 'the subject around which all other subjects should revolve'. Based on such an understanding of girls' future domestic roles, there was, even within the same stream, less time given to girls than boys for maths and science – a curriculum already highly restricted by social class, was thus further restricted by gender. Interwoven with the emphasis on domesticity was the pathologisation of the working-class girl – our main 'educational' task was to learn how to perform our future roles of wives and mothers: 'the curriculum for girls [was] also based on an uncomfortably and often hostile image of the working-class girl. Such girls, it was widely asserted, were generally rebellious, sexually promiscuous, and a danger to society' (McCulloch, 1998, p. 121).

In my school, there was a lot of needlework and domestic science. I learnt to make starch for stiffening shirt-collars, to iron 'correctly', bake cakes, repair electric plugs and practise domesticity in the school apartment, where we spent the day cleaning and preparing a 'high tea' for our guests – our mothers. (Neither the concept of high tea nor the menu was typical of home.) The curriculum was further reinforced by the building itself: the girls' entrance was framed on one side by the two large domestic science rooms and the school apartment, and on the other side by two equally large needlework rooms. My school reports show the domestic science teacher's pleasure that, at age 14, I was 'developing into a very pleasant girl' and at 15 into 'a responsible girl'. (This particular working-class girl's 'rebelliousness' and potential 'dangerousness' were clearly being 'domesticated'.)

Whereas the 11-plus guarded the gateway to grammar schools, the new Year 11 exam, the General Certificate of Education (GCE), guarded entrance to higher education; secondary modern schools were not allowed to let their pupils sit the grammar school exam. It was feared that, even with 11-plus filtering and the restricted curriculum, there would still be increasing numbers that would qualify for higher education – more than were needed by the labour market. Over-qualified and under-employed people would lead to social instability. Hence, Circular 103 of 1946 announced regulations that would 'prevent schools *other than* the Grammar schools from entering *any* pupils for *any* external examination under the age of seventeen'. Such an explicit directive was subsequently replaced by less obvious barriers: the new GCE could only be taken at age 16, one year after the school leaving age, and the standard of the examination was high, 'thus excluding Secondary Modern children':

> Even under a Labour government, elected with a massive majority, the mediation of existing class relations was still seen as the major function of the education system. (Simon, 1999, p. 115)

I stayed at school past the leaving age of 15 and, despite promises that I would be able to take some GCEs, this never materialised and so I sat a very local, secondary modern exam that no one now, or then, has ever heard of. We were to have no transferable cultural capital whatsoever. These local exams were worse than nothing – rather than give an indication of what we might be capable of, they instead suggested the limit of what we could do.

Teachers' expectations were very low. The exception was an English teacher who joined the school in my last years and argued that some of us in the C stream should be allowed to sit the English language GCE; with very little preparation we did, and two of us passed.

The rigid interpretation and implementation of policy within my school illustrates the way in which a national education policy is simply one part of the policy cycle, for the local authority and the school reconstructed the policy quite differently from some other authorities and schools of the time. The GCE exams also illustrate the time-lag between policy debate and practice, for in 1958 (that is, six years before my Year 11), despite the government pressure for grammar exclusivity, over 25 per cent of secondary schools had entered GCE candidates (some may have entered for just one exam). This trend was strongly resisted by those who feared this would devalue the grammar exam and by those who feared that too many young people might qualify for 'better' positions within the labour market. For instance, the Chief Inspector of Schools wrote in 1958 that the secondary moderns were becoming increasingly aware of the needs and aspirations of their more able pupils and were threatening to blur the lines of distinction between grammar and modern.

There remained, however, difficult issues concerning those on the borderline of secondary modern and grammar. Newsom wrote in 1955 that it was 'difficult to distinguish' between the pupils at the top of secondary modern and those at the bottom of the grammar. He pointed out that whereas the parents of middle-class 11 + 'failures' could send them to an independent school where they often go on to pass four or more GCEs, the parents of the working-class child were unable to do this. In 1959, the Crowther Report acknowledged that there were secondary modern children whose 'knowledge [was] comparable to that of many Grammar school pupils' and suggested they sit external examinations, for these were 'the Modern school's potential GCE candidates, and must not be robbed of their chance'. However, the policy response to these concerns was not secondary modern access to the GCE and its grammar curricula but a new purpose-built examination for the 'less able' – the Certificate for Secondary Education introduced in 1962 and first sat in 1965 (the year after I left school) (SSEC, 1960; Lowe, 1997). Exclusion from the grammar GCE exam meant exclusion from higher education. The Robbins Report on Higher Education (MoE, 1963) identified class as the main factor of inequality: only 2 per cent of children of semi-skilled or unskilled workers went on to higher education despite representing 22 per cent of the total population, as contrasted to the 45 per cent of those from higher professional families.

The discourse around this level of accreditation has changed; but consider the current English situation, where some are entered for A–C grades and others for C–E with no possibility of achieving the higher ones – a decision frequently made in Year 8 or 9 with little parental or pupil involvement or awareness. Is this really any different?

Beyond the curriculum, the locality and social relations of the school also contributed to the construction of identities. Whereas those at grammar school travelled across the city, thus expanding their spatial and cultural knowledge, my school served the neighbourhood catchment area and I walked. The curricula barrier was replicated socially; good at sports, I played in a team where everyone else was from the grammar stream. Such fraternisation was frowned on – the grammar girls were 'other' to the modern, and to be seen with them was a betrayal of my 'own', an aspiration to the 'other' – a marginal position reinforced by being 'top of the class'.

Though the policies of the 1950s/early 1960s reflected clear and unambiguous class, gender and 'race'/ethnic interests, the construction of class, gender and learner identities is not static or singular, not solid and unmovable, but complex and contradictory. We are not totally passive to the constructions of others for we ourselves move, resist and take on multiple and changing identities (Griffiths, 1995), for within the class-based constructions of the school I unwittingly played/struggled at the edges of the class and learner divide. However, despite my attempts to confront and move beyond the constraining structures, and despite my practices of passive resistance, I was constructed by the school as a working-class girl who, despite academic and social aspirations, was destined not for the sixth form and university but for the labour market first (for the nursing cadet that I began with or the office worker that I quickly became) and later, for the domestic market of housewife and mother – which with many women of my generation I instinctively fought against, and later, through feminism, theorised.

The linkage between secondary modern education and the labour market is clearly shown in the 1945 Ministry of Education pamphlet *The Nation's Schools: Their Plan and Purpose*, which points to 'repetitive and routine process work [that would] not demand any measure of technical skill or knowledge', emphasising instead that the working classes should be 'trained in character' and 'adaptable' (quoted in McCulloch, 1998, p. 61). Within the policy-making process there were others who similarly held a pathologising view of secondary modern working-class pupils, speaking of the need to 'instil standards and values, responsibility to community, tolerance, dependability and absolute honesty' (McCulloch 1998, p. 130).

Conclusion

Throughout the years of my secondary schooling, society was changing and perhaps my frustrations were symptomatic of those changes. As epitomised in the 1944 Act, the rigidity of selection and the narrowness of meritocracy reflected an explicitness of class interest that would, over the ensuing decades, go through significant discursive shifts which would nevertheless leave the materiality of class privilege and oppression intact and, in some instances, strengthened. For instance, since the 1950s there have been many educational reforms in which there are discernible shifts in the class discourse. Yet the basic idea of (multiethnic) 'working class' equals 'low academic ability'; of working-class people being more naturally vocational; and, of course, the general pathologisation is as evident now as it was then. Consider, for example, the proposed specialist schools, the discourse on teenage mothers and unemployed people.

There is, then, a relationship between my experience of schooling and my belief that education is political, structurally benefiting some to the detriment of others. Education as an instrument of government policy is powerful, it has the potential to fail people, to *under*-educate; but, as Freire (1972) and others remind us, it can also empower and even liberate. Educational research can identify and interrogate these processes, bear witness to their effect and occasionally contribute to the policy-making process.

My biography informs my research interest in policy, first, in its discursive construction and its practical implications for relations of class and gender power – for the ways in which it limits people's lives; and second, in the agency of people and institutions, in the many ways in which, individually and collectively, we positively use, resist and reconstruct that policy. Policy and agency are both contextualised by the specificity of time and place.

References

Bauman, Z. (1999). *Thinking Sociologically*. Oxford: Blackwell.
Board of Education (Norwood Report) (1943). *Curriculum and Examinations in Secondary Schools*. London: HMSO.
Bourdieu, P. (1990). *The Logic of Practice*. Cambridge: Polity.

Bourdieu, P. (1997). The Forms of Capital. In A. Halsey, H. Lauder, P. Brown, and A. S. Wells (eds) *Education, Culture, Economy, Society*. Oxford: Oxford University Press.

Brine, J. (1999). *Under-Educating Women: Globalizing Inequality*. Buckingham: Open University Press.

Crompton, R. (1998). *Class and Stratification: An Introduction to Current Debates*. Cambridge: Polity.

Freire, P. (1972). *Pedagogy of the Oppressed*. Harmondsworth: Penguin.

Gillborn, D., Corbett, J., and Beraton, G. (2001). The New Eugenics: Race, Class, Gender and Disability Inequality in Education. Paper presented to International Sociology of Education Conference, Sheffield, 3–5 July.

Goodson, I. (2000). Developing Life Histories. Paper presented to the Conference on Current issues in qualitative research, held at CARE, University of East Anglia, July.

Hall, S. (1990). Introduction. Who Needs Identity? In S. Hall and P. DuGay (eds.), *Questions of Culture and Identity*. London: Sage.

Hammersley, M. (2000). If the Social World is How Qualitative Researchers say it is, What Impact Can Their Work Have on Policymaking and Practice? Paper presented to conference on Current Issues in Qualitative Research, CARE, University of East Anglia, July.

Harvey, D. (1989). *The Condition of Post-Modernity*. Oxford: Blackwell.

hooks, b. (1994). *Outlaw Culture: Resisting Representations*. London and New York: Routledge.

Howe, M. (1997). *IQ in Question: the Truth about Intelligence*. London and New York: Sage.

Kuhn, A. (1995). *Family Secrets: Acts of Memory and Imagination*. London: Verso.

Lowe, R. (1997). *Schooling and Social Change 1964–1990*. London and New York: Routledge.

Mahony, P. and Zmroczek, C. (1997). Why Class Matters. In P. Mahony and C. Zmroczek (eds.) *Class Matters: 'Working-Class' Women's Perspectives on Social Class*. London: Taylor and Francis.

Marcus, L. (1998). The Face of Autobiography. In J. Swindells (ed.) *The Uses of Autobiography*. London: Taylor and Francis.

McCulloch, G. (1998). *Failing the Ordinary Child? The Theory and Practice of Working-Class Secondary Education*. Buckingham: Open University Press.

Ministry of Education (Newsom Report) (1963). *Half our Future*. London: HMSO.

Ministry of Education (Robbins Report) (1963). *Higher Education*. London: HMSO.

Munro, P. (1998). *Subject to Fiction: Women Teacher Life History Narratives and the Cultural Politics of Resistance*. Buckingham: Open University Press.

Reay, D. (1997). The double-bind of the 'Working-class' Feminist Academic: the success of failure or the failure of success? In P. Mahony and C. Zmroczek (eds) *Class Matters: 'Working-Class' Women's Perspectives on Social Class*. London: Taylor and Francis.

Secondary Schools Examinations Council (Below Report) (1960). *Secondary School Examinations Other Than the GCE*. London: HMSO.

Simon, B. (1999). *Education and The Social Order: British Education since 1944*. London: Lawrence and Wishart.

Swindells, J. (ed.) (1995). *The Uses of Autobiography*. London: Taylor and Francis.

134 *Jacky Brine*

Walsh, V. (1997) Interpreting class: auto/biographical imaginations and social change. In P. Mahony and C. Zmroczek (eds.), *Class Matters: 'Working-Class' Women's Perspectives on Social Class.* London: Taylor and Francis.

Weiner, G. (1994). *Feminisms in Education: An Introduction.* Buckingham: Open University Press.

Wright-Mills, C. (1970). *The Sociological Imagination.* Harmondsworth: Penguin.

8
Gender, Identity and Social Change: Understanding Adults' Learner Careers

Sue Webb

Introduction

It has become commonplace to assert that widening access, rather than just increasing the numbers entering higher education, is essential if the gap between the information-rich and the information-poor is to be reduced. Graduation is seen to confer a number of advantages because, in addition to increasing an individual's earning capacity, it is regarded as enabling individuals and societies to compete more effectively in global markets (Dearing, 1997). In other words, widening access to higher education has become synonymous with strategies to solve social exclusion and reduce economic, political, social and cultural inequalities. But what has this meant for different groups of adult learners? What has been their experience of higher education? Many research studies have identified the positive and transformative aspects of returning to education for mature students and there has been an assumption that gaining a higher education qualification increases adults' employment and other life-chances. But relatively few studies have examined these new learners' changing identities, experiences and opportunities in relation to gender and class.

This chapter addresses this by discussing the findings of a recent longitudinal qualitative study based initially on 92 access and alternatively qualified mature entrants to full-time study in seven higher education institutions in the UK in the early 1990s. It examines the experiences of 33 of these learners (the majority of whom were women) and charts their lives since graduating. The concept of learner career (Bloomer and Hodkinson, 1997, 2000), which captures transformations in learners' dispositions to learning over time, helps us to understand two issues: how these women and men experienced their studies and how they negotiated their moves into employment or other activities following graduation. The chapter argues that transformations in the disposition to learn and in the lives of these learners post-higher education are contingent on the different economic, political and social circumstances and milieux in which these graduates move and the sense they make of these experiences. The chapter is informed by Bourdieu's work on habitus (Bourdieu and Passeron 1990), which links developments and changes in people's dispositions and their structural positioning to their social interactions. The chapter argues that an appreciation of how gendered subjectivities intersect with the development of dispositions to engage with formal education is needed in order to understand different women's and men's decision-making. This is because their decisions are informed by their perceptions of events or phenomena as opportunities for change or reasons for not taking risks. The findings from these adults' stories suggest that although policies to widen access may temper some inequalities, gender and social class are persistent determinants of the post-higher educational opportunities of adult learners.

Telling educational stories

A central focus of this longitudinal study are the transformations in identity, or what others have called learner careers (Bloomer and Hodkinson, 2000), that adult learners experience in gaining access to higher education in the early 1990s and in achieving their ambitions to improve their labour market positions after graduation. Previous analysis of interviews with the 92 students during their first year of university showed that different educational identities were produced at different times through narrative accounts of initial schooling and post school experiences of family, paid work and education (Green and Webb, 1997; Webb, 2001). The stories these learners told showed how they were re-inventing themselves, adjusting and shifting their identities, and redescribing the past from the perspective of their new position as higher education students. This analysis showed that similar events, the birth of children, divorce, unemployment, domestic and occupational boredom for example, had different meanings for individuals and linked with their changing educational identities in quite different ways. Social categories such as 'mature student', 'lone parent' or 'school failure' took on different meanings and explanatory potential in the different educational stories produced through the research interviews. In other words, 'the meaning of experience originates from the narrative and discursive contexts in which individuals find themselves and which help to organise their lives' (Wildermeersch, 1992, p. 25).

This approach to storytelling focuses on the social role of stories, the political processes through which they are produced, the work they perform in the wider social order and how they change and under what circumstances. These educational stories are not taken as providing pure, unmediated accounts of the learners' experiences, but rather they are regarded as 'an empirical social process involving joint actions in local contexts themselves bound into wider negotiated social worlds' (Plummer, 1995, p. 24).

Higher education entrants' narratives

When they first entered higher education, there were three main ways in which the learners described themselves and justified their educational attainment at the point at which they left school. These were articulated through three educational narratives, access denied, untapped potential and wasted potential that linked the students' experiences in different ways to social, public and cultural narratives. How the students positioned themselves within the three educational narratives provided some insight into whether these events were significant or not in relation to their educational decision-making. Elsewhere (Webb, 2001), I have argued that central to these accounts was the predominance of exclusionary or inclusionary notions about the 'fitness' of the narrators to become students in higher education. The narratives included, on the one hand, those that highlighted their exclusion from higher education at the time they left school, by invoking political, ideological and socio-economic constructions of their 'otherness' to explain why access had been denied. On the other hand, there were those who problematised their not progressing to higher education when they were 18 by focusing on the attributes that they lacked. In these ways this second group constructed a deficit model of themselves which drew on meritocratic notions of education, although this took two forms: untapped potential and wasted potential.

Gender, social class and ethnicity cut across these storytellers in interesting ways. The working-class[1] students were most likely to tell the access denied story and this was an exclusively working-class tale, with women slightly more likely to tell this than men. Identifying with untapped potential was more likely to be a female than a male story, whereas men were the most likely to describe wasting their potential. Perceptions of whether one had untapped potential or whether one had wasted it at school were divided by social class, and the former included more working-class than middle-class students, whilst the latter was exclusively a middle-class narrative. Ethnicity was in part a category of division within these narratives. The majority (nine out of ten) of the ethnic minority students interviewed (representing more than 11 per cent of the sample) told stories of their exclusion from higher education at the point which they left school because they had been 'denied access' or had 'untapped potential'. Only one entrant, who identified himself as a male Black African, talked of having wasted his potential.

I (Webb, 2001) have argued that this focus on the transformations in educational identities shows that what the policy literature describes as situational, institutional and dispositional barriers (Cross, 1981) and constraints to educational participation operate in complex ways. These cannot neatly be regarded as applicable to women or men, or one social class as against another. In the narratives there were some factors that were more or less likely to appear in the accounts of women rather than men, but there were also exceptions. Simple, dichotomous models of behaviour and decision-making were not present. Events that, on one level, are the same, such as becoming a parent, gaining or losing a job, or experiencing marital breakdown or ill-health, took on different meanings not just between women and men but also among women and men. The focus on the individuals' biographies of self and their educational identity showed that the discourses of femininity and masculinity had been reinterpreted or incorporated in individualistic forms.

The earlier analysis (Webb, 2001) showed that discussions of employment experiences and of family and home life were key elements in the learners' narratives, but these were presented in positive or negative ways. For those who talked of their wasted potential, employment figured largely in the accounts, more so than discussions of their personal lives or domestic and family concerns. In these accounts positive

Table 1   Alternative entrants' identities on leaving school

	Women	Men	Total
Access denied	36 (57%)	14 (54%)	50
Untapped potential	22 (35%)	7 (27%)	29
Wasted potential	5 (8%)	5 (19%)	10
Total	63 (100%)	26 (100%)	89

Source: Interview data from Alternative Entry Project (Green and Webb, 1997).

employment experiences were presented as the spur that pushed them towards realising their selves. This often occurred after a period of reflection, which suggested that the decision to enter higher education was an active step in their self-actualisation. Frequently, this transition was achieved fairly speedily and all these storytellers could be described as fast-tracking, taking no more than one year to gain access. In contrast, in the access denied and untapped potential narratives, employment was often seen as something to escape from and this, together with caring for others, rather than seeking to fulfil personal goals, were the common elements as they began to identify their latent or submerged interest in further study. As a consequence, their transition to higher education tended to be slower than that of the other narrative. Not surprisingly, those students who had adopted the narratives of access denied or of untapped potential were more likely than those who regarded themselves as having wasted their potential at school to be older, to be women rather than men, and to have come from working class backgrounds. However, the presence of the younger women with children from working-class backgrounds as tellers of the wasted potential story, and of older men in the access denied group, who in some cases were concerned about their caring responsibilities, suggested that the three narratives were not completely gendered.

Interestingly, analysis of quantitative data derived from the full population (from which the interview sample was obtained) of alternative and access entrants to seven higher education institutions in 1991, showed that students from ethnic minority backgrounds experienced a shorter break in their formal learning between leaving school and entering higher education (Webb *et al.*, 1994a), irrespective of gender. In other words, these entrants were more likely to adopt a fast track into higher education (Webb *et al.*, 1994b) and were more likely than white students to progress to higher education directly from employment. Moreover, when they described further education as a turning-point in their learner career, as was overwhelmingly the case for Black Caribbean and other Black students, the length of time spent in further education was very short in comparison with the majority of white alternative and access entrants, often just long enough to complete an access course (Webb *et al.*, 1994a).

Graduates' narratives

In 1999, four years after these students had completed their full-time higher education undergraduate studies, they were contacted again (using their last known address) and 33 responded, expressing a willingness to be re-interviewed. The overwhelming majority of these were women, more than in the original sample, and this in itself raises some questions. Are women more likely to respond positively to such a request? Are women more willing to tell their stories; or are women less mobile and so easier to track down than men? If so, what might this indicate about the impact of a degree on adult learners' lives?

More specifically, if women seem more willing to tell their stories, to what extent is this linked to wider political processes and gendered subjectivities? In the original sample men were more likely than women to identify themselves as having wasted their potential at school. In other words, for many of the men, their educational story was one in which they had merely delayed taking up their rightful place in higher education. There was no sense of having to tell a story to name their history or shape their identity. As hooks (1989) asserts, there was no sense that they were oppressed people resisting through telling their stories, in contrast to the majority of the women's stories about their denied access and untapped potential. Alternatively, more of the women may have been successful students and ready to tell their story, supporting the view that 'the power to tell a story, or indeed not to tell a story, under conditions of one's own choosing is part of the political process' (Plummer, 1995, p. 26). Not surprisingly, therefore, the analysis of the educational stories of this latest sample is beginning to suggest that, first, women have been less mobile than men since graduation and so have been easier to re-establish contact with. Second, since the majority with whom contact has been re-established were originally categorised as access denied and untapped potential storytellers when they left school, it also suggests that those who defined themselves as excluded from higher education are more likely to want to continue to tell their story. Detailed analysis to date of all those re-interviewed from one region (11 interviews) shows that although the sub-sample is small, and over-represents the experiences of women (ten women, one man), in other respects its composition reflects the original sample. The sub-sample reflects the wide spread of age groups interviewed in the earlier study, from 25 to 54. It does not include the small numbers of students aged 55 and over in the original sample. The ethnic minority group composition of the sample (18 per cent) also reflects the original sample for this region (nine white, one Black Caribbean, one Pakistani) and similarly the disability composition with one disabled person (9 per cent).

Other interesting features of the sample were that they were all still living in the region where they had studied for their first degree. They had all successfully gained a first degree and the majority had gained further qualifications (eight people, or 73 per cent). The majority had obtained postgraduate level qualifications (six people, or 55 per cent) and all these were women. Incidentally, the one man in the sub-sample had gained additional pre-degree level qualifications only. They were all in paid employment. Moreover, they all retold the educational story of leaving school believing that higher education was not for them because either *access was denied* or they had *untapped potential*. Finally, at the point they left school all but one originated from families that fell within the skilled manual or semi- and unskilled manual working categories and the exception fell within the routine non-manual and service category.

Gender, learner narratives and employment career decisions

Four years after graduating, gender and age still emerged as a significant though not the only factor of difference between the storytellers when they described their attitudes towards learning in higher education and their decisions to make risky choices to pursue their career aspirations. Although they all described their experience of higher education as valuable, differences between learning for self-development or for more instrumental reasons continued to be part of the learners' identities. To some extent these differences were associated with age and gender, with younger women, often single parents, and young men more likely than older women to link learning with instrumental self-interest rather than with self-development.

For example, Ellie (35–39 age group), who was 27 when she started her Access course, is now working full-time as a school teacher. She saw her degree as an enjoyable experience but she still prefers learning to be purposeful and not just for interest. She said:

> The fact that I did the environmental science degree was a good choice for me, I did enjoy the experience . . . I had a brilliant time, I really enjoyed the going and learning and doing the research and having time to spend to do this because unless you are actually made to do this, I am probably not the kind of person to do this just because I felt like it. My husband reads all kinds of things, because he is interested in different things. I wouldn't never even dream of

picking up a book just to find out about something, unless there was a purpose to it.

Nevertheless, some women and the one man differed in relation to whether the purpose was to enhance their own self-interest or that of their families or communities. Women were more likely to identify with the latter, even when they linked learning to pragmatic reasons (see Purcell and Pitcher, 1996, for a typology of career choice – hedonistic, pragmatic and fatalistic). Diane (30–34 age group), who undertook further nursing qualifications and postgraduate study following her degree in Sociology and Social Policy, suggested that

> I wanted to have a career basically because of the children. It enables me to have the skills to teach them as well as a career where I can have a reasonably comfortable life financially.

This twofold approach to learning, that is, learning for pragmatic employment reasons alongside justifying learning for the development of self and others, appeared in a number of the women's narratives. This suggests that the women who originally identified with the narratives of exclusion from higher education are likely to link the story of their success in gaining access to higher education and progression to professional employment to a reflexive view of the place of learning in their lives and those of others like them. Such learners were found to talk of re-presenting their learning stories to work colleagues, family and friends to encourage the learner careers of others: As Sue (50–54 age group) said:

> There's a helper at work and she's 35 now and she left school with few qualifications and she's seen me. I told her about me and told her if she wants to do it, then just to take one year at a time.

This reflexivity was also linked by some to a more overt political and social consciousness as Diane, a Black Caribbean woman and a single parent, said:

> I feel positive because I see things from a black perspective, so I'm lucky my strength comes from that and because of my academic achievements I'm able to help my children . . . . [both her children are doing well at school and] I'm involved with a study group on Sunday, it's more about black awareness . . . there's a lot of learning . . .

I'd always encourage people to do degrees. I think you find it can bring out skills that you didn't know you had and it can lead you in other directions. Even my last partner I was with, he did a degree through me.

In contrast, instrumental interests were more self-, rather than other-, directed in the case of the one man in the sub-sample. He recognised that learning and educational qualifications could advance his career, but this did not always make learning palatable. Rob (30–34 age group), who had left school to work in the construction industry, joined an Access to Law course with the sole intention of improving his career prospects. He described himself as 'single-minded'. When reflecting on how he gained his current appointment as an information technology services delivery manager at an organisation where he had been working on an unpaid placement after he had graduated, he identified the importance of the degree to the employer, but regarded his learning experience in higher education as unsatisfactory:

I'm pretty sure that had I not had the degree, [pause] I was looked at more favourably, they were better disposed towards considering me. They were really impressed I had the degree...At the basic level it increased my starting salary...[the senior manager] sees me as having an interesting background, went from the construction industry to this. I have a certain life knowledge which demonstrates a certain flexibility and a certain degree of intelligence to get the degree, so it has helped me to be taken seriously.

Interestingly, given this acknowledgement of the use-value of the degree, Rob drew distinctions between the requirements of learning academic knowledge for a degree and learning for practical reasons because one wants to know something. The former may give one status but little personal satisfaction. He said that when he was at university, he 'did just enough not to get thrown out' and 'only got a pass degree'. He regarded his university experience negatively, not only

the financial aspect...[but also] it can be quite boring a lot of the time. Maybe it was the subject itself, law, I didn't like it when I was younger and it still didn't feel any different at university...sometimes I felt the lecturers were paid a lot of money and all they had done was learn the subject like I had [from books] and hadn't really practised and never applied it. I thought I could be doing that...

I always prefer to learn what I want to learn in my own time than what I'm told to learn. If I'm interested, I'll go and find out for myself . . . [whereas the law degree had been] too dry, too much of an academic approach to something practical.

Thus even though the sample discussed here is small, it lends weight to an emerging thesis that 'there does not appear to be a specifically female or male orientation to education, rather, women and men simultaneously hold instrumental and self orientated attitudes' (Britton and Baxter, 1999, p. 191). Indeed, in this study, age rather than gender was a more likely indicator of different attitudes towards learning. Several of the older women expressed a self-development rather than an instrumental orientation and, as I have reported elsewhere, this was also a perspective associated with some of the older men (Webb, 2001). For example, Sue (50–54 age group) suggested that although she 'had always enjoyed school. I had always read a lot, even though sometimes it was trash, I wasn't happy unless I had a book in the house from the library'. Her access to higher education had been denied in the 1960s because girls like her went into office work. She said, 'I left school with 5 O-levels, that was in 1963, which was considered quite sufficient for a girl at that time.' She worked in an office for 13 years until the birth of her son and then took up part-time cleaning work in a residential home near her where she lived. However, the breakup of her marriage was the trigger to encourage her to return to education: 'This was a crisis point in my life and I decided what happened to me was either going to make or break me.' She described going to university as a decision to do something that 'I really wanted to do . . . it was a morale booster. I'll show him, I'm going to do something with my life, I'm not going to stop as a cleaner.' But this decision was less focused on a specific career move than others in the sample. For Sue,

it was just the fact that I was there, that was such a great buzz . . . I don't think I gave that amount of thought as to directionalise myself at all . . . I found the whole experience wonderful. The atmosphere of learning again, having to meet deadlines for essays, etc. and being with people again often in the same situation.

A second theme that runs through these learner narratives was the level of support learners felt they received during their degree studies and in their pursuit of employment. Their narratives revealed differences in their financial position and in their family's and friends' attitudes and expectations about higher education and employment options: what others term the learners' habitus (Bourdieu and Passeron, 1990) or social and cultural capital (see Baron *et al.*, 2000). The narratives showed that learners' perceptions of family attitudes and social contexts played a critical part in their career decision-making process. (See also Jenkins *et al.*, 2001, for a discussion of this in a similar study.) All the sub-sample suggested that their financial position both before and during their university studies had been weak. Interestingly, in the light of current UK policies on undergraduate funding, a number of these learners were been able to consider studying full-time only because, at the time they entered HE, the state funding of tuition fees and grants meant that their incomes were little different from their previous earnings in low-paid, part-time work or as unemployed people. As Barbara (35–39 age group) put it:

> Before I went [to HE] I was working part-time as a cleaner so when I got the grant we were better off so it really made a big difference to us. I don't know how it works out for people now there isn't a grant.

Reflecting on their career trajectories, for some, the process was described in positive ways in which postgraduate study or the securing of their first graduate employment followed rationally from the undergraduate study in spite of the financial risks this involved. For example, Diane, who completed a specialist mental health nursing qualification and a postgraduate Diploma in Counselling following her undergraduate degree said:

> Only just now feeling better off because until I finished in March I'd been working part-time in an agency while I studied, so my finances have greatly improved after being a student for so long ... before [the first degree] worked in catering jobs, a bar, and part-time jobs in a hospital, so yes, far better off.

Another of the interviewees (Neema, 25–29 age group) suggested that gaining the degree itself changed the way they viewed their options and that this, in turn, has had financial as a well as personal benefits,

> Having gained the degree it has changed my outlook on life, I don't have to do any job now, I have more choice. I know that doing my BEd, it would lead into what I wanted to do, but yes

I feel I have a choice, I have a career and I have a goal. It was very positive experience. Financially, the degree has benefited me. I have my own house; I'm getting married again soon. I have my own money. Being in employment has its benefits for the future, i.e. a pension. I wasn't in any pension scheme with my other employment, so this is a benefit. My previous jobs were to enable me to have money to live from day to day. I couldn't have planned for the future before.

In contrast, others regarded the risk of further debt as too great to contemplate, especially if they were older women. For example, Stephanie regarded herself as the main breadwinner in her relationship and said that she could not afford to undertake postgraduate study for her chosen career in probation work because of the financial risks involved. Instead, she had resigned herself to an administrative position with the civil service, within the penal system, which she did not particularly like and regarded as underpaid, but the advantage was that she would have an occupational pension. For Stephanie, the degree 'didn't open doors' because she thought the financial risks of further study were too great to contemplate because of her age (she completed her first degree in her late forties). Nevertheless, there were examples of others taking financial risks at a similar age. Pat (45–49 age group), who left school with no qualifications at 15, 'always felt that something was missing'. She completed a Master's degree before embarking on a career as an occupational therapist, even though this involved taking out a student loan of £2,000, which she is still paying back. Pat acknowledges that not everyone would be prepared to take such a risk, and that the support of her husband had been critical to enabling her to pursue further study:

I think I was quite fortunate at the time. Vic backed me because I didn't know and he didn't know either if I would achieve. You're actually giving up an income and you don't know if at the end of it you will get it or not, and I had two boys then.

Pat went on to describe how important financial support is to mature students and without the type of support that she had, they may not be able to enter higher education:

[One work colleague] she's actually being sponsored but she's done some stepping stones so she's been on a one day a week Access course. And there's also some of the auxiliaries, and she's been working nights and studying, and she's been accepted at [name of university] but she might not take it because of the money.

Clearly, for some potential learners, material circumstances may vary or be perceived differently and their views of financial risks seem different, which would have different effects on their dispositions to learn. For Pat, having a supportive husband, if not a supportive wider family, helped her to take the financial risk of giving up working as a secretary to spend ten years in further and higher education, whilst going into debt. She said:

> My parents, really I still don't think they fully understand, my husband's parents...I think they thought I was perhaps putting too much of a burden on their son. Now it's all sort of finished but the reactions were quite interesting. I don't think my parents thought much about it one way or the other. I don't think education means much to them.

For others, the lack of an understanding family or a supportive partner, even where there was a partner's income, meant that financial risks had to be minimised. Frequently, these risk-minimisers talked of the transition to employment as one of disappointment, frustration and making the best out of limited options, in spite of having dispositions to learn similar to the risk takers. For example, Lucy (45–49 age group), a single parent, had family networks in which her move to higher education was little understood. She said that her mother thought that when she was taking her degree it was just an extension of the classes she had taken at the local college and that her sister had been taking to improve her cake decorating skills. Yet she described her decision to return to further education and ambitions for higher education in terms of 'going to get some real good qualifications and work with people'. However, seven years on, following an abortive attempt to find funding for postgraduate training for social work, a failed attempt to find work as a medical practice manager (in spite of taking a further qualification in this field) and redundancy from work as an administrator with a charity that folded, she was working once again as an accounts clerk. Unlike the other cases described, Lucy was deliberately disguising the fact that she has a degree in her applications. So she has probably further limited her opportunities to move on to a job she would prefer. In other words, financial pressures have begun to limit the risks she is prepared to make in her job searching. She said:

> When you're my age and have a degree... if I send in an application for something that needs a degree when I've got nowhere, I've rung them up and they say we were very impressed with you and thought you did well at the interview, but this job will progress for a long time, and we want someone who can move along with it, and I know that they want somebody younger. And if I go for the sort of job that I know I can get where a degree isn't really necessary, and if you put this on your application form I think you can be seen as a threat.

Understanding adults' learning and work careers

To understand what might have been going on, and why these graduates had not all experienced the occupational success that they expected being a graduate to confer, Riddell *et al.*'s (1999) reworking of Putnam's use of social capital is useful. This is because it emphasises the negative as well as the positive aspects of social networks through the concepts of bridging and bonding. Arguably, although these learners had acquired a number of qualifications (or human capital) as adults, in spite of leaving school with little or no expectation of taking up further study, their similar working-class backgrounds did not structure their subsequent experiences as graduates seeking employment in the same way. To understand what changed as they progressed through adulthood and gained first degrees, and why their subsequent career trajectories varied, the concept of learner career helps to understand why some were more disposed than others to continue with postgraduate study. However, linked to this, an appreciation is needed of their perceptions of their material circumstances and their social and cultural capital: although they all valued learning they did not all choose further study, even when they knew that this would be necessary to secure the work career they aspired to. The material circumstances of all the learners was limited, but when they experienced support in their families and communities or had networks that bridged them into the world of graduate employment they were more likely to take financial risks and continue engaging with formal learning for instrumental reasons. Whereas if they had little financial and emotional support, and their family and friends' understanding of the world they were entering by engaging in higher education was limited, they were less able to contemplate financial risks. In addition, if they had embarked on higher education in the first place purely for personal development, with little instrumental thought given to future economic gains, they were less prepared to go into debt to gain postgraduate qualifications, even though they enjoyed studying.

Clearly, for some graduates, the transition to employment was experienced as an unbroken and positive career trajectory in which they were able to plan and where necessary take risks, and even go into debt to undertake postgraduate study. Whereas, for others, such risk-taking could not be contemplated and their career trajectory was more a case of getting a job to make a living rather than finding fulfilment through work. In the space of this chapter it is not possible to delve more deeply into the qualitative data to develop these arguments further, but the interesting issue that emerges from the examples cited so far is that these learning and work career trajectory differences cut across age and gender. Therefore, other factors need to be examined to understand why risk taking does not neatly map onto actual disposable income levels or onto other lifestyle differences such as marital status, the existence of caring responsibilities, or being a single parent. Evans *et al.* (2000, p. 124) in their studies of the work career trajectories of young people found similar differences in risk taking: they explain these in terms of people's 'past socialisation in family and school but also their identity formation linked to challenging and rewarding experiences in the passage to employment itself'. In the sub-sample, there was evidence that those with broken employment career transitions, and family networks in which their move to higher education was little understood were less likely to take learner career risks. Stephanie (45–49 age group) was a key figure in her local community, organising events for others on her local estate, but ironically these voluntary activities bonded her more closely to her neighbourhood and discouraged her from applying for higher grade civil service posts at the other end of the conurbation. There are clear similarities here with Reay and Ball's (1998) discussion of class differences and the importance of localism in working-class decision-making when choosing children's secondary school. Reay and Ball argue that in the context of educational decision-making the child is positioned as an expert in families where parents' knowledge is limited. As a consequence, it is likely that in working-class families the child's preferences for remaining with their friends will be more influential than in middle-class families, where parents ensure their children accept the norm that the best school to secure a good future must be chosen. Arguably, in a similar way, working-class adult learners are the educational experts within their families. Yet the choices they have to make on graduation have more financially far-reaching consequences than those of 11-year-olds. So unless they have other networks to support them in taking riskier decisions, people such as Stephanie may find it difficult not to go back to the positions they held before going to university.

These working-class graduates experienced their social networks, the attitudes of friends and family in different ways. Although there were notable differences between women and the one man, younger women were more likely to talk of taking on debt to pursue their work careers than older women. Nevertheless, age was not the sole factor regarding these differences. Rather it was the case that more of the older women than the younger women were more embedded into the social networks of their families and communities of origin, which made moving away from these influences more risky. In contrast, those that had less broken employment career trajectories after graduation cited the importance of the support they received from their families or activities in wider community networks which made change less difficult. Interestingly, not all of these cases involved younger women and men. There were some older women who had support for their studies from their immediate family, and they developed what Evans *et al.* (2000) described as action competencies or interdisciplinary competencies through networking with others in their chosen field of employment.

Barbara (35–39 age group), who had worked part-time as a cleaner before going to university, had two children and a supportive partner, and worked as a postwoman, may have been helped to obtain her current position following her postgraduate course because she kept in touch with fellow graduates, who have each moved into employment within the legal profession. Thus, she developed new social capital that bridged her into a world of professional employment and yet she was able to retain her working class networks because these understood and were supportive of her network crossing.

In a similar way, Sue (50–54 age group), as a single parent, who had also worked as a cleaner prior to going to university, chose to position herself so that she would be able to apply for certain jobs in the public sector where she felt there might be less age discrimination than in the private sector. In her final year at university she applied for and obtained relief work in the library service of the local authority with the prime intention of gaining access to the internal vacancies list. She said, 'I knew this was a foot in the door . . . I would have access to the internal job vacancy lists and I thought this would make things easier.'

Conclusions

I have argued that whilst material circumstances were important to enabling the learners to return to study and give up their previous paid work or their search for a job, their different perceptions of the risk involved were significant. These risk perceptions linked closely with their learner identity and their ambitions but they were also informed by the levels of support they had from family and friends and the knowledge they had of what was possible. Learner identity did not neatly divide along gender lines with women more likely to express an interest in personal development and men more likely to be concerned with their future career opportunities. Differences were found within the sample of women and many especially the younger women were as likely to be interested in learning for its own sake as for the benefits that qualifications may bring. These accounts would suggest that the relationships between gender, and educational identity are complex and frequently influenced by age, class and milieu. We should be cautious about presuming the continued relevance of the findings of studies conducted in very different and earlier contexts. These suggest that women returners see education as a means to self-fulfilment and men regard education as a means to gaining credentials (for an example of this work, see Pascall and Cox, 1993).

However, the extent to which learners in this study took the risks needed to take up professional roles following graduation varied with their gendered experience of social capital. For many of these learners family support was crucial, but equally, for some, severing ties with the immediate family through a divorce was a key trigger for change, especially for women. Indeed, Field *et al.* (2000) quote Pahl and Spencer (1997, p. 102) who suggest that strong family ties can be inward looking and may prevent adults from learning 'to cope with a risk society and gain full opportunities from a flexible labour market'. This chapter suggests that this would seem to be particularly the case for many of the older women in this sample.

In order to make the transitions needed not just to enter higher education, but also to move on to professional employment, 'bridging ties' that link learners into other communities of interest are necessary to access resources such as funds for postgraduate study, job vacancies, and the knowledge of how to appear employable. Given the family backgrounds of these learners, some of these resources are unlikely to be available within the family and others, if available, would require the reprioritising of other needs within households. For some, such as Lucy, a single parent with a disabled mother who required regular support, and thought Lucy's degree study was an extension of a cake decorating course, the strong ties that their immediate families hold over them may restrict their opportunities. These ties can constrain learners' time, withhold emotional support and influence students' perceptions of whether they can take financial or other risks. It would seem that these social networks are experienced in part in gendered ways and many older women are more likely to identify them as constraints than younger women or men. Therefore, recognising the gendered and aged basis of social capital will go some way towards understanding differences in adults' learner and work careers.

Note

1 Three of the 92 interviewees had always intended to study in higher education and categorised themselves as middle-class. They were accepted following initial rejection, with qualifications other than two 'A' levels, in spite of being under 21 years of age at the time. Their stories have not been used in this analysis.

References

Baron, S., Field, J. and Schuller, T. (eds.) (2000). *Social Capital, Critical Perspectives*. Oxford: Oxford University Press.

Bloomer, M. and Hodkinson, P. (1997). *Moving into FE: The Voice of the Learner*. London: FEDA.

Bloomer, M. and Hodkinson, P. (2000). Learning Careers: Continuity and Change in Young People's Dispositions to Learning. *British Educational Research Journal*, Vol. 26, No. 5, 583–99.

Bourdieu, P. and Passeron, J-C. (1990). *Reproduction in Education, Society and Culture*, second edition, London: Sage.

Britton C., and Baxter, A. (1999). Becoming a Mature Student: Gendered Narratives of the Self. *Gender and Education*, Vol. 11, No. 2, 179–93.

Cross, K.P. (1981). *Adults as Learners*. San Francisco: Jossey-Bass.

Dearing, R. (1997). *Higher Education in the Learning Society*, National Committee of Inquiry into Higher Education. London: HMSO.

Evans, K. Behrens, M. and Kaluza, J. (2000). *Learning and Work in the Risk Society*. Basingstoke: Macmillan.

Field, J., Schuller, T., and Baron, S. (2000). Social and Human Capital Revisited. In S. Baron, J. Field and T. Schuller (eds.), *Social Capital, Critical Perspectives*. Oxford: Oxford University Press.

Green, P. and Webb, S. (1997). Student Voices: Alternative Routes, Alternative Identities. In J. Williams (ed.) *Negotiating Access to Higher Education: The Discourse of Selectivity and Equity*. Buckingham: SRHE and Open University Press.

hooks, b. (1989). *Talking Back, Thinking Feminist, Thinking Black*. Boston: South End Press.

Jenkins, A., Jones, L., and Ward, A. (2001). The Long-term Effect of a Degree on Graduate Lives. *Studies in Higher Education*, Vol. 26, No. 2, 147–61.

Lee, D. J. and Turner, B. S. (1996). *Conflicts about Class, Debating Inequality in Late Industrialism*. London: Longman.

Pascall, G. and Cox, R. (1993). *Women Returning to Higher Education*. Buckingham: SRHE and Open University Press.

Plummer, K. (1995). *Telling Sexual Stories*. London: Routledge.

Purcell, K. and Pitcher, J. (1996). *Great Expectations: The New Diversity of Graduate Skills and Aspirations*. Manchester: CSU Ltd.

Reay, D. and Ball, S. J. (1998). Making Their Minds up: Family Dynamics of School Choice. *British Educational Research Journal*, Vol. 24, No. 4, 431–48.

Riddell, S., Baron, S. and Wilson, A. (1999). Social Capital and People with Learning Difficulties. *Studies in the Education of Adults*, Vol. 31, No. 1, 49–65.

Webb, S. (2001). I'm Doing it for All of Us: Gender and Identity in the Transition to higher education. In P. Anderson and J. Williams (eds.) *Identity and Difference in Higher Education: Outsiders Within*. London: Ashgate.

Webb, S., Davies, P., Williams, J., Green, P., and Thompson, A. (1994a). *Alternative Entry to Higher Education: Final Report*. Unpublished report to Employment Department and the Further Education Unit.

Webb, S., Davies, P., Williams, J., Green, P., and Thompson, A. (1994b). Access and Alternative Entrants to Higher Education: Routes, Tracks, Triggers and Choices. *Journal of Access Studies*, Vol. 9, No. 2 197–214.

Wildermeersch, D. (1992). Ambiguities of Experiential Learning and Critical Pedagogy: The Challenge of Scepticism and Radical Responsibility. In D. Wildermeersch, and T. Jansen (eds.) *Adult Education, Experiential Learning and Social Change: The Postmodern Challenge*. Gravenhage: VUEA.

9

Diverse Identities in Postgraduate Research: Experiencing Gender and Class

Sue Clegg

Introduction

This chapter focuses on two closely related themes in postgraduate research: the experiences of non-traditional students and the challenge of diversity. The idea of inclusive education at PhD level is barely developed. However, increased diversity in the backgrounds and purposes of students studying for a research degree potentially destabilises notions of the autonomous scholar (Bartlett and Mercer, 2000; Johnson *et al.*, 2000). The 'scholar' in the traditional discourse of the PhD internalises the authority of the academy (Hindess 1995) through submitting to intellectual mastery (Bourdieu, 1990) rather than opposing it. In this chapter I show how some research students come to see themselves and the university system in a more equivocal light. The second theme relates directly to the experiences of non-traditional students. Traditional PhD students are assumed to be full-time, funded, recently graduated and oriented towards entry into academic or other research careers. In contrast, non-traditional students are post-experience, working, part-time and often self-funded. The chapter explores how diverse individual research students draw on gender and class identities in describing their route into postgraduate research. Their identities as research students are mediated through locations outside the academy in ways that render the idea of the autonomous individual being initiated into the academic realm problematic.

Background

Diversity is now a recognised feature of university systems internationally (Brennan *et al.*, 1999). The challenges in confronting this diversity are both social and epistemological, involving a recognition of the ways in which such terms as 'research degree' and 'research' encompass different practices and truth claims (Winter *et al.*, 1997; Gibbons, 1999). The range of students, and their motivations for participation, are expanding and becoming more fluid (Weil, 1997). Increased diversity (Deem and Brehony, 2000; Humphrey and McCarthy, 1999) among research students is of particular interest because of the importance of research to the academy (Johnson *et al.*, 2000). Research students are significant in the definition of a university beyond their numerical proportion (Becher *et al.*, 1994; Noble, 1994). By recruiting research students and awarding higher degrees universities seek to ensure continuity and renewal of intellectual capital and their pre-eminent role in the generation of knowledge as well as transmitters of tradition (Bourdieu, 1990; Clark, 1993).

Postgraduate research students are not a homogeneous group. There is considerable variation in concentrations of research students across institutions and within discipline areas, and differential pressures on recruitment and retention. In England traditional full-time, academic PhD students still dominate in many older universities, particularly those with a strong research base (Burgess 1997; Berrell, 1998). Moreover, in elite areas of the physical and biological sciences there are worries about a short-fall of research students and a weakening of the international competitiveness of British science (Newbound and Phillips, 2000). The universities of the post-1992 sector, with their polytechnic past, have newer research cultures and are not as well funded as their more established competitors. These institutions have used their new research degree awarding powers to attract more part-time research students (Hutchinson, 1995), many of whom are mature professionals whose interest in research is detached from the aspiration to become an academic or full-time researcher. Some of these students are involved in 'practice-based' rather than traditional academic PhDs (Winter *et al.*, 1997). Practice-based PhDs involve a wide range of professions in reflexive enquiry into their own work-based practice, notably in areas such as health and education where practitioner research has a high profile in the improvement of practice. The emergence of this second group of research degree candidates has taken place at a time when there has been increased debate about the nature, purpose and functions of the PhD, both nationally and internationally (Zuber-Skerritt and Ryan, 1994; Harris, 1996).

Other researchers (Salmon, 1992; Denicolo and Pope, 1994; Deem and Brehony, 2000) have reported findings from case studies of research students with differing backgrounds and challenged the stereotype of the full-time, funded and typically young research student. These studies problematise the categorisation of mature, busy professionals as 'non-traditional' by pointing out that such students in fact constitute a large and important part of the student population. However, Weil (1997) points out although there are many post-experience postgraduate students:

> ...as they dance closer to the borders, they can confront sterile dualities between theory and practice, objectivity and subjectivity, disciplinary purity and problem centredness, universalised and contextualised truths. For such candidates, the psychological and social costs of re-engaging with the assumptions, practices and traditions of the formal system – merely for the sake of a qualification – may be too great to warrant investing time, energy and spirit.

Weil makes clear that engagement involves competing sources of legitimation and issues of epistemology, not simply students' understanding of institutional structures. Moreover, as Johnson *et al.* (2000) have argued, the PhD is predicated on the idea of an autonomous self, which is '*always-already*' present prior to the engagement with the PhD process. They argue that this autonomous rational self who is capable of making an independent contribution to scholarly knowledge is the masculine figure of enlightenment philosophy (Lloyd, 1984). Moreover, the central supervisory relationship is redolent with metaphors of power (Bartlett and Mercer, 2000). Diversity and inclusion are, therefore, more than just the incorporation of people from 'non-traditional' backgrounds into the formal and tacit protocols of the PhD (Parry, 1998). It challenges academic staff and members of the research community to engage reflexively with their own practices (Berrel, 1998; Bartlett and Mercer, 2000). Reflecting on the experiences of students from diverse backgrounds can help expose the regularities of the academic habitus. Habitus, as understood by Bourdieu (1992), generates practices and behaviours of 'reasonableness' and 'common sense'. Being part of the habitus as an insider presents special difficulties of breaking with experience and reconstituting it in an objectifiable form for research (Bourdieu, 1990). Looking closely at the different common senses of individual research students can thus also help in making visible the 'reasonable' practices of academics to themselves.

In presenting the analysis I have organised the discussion in relation to gender and class. Neither of these is a pure category: gender is lived through class experience and class experience is lived as gendered being. Moreover sexuality, experiences of parenthood and disability, the experience of being normalised as white or racialised as other (McClaren and Torres, 1999), are all elements of our lifeworlds. I have focused on class and gender because these were the areas that emerged most forcibly from the study. Any full discussion of inclusion must extend the possible range of categories beyond that, and in particular explore the ways in which identities become racialised within the dominant discourse. The chapter deals with the identities and lives of particular actors. The conditions that shape these diverse identities are created by the emergent powers of the underlying mechanisms of class, gender and other oppressions. These structures of oppression are not directly analysed in this chapter; rather, my focus is on students' own accounts. The research did not begin by looking for particular categories of experience; rather it started as a quest to understand the lifeworlds of individual research students in a particular time and place, to explore their understanding of their research and how they came to be doing a research degree. The motivation was with understanding difference itself rather than the categories that might describe it.

The empirical study

The chapter draws on data from a study of research students from one English university. The case study institution is typical of a large 'mass' university concentrating predominantly on teaching (Scott, 1995; Huisman, 2000). Research students in the study institution differed from the national profile of research students in that they were older, were more likely to be part-time students and included slightly more women (Clegg *et al.*, 2000). The data used for the analysis in this chapter involved 34 in-depth interviews. Demographic data about the students were not recorded beyond gender (half those interviewed were women), and students were free to self-identify their class, age, sexuality or ethnic identity as seemed relevant to them. Only one student identified herself in ethnic terms, describing herself as Chinese. This reflects the predominantly white intake at PhD level, and the uncommented character of 'whiteness' as a category of experience. None of the students identified themselves as disabled, but one student described caring for a disabled partner. The design of the interview was intended to explore the research students' own framing of their experiences. The interviews were preceded by a pen-and-paper instrument based on the work of Denicolo and Pope (1994). This involves using open-ended mapping of a journey, and open questions as prompts that reflected the lifeworlds of the students we were interviewing, rather than imposing premature closure on categories of experience (Ashworth and Lucas, 2000). The interviews typically lasted about an hour, and were conducted by a peer rather than by someone identifiable as an academic. The design of the interview was based on asking research students to describe the process whereby they came to be a research student and their current views and experiences on being a research student. The sample was drawn by writing to research students asking them to volunteer, and although no attempt was made to create a representative sample, we checked that our sample included a balance of women and part-time students which matched the institution's profile. Our sample included slightly more women and part-time students. The areas in which research students work include leisure and sports studies, applied social studies, public policy, business, health, information communication technology (ICT) and engineering, fine and applied art and architecture, cultural studies, and teacher and continuing education. Our sample reflected the overall profile of the university. All 34 interviews were fully transcribed and rigorous assurances of confidentiality were given to the research students who participated in the study. Pseudo-names have been used in writing this chapter.

In this chapter I explore how particular individuals made sense of their backgrounds and current social location, and how these factors combined in informing their understanding of the PhD and their relationship to the university. I present a detailed analysis of four students. First, Jan who had received funding for a full-time PhD but is finishing her degree part-time. Jan is researching teachers' classroom experiences where she was active professionally until her retirement. Second, Viv, in her forties, a part-time student, who works part-time at another academic institution and is researching sexuality. Third, Liz, who came to higher education later in life as a part-time research student, is researching a community organisation where she is employed. Lastly, Alan, who worked for many years in an accountancy firm and entered higher education late, is now doing part-time action research in the area of information technology use. These four students have been chosen to reflect the particular social locations described not for their typicality, either among the students interviewed, or among the larger population of research students. This focusing down on individuals is legitimate and important if the complexity of different ways of construing the PhD is to be understood. However, the selection of the students was not arbitrary. It is grounded in an analysis and close reading and indexing of the whole data set (Clegg *et al.*, 2000) which created the interpretative framework for understanding diversity.

Gendered lives – 'Typical women's story isn't it?'

The quote above describes how Jan summed up her experiences. In answer to the question of how she came to do research she went back unprompted to her childhood and how she was brought up to value education. Her experience of getting to where she is now is her *'typical women's story'* of the long route to a PhD, which she is only just completing in her (early) retirement. After finishing a degree she did a teacher training course under pressure to have *'some sort of career'* so that her ideas for research and creative writing were put on hold. This 'on-holdness' continued when she met her husband and decided to have children. Once her children were in school she applied for a Master's degree at the same time doing some part-time teaching. She then experienced a series of temporary contracts:

> I was intending to do the Master's but having taken on a new job, that was my first priority and I then had to keep re-applying for work here and the terms of my employment kept shifting and therefore I was involved in different courses so therefore my interests kept shifting ... so again every time I got paid work that was the priority because I felt that I needed to learn the job basically ...

In terms of her lifeworld, the interrupted nature of paid employment underpins her claim to typicality. Her self-knowing commentary on her own position is presented as the way in which gender is lived by many women. The significance of these breaks in the lifeworld of an individual researcher is more than just a matter of conditions of employment. Her experiences of fractured employment broke the intellectual continuity of her development as her interests followed the pattern of her job movements. This shifting of interests in relationship to jobs is not how academic knowledge and reputations are traditionally organised. The habitus of academic scholarship and interests are characterised by their cumulative pattern across a research career, with the progression from PhD to publication, and reputation based on association with a particular field of research. Consistency of employment underpins, therefore, not only continuity of cultural association but also epistemic position. So although Jan experienced the desire to be involved in research-type activity as fundamental to her value system from childhood, the practical possibility of achieving this is deflected by her experience of a typically gendered set of opportunities. Most starkly, she describes being denied the possibility of submitting her Master's degree by being out of time, which she explained in terms of a new job and hence a new set of learning priorities.

Jan's positioning outside the academy for long periods of her life gives her a particular set of values she draws on in doing her research. Values, which she describes as being deeply held, *'about what I think education should be about and what research should be about'*. The nature of these values gives her a critical perspective on the university:

> I think there are some strands of thinking within the institution which see research as very much more utilitarian – either for the researcher and the researcher's career or for the institution and the institution's well-being/future or instrumental in terms of the subject being researched...

Drawing on alternative experiences as a basis for a critique of institutional values and arrangements is not solely a gendered experience. However, Jan's account of her different 'jobs' contrasted with the 'researcher's career' is indicative of the ways this contrast is concretely lived. She draws on a broader set of values rather than utility for the 'institution' to contextualise academic practices. Jan describes her primary motivation as the research itself. While the traditional ideal of the university might be thought to uphold the ideal of the value of scholarship in and of itself, more recent work (Prichard and Willmott, 1997; Trowler, 1998; Enders, 1999) on managerialism suggests that the traditional values of the university are in practice being remoulded towards a different set of targets and goals, which become measurable and controllable outputs from the system. It is these new 'facts' of academic life that practically confront research students in relation to their personal values about research. In Jan's lifeworld the achievement of the degree itself is almost an afterthought. She is confident about her own capabilities and her values, and how the beneficiaries of her work should be teachers and the education system as users of her research. She also feels that her activity has importance in the symbolic realm and for her own identity as an older person. She describes the importance of achieving a PhD as being for *'senior citizens of the world'* in showing that it can be done. But, as with the Master's, the completion of the PhD is organised around different symbolic and practical timescales from those envisaged by the university's regulations. There are tensions with the university's systems and targets in respect of completion. Jan initially had a three-year bursary, but has now funded herself as part-time for two years. She describes her motivation for completion in terms of her own 'life space' – '*I think it's time now I got it finished and re-ordered my life space*'. Her experiences and ways of understanding the degree are as a moment within the flow of her life and her ongoing commitment to a set of values and research. The PhD does not figure as a single event or a means to an end assumed by the understanding of the research degree as a route into academic life. Nor does the PhD mark a rite of passage; its symbolic significance for her is the centrality of the values to her identity and for others outside academia.

Viv also expresses the significance of life experiences as a source of alternative values. Viv now works part-time as an academic at another institution. Like Jan her experiences as carer (as a single parent and now carer for a disabled partner) mean that she has not had an established career. Her current employment situation is '*casualised work*', which she characterises as involving no payment in the summer and no sick leave, and she rates her chances of getting full-time employment as slim. However, her employment situation gives her autonomy in relation to her research, which is focused on issues of sexuality:

> and still, I mean if somebody told me I couldn't get a PhD if I continued this line of research, the chances are I would still follow this line of research. And still if it comes to a tug I will work in Sainsbury's [a large supermarket chain].

The autonomy of casual work gives her important symbolic and personal independence and it is clear from the quote that she does not see this independence as a tradable commodity for other life chances. While she recognises the PhD could be useful in trying to get a full-time job, her assessment of the likelihood of 'success' (based on age and employment history) leads her to reject a pure means end logic. The symbolic significance of the PhD, while having a potential external currency, is for her primarily personal and about the assertion of particular values.

Viv's orientation towards her research, in parallel with Jan's description of her values dating from childhood, is located in the past. Viv attributes her desire to control her research as coming from her experiences at school:

> it's also a response to me and I was – as a child I wasn't successful in school and I have very often felt that the things I wanted were – I was

always asking the wrong questions and at the time I thought it was because I was stupid – and now I just think I saw things differently.

The theme of failure at school is reiterated at various points in the interview and in relation to her determination and own personal drive to succeed in terms of the research. This personal drive is different from the 'always already' constitution of the individual. The notion of 'always already' PhD students assumes that there are people already inside the system who, because of their capacities, can achieve the PhD. They need little support to achieve a PhD because they are part of the *habitus*. The model of the person that is involved is part of the discourse of rational individuals who, in terms of MacPherson's (1968) classic depiction of 'possessive individualism', own their intellect as an alienable commodity. The PhD is simply the cashing in of pre-constituted intellectual capital. Viv's sense of individualism does not position her in this way. It is experienced as difference and otherness. She describes herself, not as '*stupid*', but as seeing things differently. In part, she recognises her difference in contrast to the men in her family who she describes as having more power and status despite her qualifications. This 'difference' includes her sexuality, but in articulating her experiences, she prioritises gender rather than sexuality. Her gender and responsibilities (she did her degree as a single parent when her children were young) drive her to a fierce determination to succeed, but in ways that escape the traditional definition of an academic career.

Neither Jan nor Viv fits the model of the creation of the autonomous scholar (Bartlett and Mercer, 2000; Johnson *et al.*, 2000). Both locate their social identities and values outside the academy. While their highly personal values stress the intrinsic importance of research, the form of self-identity and individuality professed by Jan and Viv are lived in ways that are in tension with the modern academy. In Viv's case even the 'I' of the PhD is destabilised. She describes how she discussed with her female partner[1] the idea of life stories which form the basis of her research on sexuality: '*and we worked out a kind of – this is what I would be interested in and this is how we would do it*' [my emphasis]. The intellectual and social commitment and contribution of her partner to the project constitutes an important social and symbolic location for the research, rather than Viv seeing herself as constituted simply as an autonomous individual within the academy. The lifeworlds of both Viv and Jan, as described by them in terms of their relationship to gender, parenthood, age and sexuality, position them outside the dominant discourse of the PhD as a route into academic life. Both are partial outsiders by virtue of their life experiences. Both women use their understanding to assert an independence from the dominant values of academia, and in the process of doing so create potential challenges for the system. Their inclusion certainly does not involve a seamless assimilation into the values of the institution, rather their own values are asserted as in tension with the dominant discourse.

Both women experienced some difficulty in gaining acceptance onto a PhD programme. Viv in particular, whose work deals with sexuality, described the responses she experienced: *'interesting proposal, write it differently and we will think about it'*. The suggestion to *'write it differently'* was experienced as an invitation to reformulate her proposal in more conventional discipline based academic terms. This is 'reasonable' advice (Bourdieu, 1990). Most academic work is still framed by the protocols of 'normal science' which determine sets of proper choices of methodology and the formulation of problems. Some research may have escaped the corset of the disciplines (Gibbons, 1999). However, the PhD as an apprenticeship into academia remains intellectually bound by the 'common sense' of scholars as to what constitute appropriate ways for formulating research and, as Salmon (1992) and others have pointed out, unconventional PhD students, while immensely rewarding, present challenges. Viv eventually enrolled having found a (feminist) supervisor who responded directly to her. She accepted a place at the institution, despite some reluctance, having described the way in which she had previously felt badly treated by them. Jan experienced similar difficulties gaining access. She felt confused by how she had been finally offered a place, and had some reluctance about re-establishing contact with an institution where she was already known and felt pre-judged. The institutional responses experienced by Viv and Jan suggest that students whose intellectual orientations and personal circumstances are perceived as 'different', in whatever way this is understood, present challenges for institutions, a point I will return to at the end of the chapter.

The hidden injuries of class

Jan and Viv did not talk about their own class location directly, although both of them identified financial pressures as an issue in pursuing their studies. In contrast Liz and Alan placed class at the centre of their understanding of their research careers. Liz said:

> I left school at fifteen with no O levels [national qualification], abso-
> lutely nothing, I had enough of it and was one of those truants, one

of those disaffected young people I work with now . . . I hated it . . .
I was in one of those girls' grammar schools [selective school] that was
pretty posh and I was from a poor, working-class background and
I did not fit in. I didn't even speak the same as everybody else. So I left
school and was married within a year and had a baby a year later.

This quote comes from early in the interview with Liz. On being asked
about when she first thought about doing research, Liz immediately
explained that she had not got a first degree and went back to her
school days. Only once this had been explained did she go on to
describe how she got back into education. Her experiences are in many
ways similar to those of Viv and in terms of the lifeworld Liz also
describes the significance of gender identity. I have chosen to emphasise
the 'hidden injuries of class' aspect because of the central importance
she gives it in making sense of her subsequent educational and personal
trajectory.

Like Viv and Jan, Liz was older when she embarked on her PhD. She
was forty when she decided to do a first degree, but having already
attained a range of non-degree qualifications she went straight on to do
a Master's. Although she had identified a research topic, the route to
the PhD was far from simple. She experienced being 'patronised' by a
woman who interviewed her for a PhD. Liz describes this academic as
using a language she was not used to, echoing a similar point she made
about school and not speaking the same language. She experienced this
as a major 'blow' to her self-esteem *'I was shaking like a jelly when I came
out – I get a bit emotional speaking about it'*. The feelings are powerfully
felt, even in the retelling. The language of academics, including ways of
speaking, bodily postures and codes, is core to the *habitus*. The pain of
being confronted by them for Liz meant that she nearly did not
continue. She experienced considerable difficulty overcoming the
'blow', and only by drawing on the support of her daughter, who was
also studying for her degree as a mature student, did she continue her
search for a supervisor who she experienced as more supportive.

The strangeness of academic ritual for those positioned outside the
academy for lengthy periods did not end with the admission process.
Liz describes the importance of contact with other students (as part of
the research training) because:

although I had read about it, I only know one person who has done a
PhD, and it is not as if I am in that university type work in that it is
part of an ethos – it isn't.

Her experience is of coming from outside and of the difficulties of identifying the ethos – what it *is* to do a PhD not just how to do it. For her, the culture of 'university-type work' has to be deciphered from the outside. She does not experience the ingrained sense of 'rightness' of the everyday subjectivity of the *habitus*. The academy is only made more approachable through contact with other students in a similar position as noviciates. She does not easily feel herself as part of it.

This experience of being an outsider fits her orientation to the PhD, not as a route into academia or as a qualification, but as *'definitely for me'*. She describes it as a hobby *'not belittling it – what I'm saying is that it is an integral part of my life'*. The *'not belittling'* the symbolic place of the PhD as leisure and being part of her whole life is a recognition that, in the usual public/private dichotomy, prestige and mastery are located within the public domain of work. Liz reverses this; her lack of rational instrumentality gives the experience more significance in her life, not less. She identifies her own experiences as being fundamental to her research and her life:

> I have seen more of life than perhaps I would have done if I had gone down the other track which is from school to university and maybe staying at university – I don't know.

Her experience of 'life' is valorised in comparison with staying in the education system (although tentatively so). Her research and her practice are intimately linked and, as the quote suggests, the university represents another cultural space one she only partially shares. In both employment, and as part of her research, class remains of central importance to her self-definition.

Class is experienced as the ever-present threat of exclusion by Alan who described thinking that because he had no school qualifications he *'would not be allowed to do the degree'* (my emphasis) when he was first accepted on his undergraduate degree course. At the time, he had been married a year and had his first child and he

> just had a job…I hadn't thought about a career, the people I knew didn't have careers they had a job and so it was just a closed world to me.

He makes the distinction between 'job' and 'career' based on the different expectations of people from different class backgrounds – the fear of not being allowed access is linked to his perception of the differential opportunities which shaped his own experience and the 'closed world' education represented. In describing his decision to leave school at 15 years, he refers to his 'best mate' and their interests as overriding the cautions of his parents. The experiences of 'job' and 'mates' set the original boundaries on his aspirations. The significance of both suggests a strong gendering of his experience of being a working-class young man. While his descriptions of his own experiences appear matter of fact, he voices a degree of anger about his own background and the fear that his own children might be excluded from opportunities:

> but I want my children to be aware that there is this life and you can go down this road and you are not excluded from it. Whereas looking back and analysing it then very much I think the way I grew up and the community I grew up in, it wasn't something that was – it was an exception to go to university so it wasn't part of your life and that annoys me that is the way society is.

His own life experience has shaped his passionate belief in the importance of education and access to it. Alan described himself as just not being able to stop studying, while still working for the original firm in which he had a 'job' when he started.

The outsider tension persists for him, however. He described experiencing difficulties with one academic who questioned his credentials for a Masters. Alan got *'wound up'* and *'made a fuss'*. Although apparently less hurt than Liz's experience of a 'blow', the mention of these incidents suggest that the experiences of hostile or indifferent behaviour from academics have an emotional impact and carry the implication that, despite qualifications, some people are still outside academic culture and the bounds of the habitus. In Alan's case this experience drove him to a determination to prove the person wrong, however in discussing the significance of the event he re-described his experience of leaving school as a factory worker at 15. All through the interview Alan shifts back to his early life experiences. The experience of setbacks is lived in relation to his understanding of his own class-based opportunities and his strong feeling of the *'injustice of society'*.

Alan's orientation to the academic is both enthusiastic about the values of education, and distant, he does not see himself as entering that world. He has benefited enormously in self-esteem, but when he talks about *'my community'* he talks about the context of the declining mining industry where he lives, not the university. He wants the PhD because *'I would find that extremely rewarding – it would finish it off nicely'*. The 'finishing off' is suggestive of the end of a story, but also of a settling of accounts in relation to his perception of the educational system. His plans on completion are to take his children to America, to Disneyland, in recognition of his '*selfishness*', in terms of time and money, in studying. Like Liz he describes his PhD as a '*hobby*', but this location alludes to the central position in his lifeworld making it more important, not less, as unlike involvement in a job his research interests will not go away. This again reverses the normal public/private dichotomy, giving more importance to private desire. In terms of any impact on a 'career', he reflects back to his earlier distinction:

> my parents didn't have a career, my father was a labourer and you just had a job. My friends don't have a career as such they have what I would term as – and it's not – I don't live in an area where people have careers, a lot of people have jobs in that area so it's not the done thing.

He still describes his own work as being in the same 'job'. His employers have supported him financially, but from their point of view the PhD, in contrast to the more professionally oriented Master's, counts for little. If anything, Alan thinks it will count against him.

There is no sense that Alan's experiences of a research degree have involved the creation of a new identity as the individual autonomous scholar with a home inside the academy. This distance gives him a position to comment on and resist academics' interpretations of him, as when he created a fuss over being excluded because he had not got the right qualifications. But his identity and frameworks for constructing meaning remain firmly in the lifeworld of the community and family located outside the university system.

Reflections

I have called this final section reflections rather than conclusions because I want to speculate rather more widely about the implications of diversity for our understanding of the PhD. One way of dealing with diversity is to attempt to manage and re-frame it by asking how students can be supported into succeeding in terms of the dominant discourse. This approach reinforces the sense of 'otherness' described in the interviews. This model offers acceptance on the terms of the limited identities already available inside the academy. I want to suggest that the challenges diversity poses are not just about support and success within an unchanging system, but rather about how academics understand what counts as knowledge and the nature of knowing. The engagement of the students described above in the PhD process involves openness to values and influences from outside formal higher education. This in turn exposes what counts as legitimate ways of knowing and is, in part, predicated on the fracturing of disciplinary knowledge.

Feminist analysis and other critical frameworks have been based on breaking down disciplinary boundaries. The tribes and territories Becher (1989) describes are conservative in the sense of conserving knowledge and culture, and also placing boundaries around how new questions can be generated. The breaking down of these boundaries has perils, as Gibbons (1999) has pointed out. His description of 'Mode 2' knowledge, produced in the context of application, as trans-disciplinary, heterogeneous and reflexive are characteristics of the majority of the research topics being pursued by the research students in the study. They are outside the major paradigms as currently practised. The problem is, that whereas disciplines as the name implies have well defined procedures for making judgements of worth, newer 'Mode 2' or 'real world' investigations may not. The insistence on autonomy and external values by the research students described, therefore, presents academics with real challenges, since a more diverse student body also creates opportunities for greater experimentation and decreased reliance on academic framing of knowledge and academic 'common sense'. For example, there have been debates about the nature and shape of the thesis and experimentation with different voices and ways of writing (all pioneered by feminist scholars), and these present challenges to how to examine, preserve and expand ideas of standards in the PhD (Winter *et al.*, 1997).

The idea of knowledge claims being generated outside the academy has affinities with recent debates about open and work-based learning (Eraut *et al.*, 1998; Eraut, 2000). However, these concepts are rarely extended to encompass research degrees. While there are some exceptions (Burgess, 1997; Green and Shaw, 1999), overall, research is still conceptualised as an academic and disciplinary preserve. At other educational levels and in postgraduate study in continued professional development, there is now considerable acceptance of the idea that learning takes place outside the university (Coffield, 1998, 1999). However, despite some discussions of credit rating (QAA, 1999), at research degree level there is little formal acknowledgement of learning outside the academy. For the students in this study in contrast, the university might be conceptualised, at least in part, as being about learning which is validated outside its walls.

As well as sensitivity to these epistemological issues, however, the challenge of diversity also confronts academic staff with questions of personal sensitivity and carefulness – what Van Manen (1991) captures in his description of *'the tactful structure of thoughtful action'*. The 'blows' of encounters with patronising academics and being 'wound up' by these encounters, although specific to individuals, are existentially recognisable. The culture of higher education has been inimical to women's progress (Brooks, 1997; Asmar, 1999; Bradley, 1999; Leonard, 2001) and the idea of the hidden injuries of class has been multiply documented with reference to schools and beyond. These are not easy issues for academic staff, particularly given the epistemological tensions between the disciplinary and practice-based knowledge discussed above. The debate about what constitutes an appropriate language for conducting academic arguments and the sorts of prior assumptions made are now contested terrain (Gadamer, 1985). My own research on supervisors suggests that issues of power and emotion have a profound impact on the supervisory relationship (Clegg *et al.*, 2000). Many newer supervisors do not come from white, male, socially elite backgrounds and so they have negotiated the same terrain as their students in relation to academic cultures. Identities of interest or background do not automatically guarantee empathy. However, the extension of the PhD beyond the narrow confines of entry into the academy suggests that the practical wisdom (phronesis), *'demanding the skilful application case by case'* (Bhaskar, 1993), of supervision must be based on an increased openness to diversity. The challenge is to develop the tactfulness of the pedagogic moment in its immediacy (Van Manen, 1991).

There are, however, powerful policy drivers that may in fact be making sensitivity to diversity more, not less, difficult. There has been considerable debate about the PhD both nationally and internationally, but this has been overwhelmingly framed around the needs of full-time traditional students. The debates about the purpose of the PhD, and the balance between originality and research training (Hockey, 1991; Clark, 1993; Burgess, 1994; Clegg, 1994) have largely focused on the need to equip postgraduate researchers with broader skills in order to enhance their employment prospects. Restraints on public finance, international competitiveness, and the diversity of providers, have resulted in pressure on completion rates, and quality assurance practices (Harris, 1996; Pearson, 1999). Much of what was taken for granted about research degrees, about the nature of originality, and their function as a route into academic life, can no longer be assumed as sacrosanct (Green and Shaw, 1999). However the pressures on supervisors are primarily to ensure success and meet institutionally and externally set targets. But the research students quoted do not see the PhD in this light. Their motivations for completion are complex and they are to a large extent positioned outside the means/end logic of employability. The pressures on academic staff, therefore, may not match the interests of a diverse student body. A *'negotiated order'* (Acker *et al.*, 1994) in supervision, whereby supervisors shape their preferred style to meet external measures, such as completion rates, as well as those of individual students, may become more difficult if some students contest, rather than share, the values of the academy.

An important rider in relation to the above speculations is worth noting. The four cases cited above were from education, social science and information communications technology. These disciplinary concerns lend themselves to the formulation of a real world inter-disciplinary paradigm (Robson, 1993). The epistemological challenge may be more attenuated when it comes to large-scale science. For research scientists the full-time PhD from an established department remains the basis on which claims to competency and knowledge can be maintained (Hermanowicz, 1998). Although much science is applied, it is rarely possible for researchers to come into academia as post-experience research students with problems formulated from experience. The development of interdisciplinary science (Gibbons, 1999) in these areas is, therefore, largely a post-doctoral activity. The arguments from this study are from within specific disciplinary discourses and inside particular historical institutions. Other constructions may dominate at different times and in different parts of the system, and a full recognition of diversity must look beyond single studies to rich descriptions of multiple contexts.

Acknowledgements

Thanks go to Helen Bowman who conducted the interviews. While she was not directly involved in the analysis here she helped enormously in the many discussions we had when I was coding and reading and rereading the data. This was especially critical as for reasons of confidentiality I was working from transcripts not tapes and Helen's validation of my interpretation based on the original speech data was crucial.

Note

1   Viv described her relationship with her female partner in the interview, and also talked about sexuality in relation to her research topic, but she did not use the term lesbian to define her own identity. As with all the interviews I have used her own description.

References

Acker, S., Hill, T. and Black, E. (1994). Thesis Supervision in the Social Sciences: Managed or Negotiated? *Higher Education*, Vol. 28, 483–98.
Ashworth, P. and Lucas, U. (2000). Achieving Empathy and Engagement: A Practical Approach to the Design, Conduct and Reporting of Phenomenographic Research. *Studies in Higher Education*, Vol. 25, 295–308.
Asmar, C. (1999). Is There a Gendered Agenda in Academia? The Research Experience of Male and Female PhD Graduates in Australian Universities. *Higher Education*, Vol. 38, 255–73.
Bartlett, A. and Mercer, G. (2000). Reconceptualising Discourses of Power in Postgraduate Pedagogies. *Teaching in Higher Education*, Vol. 5, 195–204.
Becher, T. (1989). *Academic Tribes and Territories: Intellectual Enquiry and the Cultures of Disciplines* Milton Keynes: SRHE and Open University Press.
Becher, T., Henkel, M. and Kogan, M. (1994). *Graduate Education in Britain*. London: Jessica Kingsley.
Berrell, M. (1998). The Place of Research, Scholarship and Teaching in Newly Established Universities. *Higher Education Management*, Vol. 10, 77–93.
Bhaskar, R. (1993). *Dialectic: The Pulse of Freedom*. London: Verso.
Bourdieu, P. (1990). *Homo Academicus*. Cambridge: Polity.
Bourdieu, P. (1992). *The Logic of Practice*. Cambridge: Polity.
Bradley, K. (1999). The Incorporation of Women into Higher Education: Paradoxical Outcomes. *Sociology of Education*, Vol. 73, 1–18.
Brennan, J., Fedrowitz, J., Huber, M. and Shah, T. (1999). *What Kind of University? International Perspectives on Knowledge Participation and Governance*. Milton Keynes: SRHE and Open University Press.
Brooks, A. (1997). *Academic Women*. Buckingham: Open University Press.
Burgess, R. (ed.) (1994). *Postgraduate Education and Training in the Social Sciences: Processes and Products*. London: Jessica Kingsley.
Burgess, R. (ed.) (1997). *Beyond the First Degree: Graduate Education, Lifelong Learning and Careers*. Buckingham: SRHE and Open University Press.
Clark, B. R. (Ed.) (1993). *The Research Foundations of Graduate Education, Germany, Britain, France, United States, Japan*. Berkeley: University of California Press.
Clegg, S. (1994). Research Training at Leeds Metropolitan University. *Journal of Graduate Education*, Vol. 1, 39–45.
Clegg, S., Bowman, H. and Marchant, P. (2000). A Case Study of Research Students in a Non-elite Setting. *Higher Education Research and Development*. Submitted for publication.
Coffield, F. (ed.) (1998). *Learning at Work*. Bristol: Policy Press.
Coffield, F. (ed.) (1999). *Why's the Beer always Stronger up North? Studies in Lifelong Learning in Europe*. Bristol: Policy Press.

Deem, R. and Brehony, K. J. (2000). Doctoral Students' Access to Research Cultures – Are Some More Unequal than Others? *Studies in Higher Education*, Vol. 25, 150–65.

Denicolo, P. and Pope, M. (1994). The Postgraduate's Journey – An Interplay of Roles. In O. Zuber-Skerritt and Y. Ryan. (eds.) *Quality in Postgraduate Education*. London: Kogan Page.

Enders, J. (1999). Crisis? What Crisis? The Academic Professions in the 'Knowledge' Society. *Higher Education*, Vol. 38, 71–81.

Eraut, M. (2000). Non-formal Learning and Tacit Knowledge in Professional Work. *Journal of Educational Psychology*, Vol. 70, 113–36.

Eraut, M., Alderton, J., Cole, G. and Senker, P. (1998). Learning from Other People at Work. In F. Coffield (ed.) *Learning at Work*. Bristol: Policy Press, pp. 37–48.

Gadamer, H.-G. (1985). *Truth and Method*. London: Sheed and Ward.

Gibbons, M. (1999). Changing Research Practices. In J. Brennan, J. Fedrowitz, M. Huber and T. Shah. (eds.) *What Kind of University? International Perspectives on Knowledge Participation and Governance*. Milton Keynes: SRHE and Open University Press.

Green, H. and Shaw, M. (1999). Continuous Professional Development: Emerging Trends in the UK. *Quality Assurance in Education*, Vol. 7, 169–76.

Harris, M. (1996). HEFCE, London.

Hermanowicz, J. C. (1998). *The Stars are not Enough: Scientists Their Passions and Professions*. Chicago: University of Chicago Press.

Hindess, B. (1995). Great Expectations, Freedom and Authority. *Oxford Literary Review*, Vol. 17, 29–49.

Hockey, J. (1991). The Social Science PhD: A Literature Review. *Studies in Higher Education*, Vol. 16, 319–32.

Huisman, J. (2000). Higher Education Institutions: As Different as Chalk and Cheese. *Higher Education Policy*, Vol. 13, 41–53.

Humphrey, R. and McCarthy, P. (1999). Recognising Difference: Providing for Postgraduate Students. *Studies in Higher Education*, Vol. 24, 371–85.

Hutchinson, M. (1995). Postgraduate Student Numbers. *Journal of Graduate Education*, Vol.1, 94–5.

Johnson, L., Lee, A. and Green, B. (2000). The PhD and the Autonomous Self: Gender Rationality and Postgraduate Pedagogy. *Studies in Higher Education*, Vol. 25, 135–47.

Leonard, D. (2001). *A Woman's Guide to Doctoral Studies*. Buckingham: Open University Press.

Lloyd, G. (1984). *The Man of Reason, 'Male' and 'Female' in Western Philosophy*. London: Methuen.

MacPherson, C. B. (1968). *The Political Theory of Possessive Individualism: Hobbes to Locke*. Oxford: Oxford University Press.

McClaren, P. and Torres, R.(1999). Racism and Multicultural Education: Rethinking 'Race' and 'Whiteness' in Late Capitalism. In S. May (ed.), *Critical Multiculturalism: Rethinking Multicultural Education and Antiracist Education*. London and Philadelphia: Falmer Press.

Newnpound, B. and Phillips, M. (2000). UK Council for Graduate Education Winter Conference. http://www.ukcge.ac.uk/framesets/five.html.

Noble, K. A. (1994). *Changing Doctoral Degrees: An International Perspective*. Buckingham: SRHE and Open University Press.

Parry, S. (1998). Disciplinary Discourses in Doctoral Theses. *Higher Education*, Vol. 36, 273–99.

Pearson, M. (1999). The Changing Environment for Doctoral Education in Australia: Implications for Quality Management, Improvement and Innovation. *Higher Education Research and Development*, Vol. 18, 260–87.

Prichard, C. and Willmott, H. (1997). Just How Managed is the McUniversity? *Organization Studies*, Vol. 18, No. 2, 287–316.

QAA (1999). http://www.qaa.ac.uk/NQF/Contents.htm.

Robson, C. (1993). *Real World Research: A Resource for Social Scientists and Practitioner-Researchers*. Oxford: Blackwell.

Salmon, P. (1992). *Achieving a PhD – Ten Students' Experiences*. Stoke-on-Trent: Trentham Books.

Scott, P. (1995). *The Meanings of Mass Higher Education*. Buckingham: SRHE and Open University Press.

Trowler, P. (1998). What Managerialists Forget: Higher Education Credit Frameworks and Managerialist Ideology. *International Studies in Sociology of Education*, Vol. 8, 91–110.

Van Manen, M. (1991). Reflectivity and the Pedagogical Moment: The Normativity of Pedagogical Thinking and Acting. *Journal of Curriculum Studies*, Vol. 23, 507–36.

Weil, S. (1997). Postgraduate Education and Lifelong Learning as Collaborative Inquiry in Action: An Emergent Model. In R. Burgess (ed.) *Beyond the First Degree: Graduate Education, Lifelong Learning and Careers*. Buckingham: SRHE and Open University Press.

Winter, R., Griffiths, M. and Green, K. (1997). The 'Academic' Qualities of Practice: What are the Criteria for a Practice-based PhD? *Studies in Higher Education*, Vol. 25, 25–37.

Zuber-Skerritt, O. and Ryan, Y. (eds.) (1994). *Quality in Postgraduate Education*. London: Kogan Page.

10
The Corporeality of Learning: Women Students and the Body

Jocey Quinn

All I do, and for one reason only,
the working of a hammock for discreet repose
in which to dream a new self
buoy up the hefty hungry body
on leaded wings of stained glass fancy.
Here I float, there-dangle-
a nectar-sipping, blossom kissing
section of intestine that my heart has seen.[1]
Ann McKay, 'Frida Kahlo's Self Portrait with Bonito'

Introduction: meanings of the body

The corporeality of learning is a concept resonant of the changing nature of the contemporary university. Whilst the corporeal was once seen as both female and antithetical to learning, and the university itself was envisaged as the seat of a disembodied rationality that was strongly identified as male, these perceptions can no longer be sustained. The growth in the mass participation of women in higher education, so marked, that they now form the majority of undergraduates in the UK, has disrupted the mind/body, male/female dichotomy and thrown up many questions including: What happens to learning when the learning body is female? In this chapter I shall explore this interrelationship of body and learning: whilst acknowledging that they are both mutable conjunctions of materiality and meaning. My thoughts on this subject emerge from an indepth qualitative study of 21 second-year women students studying for degrees in interdisciplinary subjects in two HE institutions which have prioritised widening participation (Quinn, 2001, 2002). My sample was a diverse one, ranging in age from 19 to 62, amongst whom roughly half identified as working-class and half middle-class. In reflection of the courses I was studying, it included a small number of black and disabled students. The students were living in varied situations: with their parents, friends, children and alone, in their home city and away from home. The research explores a wide range of issues surrounding the mass participation of women in HE and the growth of feminist knowledge. One of its key concerns is the relationship between learning and subjectivity, and in this instance I wish to focus on the role of the body in that relationship.

Although obviously aware of the body as an area of contention for feminists (see, for example, Grosz, 1994; Probyn, 1996; Shildrick and Price, 1998) I had not envisaged my research as particularly contributing to this debate. I had not configured study as a corporeal issue and in this I was hardly alone, despite recent admonitions by such as Coffey (1999) not to neglect the body in considering the meanings of the 'ethnographic self'. Although the conjunction of body, gender and schooling has been increasingly addressed (see Paechter 1998) this has tended to concentrate on the fields of PE or sex education, where the body literally cannot be ignored. The broader questions of learning and embodiment, particularly in a higher education setting, are rich fields of enquiry that remain little explored. Grosz (1995) argued that in feminism: 'Analyses of the *representation* of bodies abound, but bodies in their material variety still wait to be thought' (1995, p. 31). Whilst many feminists in the fields of sociology and cultural studies have taken up this challenge, I would argue that feminist educational research has still fully to make this conceptual leap. My participants were to lead me from an abstracted idea of studying and subjectivity to an enfleshed one. In this chapter I want to discuss how this transition was made and what the implications might be for understanding both the positioning of women students and the practice of educational research. In tracing how the body imposed itself on my work, I focus on three issues: understanding the self through the body; women students as 'pliable bodies'; and the need for reflexivity about the educational researcher's body.

Studying/Subjectivity

Since universities are places where knowledge and meaning are explicitly constructed, they could be seen as privileged sites for exploration of the meanings of female subjectivity. In my research I particularly wanted to explore how, for my participants, studying in HE influenced a subjective sense of their identity as women. I focused on the intersection of studying and subjectivity, exploring their positioning in this respect as a 'location for the construction of meaning, a place where meaning can be discovered (the meaning of femaleness)' (Alcoff, 1989, p. 434). Structuring my research, so that in addition to focus groups, observations and documentary analysis it included space for indepth probing in interview and the opportunity for sustained introspection in diaries, I tried to produce the conditions where such connections might be made. The data produced were often markedly interrogative and reflective, and it seemed that studying was indeed implicated in the construction of subjectivity. Giddens argues that in late modernity individuals depend on reflexivity to constantly recreate an 'authentic self': 'A reflexively ordered narrative of self identity provides the means of giving coherence to the finite lifespan' (1991, p. 125). This was emphatically *not* the process I was witnessing amongst my participants. First, the notion that there is an 'authentic' self is drawn into question by their view of gender as a performance, a view which was surprisingly prevalent, particularly amongst working class students. Second, the vision of a linear narrative which makes order out of the chaos is the antithesis of the profound sense of rupture and disorientation with which their lives as women had left them, against which reflexivity was a feeble weapon. The discourse of the reflexive self has been critiqued as unproblematically based on male experience (Britton and Baxter, 1999). In my research the very concept emerges as schematic and reductive. Subjectivity, as my participants expressed it, was something far more fluid than such a narrative notion of identity. Subjectivity is always in process, never complete:

> The subject is not an 'entity' or thing, or a relation between mind (interior) or body (exterior). Instead, it must be understood as a series of flows, energies, movements, and capacities, a series of fragments or segments capable of being linked together in ways other than those that congeal it into an identity. (Grosz 1994, pp. 197–8)

The process of studying can be seen as an introjection into this flow, simultaneously constructing the student as a particular kind of subject and becoming part of their understanding of what it means to be such a subject. In exploring this process, four key themes emerged: learning and mothering, studying and pleasure, learning through the body, and studying as intimacy with the self. In this instance, I particularly want to address the notion of learning through the body and the interesting way in which it emerged as an issue in my research.

Body/Self

This chapter is partly a charting of my own learning process, which began with what I now perceive as a naïve and limited conception of the body. The body figured in my research preparations only in terms of including sexuality and disability within the categories of difference, which I wanted to address in my sample. To the extent that it was conceptualised at all, the body was seen as a somewhat discrete element of subjectivity. By the end of the research, it seemed that the body was not just a path to self, it was self in all its fluidity and flux: 'the very "stuff" of subjectivity' (Grosz, 1994, p. ix). How did this conceptual shift occur? It primarily emerged with the question of identity and sexuality. According to Fraser (1999, p. 11), in his later work Foucault emphasises that a truth of the self is seen primarily as a truth about sexuality: 'we are compelled to know how things are with it, while it is suspected of knowing how things are with us' (Foucault, 1990, pp. 77–8). Feminism itself, particularly radical feminism, can also be seen to privilege sexuality as centrally important to the understanding of women's position in the world. Certainly, in my research, subjectivity and sexuality were assumed to be intertwined, and I included questions about sexuality in both interviews and the diaries, which my participants kept for a week. However, to my surprise, it was not sexual identity which preoccupied them in trying to understand themselves and their positioning, but rather what it was to live in their bodies. Although very willing to discuss extremely personal issues, the question of sexuality was rarely taken up in interviews, and, when it was, the terms of engagement surprised me:

> *JQ* What about sexuality?
> *Ruth* I think it's all about confidence, sexuality and how you see yourself [*long pause*] I think part of it is accepting... We'd just moved North when I had my first period. I felt so ashamed and absolutely disgusted with myself... it was the worst thing. It's just another thing you've got to go through. I think a lot of women have their periods and a baby and all that and men have got nothing... and I get pain, nausea, headaches all that, so I think you have to associate that with sexuality and part of that is accepting it, but you haven't got a choice about it [*laughs*]. Breastfeeding, I think that's a lot how I see sexuality, it's a woman's job, get up in the night, feed the baby.

In Ruth's vision of her life, sexuality and identity are a very fleshy matter. Moreover, the body is woman's doom, bringing not pleasure, but pain and revulsion, and there is no choice involved only acceptance. This clumsy 'leaky body' (Shildrick, 1997) inserted itself in front of the rather sanitised identity politics which I had brought to the research. Amongst the majority of my participants there was an apparent lack of interest in discussing sexuality in interview; it did not seem to engage their attention. Was there a 'heterosexual presumption' (Epstein and Johnson, 1994) which led students to assume only lesbian sexuality was 'marked' as noteworthy? Hannah's response was interesting in this respect:

> *JQ* How do you feel positioned in terms of sexuality?
>
> *Hannah* I do appreciate the female form [*whispers*]. I have had crushes on female stars [*laughs*] and I still do and it's not a problem at all. And I often get annoyed with people, if I'd say I had a crush on Elizabeth Taylor and Julia Ormond – Oh I think she's absolutely beautiful! I would say that and people would go 'ah' and I'd say, 'What! It doesn't mean I want to sleep with her!' I just think she's really beautiful.
>
> *JQ* So why is the crush not sexual?
>
> *Hannah* Oh, gosh, I don't know. Because I wouldn't, I didn't, it wasn't a sexual thing, it was more that I wanted to be like that I suppose.
>
> *JQ* Right.
>
> *Hannah* . . . I think everyone's basically bisexual anyway. A member of my family is gay, so it's never been a problem.

It seems Hannah interprets my question as a search for a lesbian erotica, which she duly provides. However, she resists interpreting her '*crushes*' as sexual, losing her customary fluency at this point. Although claiming an acceptance of bisexuality, she does not permit her crushes to place her in this position. It is too easy to read her account as a denial of her 'true' sexuality, it is more that sexuality was read as fantasy, which focused on embodiment, on being in a certain kind of '*female form*', and not on a claim of sexual identity. In the diaries, which again did not seem to shy from intimacy, there was little sense of identity being predicated on sexual orientation: instead, there was ambiguity, revolving around the status of the body. The students seemed to operate as queer theorists who 'question where the limits of borderlines such as subject/object, interiority/exteriority lie and, in particular, seek to challenge the self/other dualism' (Fraser, 1999). It seemed they were signalling the body, rather than an abstracted sense of sexual identity (in other words, whether they identified as gay or straight), as a key factor in exploring their subjectivity. Embodiment, which cannot be seen in terms of a simple physical/emotional dualism, but as a fusion of both, was embroiled in learning. I tried to follow the thread of this connection, situating myself in a position of feminist 'materialist deconstructivism' (Hey, 1999, p. 180) where bodies *do* exist, but are not transparently accountable, where one must pay 'a nuanced attention to discourse, while locating it within the materialist constraints within which it is produced' (Rose, 1994).

Producing the pliable student body

Having been alerted to the primacy of the body as productive of subject-ivity, I proceeded to look at my data differently, exploring the embodiment of learning. Educational research lacks work on embodiment, although it has been addressed in terms of spatiality in schools (Shilling, 1991) or in the fields of PE (Delamont, 1998) or sex education (Lenskyj, 1990). I therefore found Potts and Price's (1995) evocation of writing whilst negotiating the physical limitations of ME a useful example of embodied learning in process. In contrast to the disembodied vision, which still tends to characterise accounts of learning, theirs was a process that was not individualised and transcendent, but marked by physical struggle and the contributions of others:

> we have attempted to inscribe our text with the traces of its genesis. Running underneath our words, underpinning our theories, are the names of those who've enabled this chapter to be written. (1995, p. 103)

The diaries my participants produced were similarly valuable, giving a sense of inhabiting the body as a student over time. I have chosen three diaries to explore here: those of three 19-year-old white women, all studying American Studies at Expanding University, providing a recurring picture of the emerging and self-regulating female student body, studying the same subject in the same place, during the same week. The diaries asked no specific questions about bodies. Amongst others, students were asked '*How do I feel about myself as a women student today and why?*' Invited to produce feelings, they responded with skin not tears. This is not really surprising, as research repeatedly indicates bodies are an obsession with young women. However, the extent to which this permeated their accounts of studying was very noticeable and the relation between body and study an interesting one.

The recurring theme was femininity and the efforts taken to produce and maintain the culturally ascribed feminine body. Interspersed with days of study were days of body regulation: an equally time-consuming process to gaining a degree. The goal of both projects initially seemed the same: the production of 'docile bodies' (Foucault, 1997, p. 138).

> Went shopping this morning and ended up spending nearly £10 on hair care products!!! If that's not a good example of the pressure on the fairer sex to look fairer than I don't know what is!!!...I guess we're all in competition with each other, which is why we are always comparing ourselves with each other. Whatever the reason, it's a bloody expensive and stressful process!! (Hannah's diary)

> I bought a hideous amount of chocolate to eat tonight. I used to fuss about my weight, not that I've ever been overweight...It doesn't bother me now, because if I want to lose weight I do it for me, not to impress men, not that I have really thought that anyway.
> I don't have a boyfriend at the moment, and it does bother me a lot when I really think about it. I sometimes think my family are, not ashamed of me, but something on that track, because I have not had a boyfriend for years. It doesn't bother me when my friends mention it though. (Laura's diary)

> I often worry about my appearance and weight, things I think the majority of girls worry about...Tonight I am going to a party and have considered not going even though originally I was looking forward to it. The reason is that my boyfriend is not going. I was thinking that this is quite interesting as I rely on him to make me feel safe when I go out. (Jenny's diary)

The diaries illustrate how the students construct themselves as 'subjected and practised bodies' (Foucault, 1977, p. 138) as women adopting the dominant discourse of femininity. Bodies take centre stage and evoke vulnerability, shame and danger and the sheer hard slog of maintenance. The students appear to watch themselves performing femininity and their imagery ranges from the parodic Bridget Jonesesque, to the abject, to the victimised: drawing on cultural narratives of femininity found in the media and popular culture. Simultaneously, the students can be observed adopting the dominant discourse of their subject. The diaries reveal how they conscientiously assimilate the values of their curricular subject and seek validation within it. Jenny consistently reflects that lectures and seminars *'made me aware of'* class or race. In the context of the course, she knows that legitimacy requires exhibiting such awareness, although not appearing to carry it through to other contexts. Hannah dutifully turns possible criticisms of pedagogy into rationalisations that her tutors are doing the right thing: *'The lecture was a little challenging (!!!) but the seminar offered us all an opportunity to explore any issues that we hadn't quite understood'*, whilst Laura demonstrates her tactics to gain reward in her study: *'I always try to study "obscure" areas for assignments of mine. I like to be different (plus it's easier to find books from the library)'*. The good student is constructed, not natural, and these students are experts in 'doing the right thing'.

Similarly, the body is something, which has to be worked up. When Laura can't decide whether she is *bothered* or not by her weight or lack of boyfriend, the rather comical way that her account seesaws from one position to another indicates one thing at least: these are issues she has learned to study. Attempts to position herself 'outside' the discourse of 'femininity' only seem to end up throwing her back in. Her account is particularly interesting because she *did* have an urgent need to attend to her body, since she had a serious congenital heart problem. Nevertheless, she persistently refused to be defined as in any way 'disabled' and projected herself as strong, powerful and in control; repeatedly reiterating: *'I wouldn't stand for it, I wouldn't tolerate it'*. Although her diary reflects on hospital visits and check-ups, Laura appears to pay far less attention to her body's physical fragility than to its status as acceptably feminine. Embodiment is not a simple matter of how the body functions but how this is interpreted, and there is some agency in deciding which symbolic categories we are going to recognise as powerful, and how we try to negotiate our positioning within them. In one sense the students cannot escape from the construction of what is acceptable and successful in terms of either studenthood or womanhood, but in another they **will** themselves to become perfected. Rather than being simply docile, they are more what Grosz terms 'pliable bodies':

> This docility no longer functions primarily by external regulation, supervision, and constraint, as Foucault claimed, but is rather the consequence of endlessly more intensified self-regulation, self-management, and self-control. It is no longer a body docile with respect to power, but more a body docile to will, desire, and mind. (1994, p. 2)

This conjunction of mind and body is very important, and historically specific. In relation to body disorders, such as anorexia, Bordo argues, 'we find the body of the sufferer deeply inscribed with the ideological construction of femininity emblematic of the period in question' (1993, p. 168). I would argue that these student bodies are inscribed with a femininity, which has been partly produced by women's progress in the field of education itself: controlled, successful, public but also precarious and unstable. Martin (2000, p. 57) expresses concern that high-achieving women students at Harvard suffer eating disorders and are obsessed with getting a male partner, noting it as a sign of the refeminisation of women in the United States – a regression to the 1950s. It seems, perhaps, more a symptom of the twenty-first century, where women are expected not only to be successful, but also perfected bodies, by any means possible. This particular bodily manifestation is connoted with youth and whiteness, and with the ambiguous position of white women students who, as my research indicates, are the new majority in HE. Yet they inhabit an educational system which is saturated with male precepts: making them, simultaneously, the 'normal' student and the stranger. Unlike older students in their fifties and sixties who claimed a new power in invisibility (significantly still a body-centred definition of self) –

Being invisible is the beginning of something wonderful, because then you start looking and there's so much that excites me. (Liz, 56, interview)

these young students are nothing if not visible. Both their pre-eminence and their vulnerability are inscribed on their body. The element of willing their learning bodies into being is also accompanied with ambiguity, self criticism and distaste, it is not triumphalist; just as my research generally shows that the mass participation of women students is hardly the triumphal march which is commonly displayed in the media. Their discomfort about their body-work could be seen as yet another act of self-surveillance, and being in their bodies is fraught with an anxiety they cannot shake. After all, these are anxieties *with* foundations: going out alone *can* be dangerous, families *can* punish women for not acquiring a partner, and critical judgements *are* consistently made on the grounds of appearance. For these reasons their consumption of the beauty industry can be seen as a constraint not a choice, even though there may be pleasure in it. If some male students are equally obsessed with refining the body through sport, this cannot be held up as a simple comparator. They are not subject to the same intense and pervasive messages telling them this is something they *have* to do, and, crucially, be seen to do: whether they want to or not; as Hannah says: *'Don't remember seeing any blokes in Superdrug!!'* One could argue that the women students are learning body lessons, which will be far more vital to their future survival than anything studied in the classroom. However, the more interesting question is how the body industry marries with the vision of the high achieving educated female to permeate the university, so that becoming the right kind of student and female body cannot be separated.

Some thoughts on the researcher's body

The research was also a bodily discovery for me. Part way through my fieldwork I fell down a hole, breaking my arm and injuring my back. Focus groups and interviews were accompanied by a plastered arm and back pain, which finally hospitalised and immobilised me for several months. Being forced to be aware of my body and its limits became enmeshed in the research, yet it was unspoken and unproblematised. I proceeded as if I did not have this inconvenient body – until I was literally forced to pay attention. Only through this unremarkable and temporary disability did I attain bodily reflection. This was appropriate enough, since in the literature on women in higher education it is only in terms of disability that the researcher's body is brought into question (for example, Matthews, 1994; Potts and Price, 1995). Honeychurch (1996) concurs that in educational research the researcher's body is too often left out of the equation, but he discusses this only in terms of the erotic when, for example, the intimacy of interview produces the unspoken possibility of sex between participants:

> It is imperative that the sexual body and the erotic be made comprehensible in the practices of social inquiry. Rather than disclaiming the corporeal as a way of knowing, the body's knowledges and desires are inescapable and constitutive to research outcomes. (Honeychurch, 1996, p. 352)

However, to focus only on the disability or erotic arousal of the body leaves a great deal out of account. Although the 'broken body' sparked my interest, it is the everyday researching body, the body in flux, in all its unremarked upon manifestations, which needs addressing. There is more to do than produce 'a fieldwork body which is both effective and plausible' (Coffey, 1999, p. 65), although this is important. Feminist educational research demands reflexive awareness, yet how far does it encourage reflexivity about the researcher as a body? Whilst Probyn offers what she calls the 'sociology of the skin' in her work on subjectivity and culture, can one produce equally bodily reflective work on subjectivity and education? 'I maintain that the body that writes is integral to the type of figuring I wish to do. It is a body that is fully part of the outside it experiments with' (Probyn, 1996, p. 6). How can I too significantly integrate my body into my research so that the artificial separation between body and mind, researcher and field of enquiry, is collapsed? When I read my research diary it was mostly the body *in extremis* I found:

Feel that an account of my day could be parodic, but it has a big impact on the fragmentary nature of my work. Kids – at this time the inability to sit down for any length of time without a lot of pain. Perched here on my hot water bottle.

If I had done my fieldwork as fully able-bodied: would I have done more, done it better? I recognise this as a research for a disembodied, neutral research, which does not exist. My search for the perfect researching body is a denial that all research is particular and flawed, just like the real bodies with which it engages. The everyday body is a body of limits. The other information about my researching body involved the body's comfort or resistance in certain spaces throughout my fieldnotes: moments when sensations and emotions seem to coalesce. For example, I felt a physical discomfort on entering the space of Environmental Studies in Expanding University which was highly defined as masculine:

Building very male . . . Lots of male presence on the corridors turning to look when seeing an (older) woman. Approach this large building over a flyover, over speeding cars. Disabled access??!! Threatening arduous approach (mobilizes my own anxieties).

This was a space in which I experienced many difficulties in gathering data, difficulty not only in functioning intellectually but physically. This contrasts with the comparative bodily ease and pleasure I felt in the same university's American Studies department, where research became 'painless'. This is surely an example of how the researching body clearly helps to produce certain outcomes, and as such its impact needs addressing, not only in my own work, but in feminist educational research in general. Feeling rather disappointed by my own lack of bodily reflexivity whilst conducting my research, I want to conclude by thinking through this issue and its broader implications.

Towards a reflexivity of the researching body

How might we become bodily reflexive as educational researchers? As St Pierre argues: 'if data are the foundation on which knowledge rests (then) it is important to trouble the common-sense understanding of that signifier' (1997, p. 176). If we are exploring body data, it is important not to assume that its meanings are instantly accessible. Just as words are not transparent, so with the body: there is no pure feeling. Even the sharpest pain is mediated by our fear and interpretation of what it means. It is important to recognise the danger that reflexivity about the body might lead to unfounded assumptions about the 'reality' of the researcher's account. Nevertheless, a research account which ignores the body must be deemed incomplete. If reflexivity is a 'continuous critical reflection on the research processes we use to produce know-ledge' (Holland and Ramazanoglu, 1994, p. 133) the corporeal element of research cannot be sidelined, it must be understood. Feminist research-ers have become adept at working through meaning, developing what Morley calls 'emotional and theoretical literacy' (1999, p. 19). Can there be a corporeal literacy? What does it mean as a researcher to be able to read and write the body?

Whilst there are inevitably traces of the body throughout any research, this needs to be brought to consciousness. Corporeal literacy needs to be ongoing and not retrospective, addressed in our research diaries, which can give a sense of the body's changeability and its relation to work in process. There should be recognition of how the interconnections between the research and the body impact both ways. Not only physical tensions, but also pleasures of the senses and the appreciation of beauty of different kinds should be addressed. The relationship between the body and methodology should be problematised. Do we avoid certain methods because we simply cannot summon up the energy to carry them out? Do some make us feel comfortable within our skin? Should we in fact be searching out those methods, which make us squirm, which add an uncomfortable but illuminating edge to our work? How do we perceive ourselves physically, in terms of age, style? How do we assume others perceive us? Is the insider conversation we feel we're having with our participants actually highly ironic and parodic on their part? There may be some unpalatable truths we have to bear.

The appropriateness of existing research methods in addressing the body needs to be questioned and the further development of innovative approaches such as video diaries (see Holliday, 2000) or the making of collages (see Seabrook *et al.*, 2001) should be encouraged as highlighting some of the dynamics of embodiment. In terms of theory, queer theorists, such as Grosz and Probyn, who have greatly informed this piece, can help educational research to break through some of its narrow parochialism and start to explore where learning through the body might take us. These are some of the things we need to think about. At the same time, we must not be narcissistic. In foregrounding the researching body there is a danger of literally disappearing up your own backside, and potential for ever more grotesque productions of 'vanity ethnography' (Van Maanan, 1988). At the risk of sounding like a stern personal trainer in same strict academic gym, reflexivity about the body must be an aid to more rigorous research, not an excuse for self-indulgence.

Conclusion

I began by posing the question: what happens when the learning body is female? Although I have demonstrated how significant this question may be for women students, it is important to stress that issues of embodiment do not only apply to female participants or researchers. There are also many more pedagogic questions that need raising around formal and informal learning and the body, about knowledge that is borne on the body into the university by students and teachers and how it can be recognised, validated and utilised. This chapter can be seen as a starting point for what is both a wide-ranging and fundamentally important debate. To return to my title, the corporeality of learning refers not only to learning as an embodied experience for students, but also points to the fact that our learning experiences as researchers, what and how we discover, are intimately affected by our bodies. Like the students themselves, we cannot learn apart from our bodies: our ever-changing, everyday researching bodes are not neutral instruments. What has this awareness of corporeality added to my work? On one level there is a more grounded and material understanding of subjectivity, which takes on added dimensions once the body is recognised and interrogated. On another there is reinforcement of the constructed and metaphoric nature of bodies and of learning. This dual perspective can add a crucial dimension to the development of a 'materialist deconstructivism' (Hey, 1999, p. 180) in feminist educational research.

Note

1 Throughout my work I intersperse fragments of my other readings, inspired by Dorothy E. Smith (1988), who speaks of a 'proxy' to the text, bringing perspectives from broader readings to expose the limits of theory. Whilst my practice is only a slight version of this project, the interrelationship between my research reading and reading for pleasure has been unplanned but illuminating.

References

Alcoff, L. (1989). Cultural Feminism vs Poststructuralism: The Identity Crisis in Feminist Theory. *Signs*, Vol. 13, No. 3, 405–36.

Bordo, S. (1993). *Unbearable Weight: Feminism, Western Culture and the Body*. Berkeley: University of California Press.

Britton, C. and Baxter, A. (1999). Becoming a Mature Student: Gendered Narratives of the Self. *Gender and Education*, Vol. 11, No. 2, June, 179–85.

Coffey, A. (1999). *The Ethnographic Self. Fieldwork and the Representation of Identity*. London: Sage.

Delamont, S. (1998). You Need the Leotard: Revisiting the first P. E. Lesson. *Sport, Education and Society*, Vol. 3, No. 1, 5–17.

Epstein, D. and Johnson, R. (1994). On the Straight and Narrow: The Heterosexual Presumption, Homophobia and Schools. In D. Epstein (ed.), *Challenging Lesbian and Gay Inequalities in Education*. Buckingham: Open University Press.

Foucault, M. (1977). *Discipline and Punish. The Birth of the Prison*. London: Tavistock.

Foucault, M. (1990). *The History of Sexuality, Volume 1: An Introduction*. trans. R. Hurley. Harmondsworth: Penguin.

Fraser, M. (1999). *Identity without Selfhood: Simone de Beauvoir and Bisexuality*. Cambridge: Cambridge University Press.

Giddens, A. (1991). *Modernity and Self Identity: Self and Society in the Late Modern Age*. Oxford: Polity.

Grosz, E. (1994). *Volatile Bodies: Toward a Corporeal Feminism*. Bloomington, Indianapolis: Indiana University Press.

Grosz, E. (1995) *Space, Time and Perversion*. London: Routledge.

Hey V. (1999). Troubling the Auto/Biography of the Questions. *Genders and Sexualities in Educational Ethnography*, Vol. 3, 161–83.

Holland, J. and Ramazanoglu, C. (1994). Coming to Conclusions: Power and Interpretation in Researching Young Women's Sexuality. In M. Maynard and J. Purvis (eds.), *Researching Women's Lives from a Feminist Perspective*. London: Taylor and Francis, pp. 125–49.

Holliday, R. (2000). We've Been Framed: Visualising Methodology. *The Sociological Review*, Vol. 48, No. 4.

Honeychurch, K. G. (1996). Researching Dissident Subjectivities: Queering the Grounds of Theory and Practice. *Harvard Educational Review*, Vol. 66, No. 2, 339–56.

Lenskyj, H. (1990). Beyond Plumbing and Prevention: Feminist Approaches to Sex Education. *Gender and Education*, Vol. 2. No. 2, 17–230.

Martin, J. R. (2000). *Coming of Age in Academe*. London: Routledge.

Matthews, J. (1994). Empowering Disabled Women in Higher Education. In S. Davies, C. Lubelska and J. Quinn (eds.), *Changing the Subject: Women in Higher Education*. London: Taylor and Francis.

Morley, L. (1999). *Organising Feminisms: The Micropolitics of the Academy*. London: Macmillan.

Paechter, C. (1998) *Educating the Other: Gender, Power and Schooling*. London: Falmer Press.

Potts, T. and Price, J. (1995). Out of the Blood and Spirit of Our Lives: The Place of the Body in Academic Feminism. In L. Morley and V. Walsh (eds.) *Feminist Academics: Creative Agents for Change*. London: Taylor and Francis.

Probyn, E. (1996). *Outside Belongings*. London: Routledge.

Quinn, J. (2001). Powerful Subjects: Women Students. Subjectivity and the Higher Education Curriculum. Unpublished PhD thesis, Lancaster University.

Quinn J. (2002). *Are Women Taking over the University?* Stoke-on-Trent: Trentham Books.

Rose, H. (1994). *Love, Power and Knowledge: Towards a Feminist Transformation of the Sciences*, Oxford: Polity Press.

Seabrook, T., Bell, P. and Green, E. (2001). Fashion and Identity: Embodied Negotiations with Marginalized Young Women. Paper presented at the British Sociological Association Conference, Manchester University, 9–12 April.

Shildrick, M. (1997). *Leaky Bodies and Boundaries: Feminism, Postmodernism and (Bio) ethics*. London: Routledge.

Shildrick, M. and Price, J. (1998). *Vital Signs: Feminist Reconfigurations of the Bio/logical Body*. Edinburgh: Edinburgh University Press.

Shilling, C. (1991) Social Space, Gender Inequalities and Educational Differentation. *British Journal of Sociology of Education*, Vol. 12, No. 1, 23–44.

Smith, D. E. (1998). Keynote speech: Theorising the Self within Social Relationships. Autobiography and the Social Self Seminar Series, Women's Studies, Universities of Lancaster and York, June.

St Pierre, E. A. (1997). Methodology in the Field and the Irruption of Transgressive Data. *International Journal of Qualitative Studies in Education* Vol. 7, 175–89.

Van Maanen, J. (1988) *Tales of the Field*. Chicago: University of Chicago Press.

Index

Lightning Source UK Ltd.
Milton Keynes UK
UKOW02f1252090615

253173UK00002B/33/P